T0162376

SAN FRANCISCO

THE UNKNOWN CITY

SAN FRANCISCO

THE UNKNOWN CITY

Helene Goupil
and
Josh Krist

ARSENAL PULP PRESS

VANCOUVER

SAN FRANCISCO: THE UNKNOWN CITY
Copyright © 2005 by Helene Goupil and Josh Krist

All rights reserved. No part of this book may be reproduced or used in any form by any means – graphic, electronic or mechanical – without the prior written permission of the publisher, except by a reviewer, who may use brief excerpts in a review, or in the case of photocopying in Canada, a license from Access Copyright.

The publisher gratefully acknowledges the support of the Government of Canada through the Book Publishing Industry Development Program for its publishing activities.

ARSENAL PULP PRESS
341 Water Street, Suite 200
Vancouver, BC
Canada V6B 1B8
arsenalpulp.com

Design by Electra Design Group
Production assistance by Judy Yeung
Cover photography by Martine Mouchy/Getty Images

Copyright for photographs used in this book reside with their owners. All photographs courtesy of Helene Goupil and Josh Krist unless otherwise noted.

Efforts have been made to locate copyright holders of source material wherever possible. The publisher welcomes hearing from any copyright holders of material used in this book who have not been contacted.

Printed and bound in Canada

Library and Archives Canada Cataloguing in Publication

Goupil, Helene, 1978-
    San Francisco : the unknown city / Helene Goupil and Josh Krist.

    (Unknown city)
    Includes index.
    ISBN 1-55152-188-1

    1. San Francisco (Calif.)—Guidebooks. I. Krist, Josh, 1972- II.
Title. III. Series.

F869.S33G68 2005   917.94'610454
C2005-904451-9

ISBN-13 978-1-55152-188-6

c o n t e n t s

acknowledgments

Thanks to:

Joelle, Regis, and Elodie Goupil, Rosemary and Jacob Whitt, William, Jesse, and Kerri Krist, Jessyca Tretola, Julie Breton, Xavier Riotte, Alex Robinson, Emma and Jason Poyner, Daniel Martinez, Randall Todd, Willie Rolling, Omar Shafqat, Johanna Chriqui, Adriana Braga, Irina and Marshall Luck, Jason Ganz, Lever Rukhin, Allison Leone, Nicole Peterson, Gregg Butensky, Michael McColl, Tyler Davidson, Lori Tenny, Adam Jones, Carolyn Blackburn, Camille Marques, Donald McDonald, the San Francisco Visitors and Convention Bureau, "Uncle Donald," the fantastic PIO at BART, and the whole team at the Job Shop.

Special thanks to Anthony Pietri and Celine Moravec for the photos they contributed; Amy Arena, James LaPointe, Bruno Navarro, and Carl Pezold, who each gave us a great introduction to the city in their different ways; Brant Herman for knowing so much about things that few people know about, and Frederick Mead for always showing us new places. Thanks to Buck Peterson, Kurt Opsahl, and J. Maarten Troost for their sage advice.

This book would not have been possible without the great people at Arsenal Pulp, thanks to Brian, Shyla, Robert, Nicole, Tessa, and Janice.

introduction

To write a book about a city as storied and complex as San Francisco is a humbling task. Everyone has their own image of San Francisco, and even though it's a world-class city, it can be very provincial.

While researching this book, people we talked to often suggested we include a particular establishment – their favorite burrito place, for example – because in their eyes, it was "the best." When we explained that not everyone might agree with their opinion, they would often reply that in the case of their "burrito place," it wasn't an opinion but a fact.

You could replace "burrito place" with bar, restaurant, landmark building, artist, historical figure – any of the people, places, and things that make San Francisco what it is today. But whereas some books offer opinions (and we have those too, of course), we give you the intriguing, behind-the-scenes facts, figures, and stories so that you can decide what's "best," or at least most interesting, for yourself.

And this city is nothing if not interesting – beneath the shards of broken illusions and common misperceptions about San Francisco, we found tons of "unknown" stories about our fair city that were alternatively funny, scary, sexy, or just plain weird. Some characters even popped up over and over again in various San Francisco tales; imagine Forrest Gump on acid....

While writing this book, we came to the conclusion that San Francisco must be broadcasting a covert message to all the truly strange and wonderful people in this world on a frequency that only they tune in to. Yes, there are stories in this book that are so bizarre even we are still scratching our heads over them, but many of the people, past and present, who live in this city seem light years ahead of us normal earthlings in their thoughts, deeds, and accomplishments.

San Franciscans also share a central tenet: that this is the best city in the world. Even if you don't agree, you'll find there's a lot more to this 49-square-mile village than meets the eye. So get out and discover an unknown San Francisco of your very own.

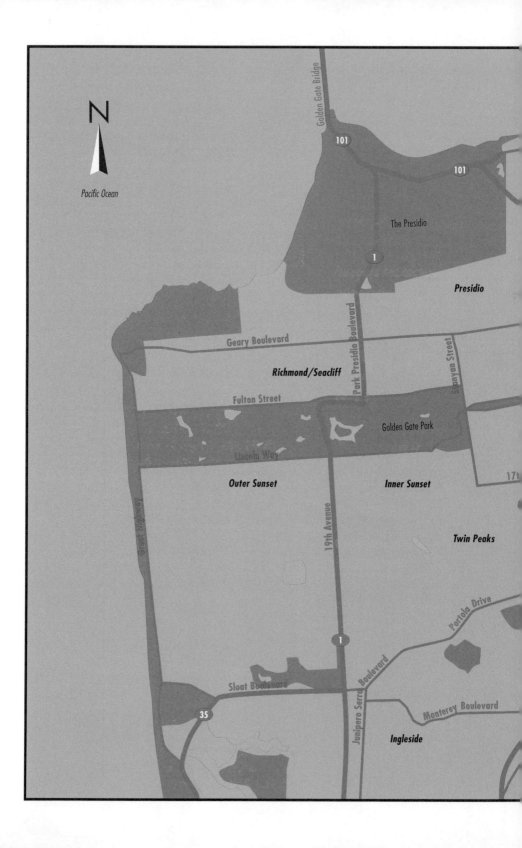

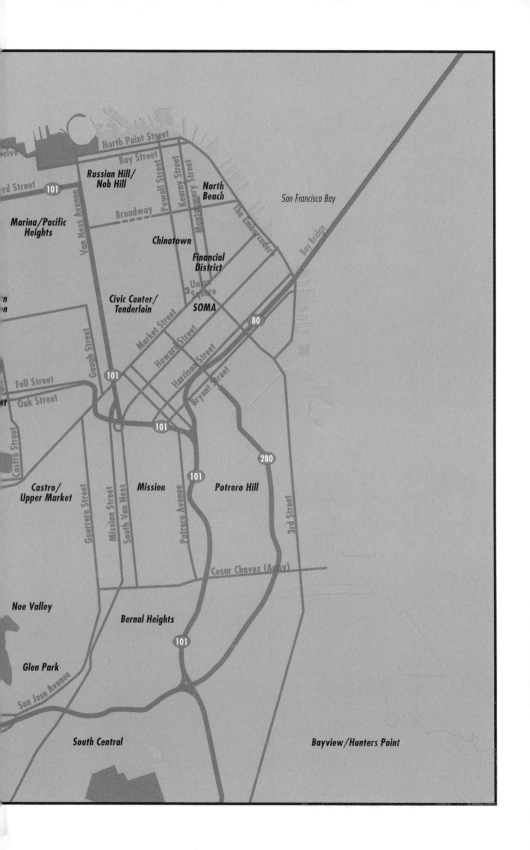

North Beach, Chinatown, & Downtown

Fisherman's Wharf

Pier 39

North Point Street

Bay Street

Coit Tower

Lombard Street

Columbus Avenue

The Embarcadero

North Beach

N

San Francisco Bay

Russian Hill

Broadway (tunnel)

Nob Hill

Washington Street

Chinatown

Sacramento Street

California Street

Montgomery Street

Battery Street

Kearny Street

Financial District

Powell Street

Bush Street

Post Street

Geary Street

Market Street

Union Square

2nd Street

1st Street

Mission Street

Howard Street

Main Street

Fremont Street

Bay Bridge

M

M

M

M

M

Van Ness Avenue

Polk Street

Larkin Street

Hyde Street

Turk Street

Civic Center/ Tenderloin

4th Street

3rd Street

5th Street

6th Street

Folsom Street

Harrison Street

Bryant Street

Brannan Street

The Embarcadero

M

SOMA

80

7th Street

8th Street

Townsend Street

King Street

Pacific Bell Park

M

M

M

101

101

9th Street

10th Street

M

Berry Street

101

280

SOMA (South of Market)

Sacramento Street
California Street
Bush Street
Post Street
Geary Street

Powell Street
Kearny Street

Financial District

Union Square

Market Street

Van Ness Avenue
Polk Street
Larkin Street
Hyde Street
Turk Street

Civic Center/ Tenderloin

101

101

101

4th Street
5th Street
6th Street
7th Street
8th Street
9th Street
10th Street

3rd Street

1st Street
2nd Street

Mission Street
Howard Street
Main Street
Fremont Street
Bay Bridge

The Embarcadero

SOMA

Folsom Street
Harrison Street
Bryant Street
Brannan Street
Townsend Street
King Street

80

Pacific Bell Park

Berry Street

280

17th Street
Mission

Mariposa Street

Pennsylvania Avenue
Indiana Street

20th Street

101

101

Mission Street
South Van Ness
Harrison Street
Potrero Avenue

N

Potrero Hill

Mission, Castro, & Upper Market

Hayes Street
Fell Street
Oak Street
Haight Street

Haight

Buena Vista Park

Castro Street

Duboce Avenue

Market Street

M

M

M

17th Street

Mission

17th Street

M

Castro/ Upper Market

20th Street

Dolores Street

Guerrero Street

South Van Ness

Mission Street

Harrison Street

24th Street

M

25th Street

Noe Valley

Glen Canyon Park

Bernal Heights

N

Glen Park

San Jose Avenue

101

9th Street

10th Street

101

Haight, Pacific Heights, & The Marina

Marina Green

Fort Mason

Palace
of Fine Arts

N

The Presidio

Lombard Street

101

**Marina/Pacific
Heights**

Divisadero Street

Steiner Street

Laguna Street

Gough Street

Franklin Street

Washington Street

Clay Street

Sacramento Street

California Street

Pine Street

Bush Street

Presidio Street

**Western
Addition**

Divisadero Street

Golden Gate Avenue

Fulton Street

Alamo Square
Park

Hayes Street

Fell Street

Oak Street

Stanyan Street

Clayton Street

Masonic Street

Haight

Haight Street

Dubace Avenue

Castro Street

Golden Gate
Park

Buena Vista
Park

Market Street

M

Landmarks & Destinations

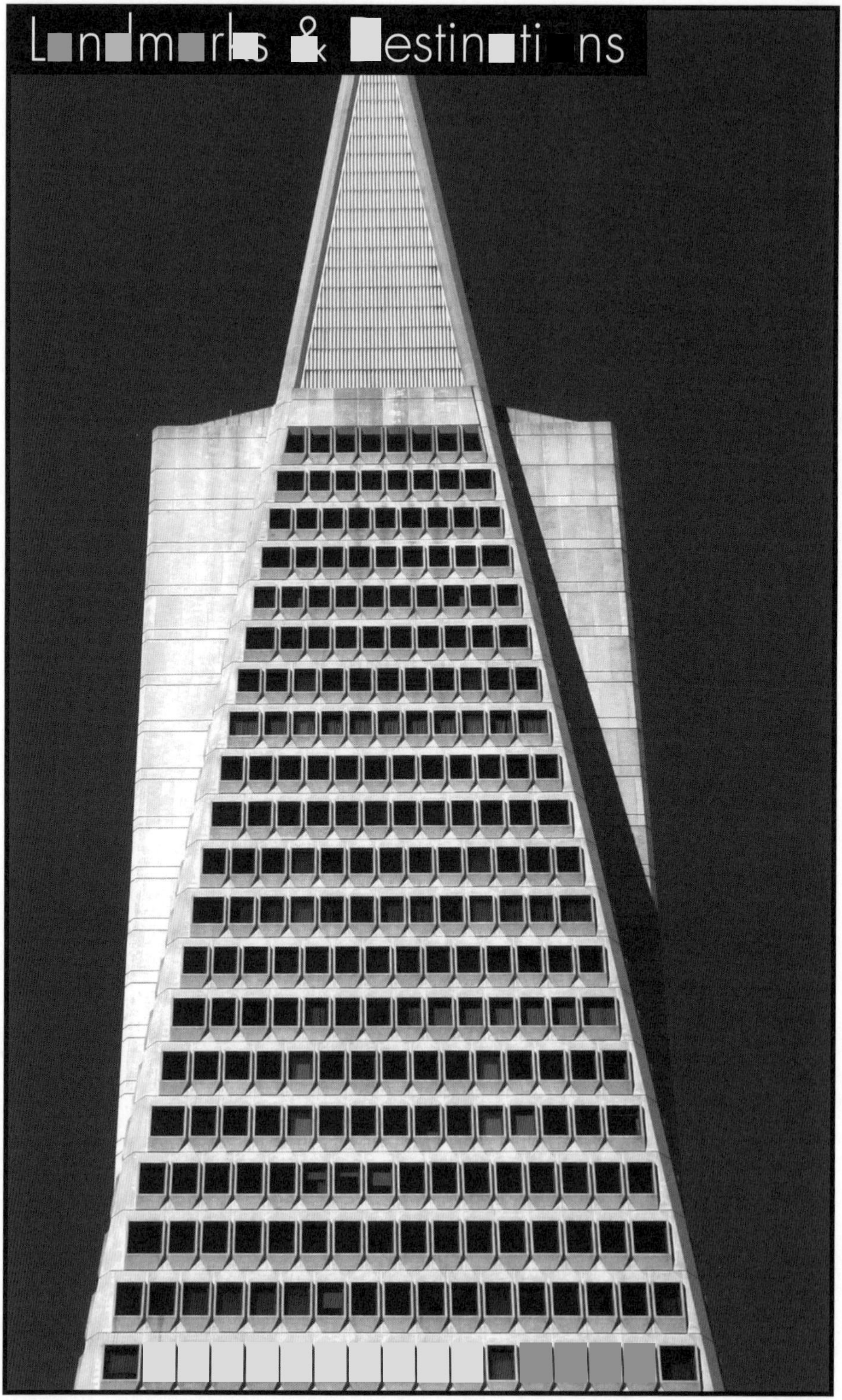

St. Francis of Assisi, patron saint of animals and the environment, and the city's namesake, has probably rolled over in his grave a few times since the small settlement of Yerba Buena cove boomed into the heart of the Gold Rush that the Chinese named "Gold Mountain." Earthquakes, fires, and roller-coaster economies have shaken up this city over and over again.

Photo: Kenneth C. Zirkel

As the Street Turns

Known as the world's most crooked street, **Lombard Street** was built in 1920 to deal with the extreme steepness of the hill. The eight-turn street, which is located between Hyde and Leavenworth, faces tough competition with **Vermont Street** (between 20th and 22nd) in Potrero Hill. Although Vermont only has six turns, the turns are supposedly sharper, but we've never measured.

The views up here among the flower gardens might be stunning but the street's past isn't so rosy. Pat Montandon, a San Francisco socialite in the 1960s, lived at the **1000 Lombard Street Mansion**, and believes that a curse put on the house by an angry tarot card reader during one of her famous parties ruined her "perfect" life. Her book, *The Intruders*, tells the story of the curse and the deaths that followed, including the mysterious death of her friend, Mary Louise Ward.

Ward was found dead in bed after a fire that destroyed part of the house. It's said that her death was not caused by the fire but was due to "undetermined causes." Chains and locks were found on the door inside the room.

Tourists flock to **Fisherman's Wharf** and **Ghirardelli Square** looking for clam chowder served in sourdough bread bowls, sweet chocolate, and sea lions. But little do they know that the real attraction in the area is hidden behind a man-made bush of eucalyptus leaves.

David Johnson, aka "Bushman," has been sitting behind his bush since 1980 yelling "ugga-bugga" to visitors walking by. The goal: to make people laugh, and get paid. Bushman, who started the first shoeshine business on Market Street, made a career change when the competition in shining shoes became too fierce. Rumor has it that Bushman is a proud taxpayer and reports an average of $60,000 in yearly income. Anyone interested in becoming the first Bushwoman?

When done perusing the shops and watching the group of seals that call the Wharf home, head over to the **Cannery** *(2801 Leavenworth St.)* for a cup of coffee and some antique shopping. The building, formerly a Del Monte peach cannery, suffered a fire in 2002 which not only did physical damage, but also hurt the shops' business because of false headlines in the newspapers indicating that the building had been completely destroyed.

SWIMMING WITH THE DEAD

After a law that prohibited cemeteries within city limits was passed, all tombs and bodies were dug up and transported out of the city. Graves and tombstones from the **Odd Fellows Cemetery** were taken out in 1901 and used to build the **Aquatic Park** sea wall *(Fisherman's Wharf at Jefferson and Hyde, 415-541-5644)*. Some of these grave markers can also be found at the foot of the Golden Gate Bridge near **Fort Mason**. Next time you're looking at a nice rock in these areas, look closer, there may be a name and date inscribed....

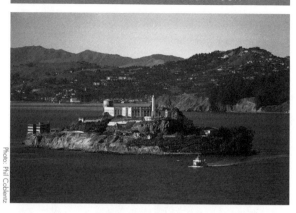

World's Most Famous Prison

Photo: Phil Coblentz

FOREVER IN BLUE JEANS

Known for its Holocaust-inspired piece of art depicting a pile of dead bodies behind one survivor holding onto a barbed-wire fence looking at the Golden Gate Bridge with determination, the **Legion of Honor** museum attracted curious visitors when in 1993, about 300 skeletons from the Gold Rush era — two of them still holding rosaries, others wearing Levi's blue jeans — were dug up from what appears to be an old pauper's graveyard. Some experts say another 11,000 bodies might still lie underneath the museum grounds.

34th Ave. and Clement St., Lincoln Park, 415-863-3330, thinker.org

Once the strongest fortress in the west, **Alcatraz** was built to protect San Francisco from foreign invaders. It was used mostly during the Civil War, and when the military left it, the island stronghold became one of the world's most famous prisons. Celebrity prisoners, an escape-proof reputation, and stories of the hardest inmates' extreme isolation fired the public imagination. Among others, D Block was home to Al Capone, George "Machine Gun" Kelly, Robert Stroud (aka the "Birdman of Alcatraz"), and Morton Sobell.

A good example of the phrase "it's not who you are but who you know that's important," Sobell was sentenced to 30 years for helping Julius and Ethel Rosenberg, the infamous Communist spies who were executed (under a cloud of anti-semitism, some say) in 1953. He spent four of those years at Alcatraz and now is living in San Francisco.

As Clint Eastwood's movie *Escape from Alcatraz* showed, some escaped the "unescapable" prison. A total of 36 prisoners were involved in attempts. Seven were shot and killed, two drowned, five were unaccounted for, the rest recaptured. In June 1962, Frank Morris and the Anglin brothers successfully escaped the prison, but no one knows if the men made it across the Bay.
nps.gov/alcatraz

If there is one must-see landmark here, it's definitely the **Golden Gate Bridge**. Named one of the seven wonders of the world, the bridge is the symbol of San Francisco. Construction started in 1933 and it opened to great fanfare in May 1937. Although there was much to celebrate on opening day, the years prior to it were not without problems. It's said that **Joseph Strauss**, the man who was given credit for the construction, spent many hours trying to minimize the work of his coworkers so that he would go down in history as the sole designer.

His coworkers, Charles Alton Ellis and Leon Moissief, were largely indifferent to his showboating until Strauss, not happy with some attention Ellis was receiving, requested he go on an indefinite vacation. After Ellis was eventually fired, he spent five months going over initial calculations because he thought that the bridge wasn't being built to a safe enough standard. He wrote a letter to the *San Francisco Chronicle* explaining how Strauss's plan for the bridge would not work (Strauss was not amused), but the construction went on. During construction, Strauss disappeared and rumor had it that he had a nervous breakdown. He divorced his long-time wife and remarried a much younger woman, a singer. When the Golden Gate Bridge finally opened, an exhausted Strauss moved to Arizona to get some rest. He died there, of a stroke, nearly one year after the bridge was completed.

Although his plan to build a statue of himself near the bridge wasn't approved at the time of construction, his widow came back to the site and was able to grant his wish. The statue, located near toll plaza 9 (on the left), reads, "Joseph B. Strauss, 1870-1938, 'The Man Who Built the Bridge.'"
415-921-5858, goldengate.org

LOOK OUT
Made famous in Hitchcock's movie *Vertigo*, **Fort Point** *(nps.gov/fopo)* is located at the foot of the Golden Gate Bridge. It was constructed by the US Army Corps of Engineers between 1853 and 1861 to prevent any hostile fleet from entering San Francisco Bay. Needless to say, the soldiers there waited for a long time.

FERRY GOOD FARE

From the Gold Rush until the 1930s, arrival by ferryboat was the only way travelers and commuters could get to San Francisco. The place where all this happened was the **Ferry Building**, at the foot of Market Street.

In 2003, after major renovations, the building reopened to host the **Farmers Market**, is now home to more than 20 bakeries, cheese shops, and restaurants. Speaking of restaurants, foodies are fawning over the city's new fave: **Slanted Door** (slanteddoor.com).

Offering a cornucopia of organic vegetables, meats, fruits, cheeses, and pastries, the Ferry Building is a great place to sample fresh Californian cuisine.
1 Ferry Building, 415-693-0996, ferrybuildingmarketplace.com

Today, the **Golden Gate Bridge** is the biggest suicide magnet in the world. The first suicide took place only five months after the opening, and since then there may have been more than 2,000 casualties – although officials stopped publishing the numbers after the 997th jump because the California Highway Patrol feared it would encourage people to try to be the 1,000th suicide.

The California Highway Patrol had good reason to fear a "final countdown." In 1973, TV crews ghoulishly hung out by the bridge waiting for the 500th suicide. Newspapers ran countdowns and bars took bets. As number 1,000 approached in 1995, a disc jockey offered a case of Snapple to the victim's family.

A 1977 rally supporting the construction of an anti-suicide barrier brought a local minister to make a speech on the bridge to his 600 followers – each protester wore an armband that bore the names of suicide victims. He explained the powers of the bridge by saying that the Golden Gate was, "a symbol of human ingenuity, technological genius, but social failure." That minister, the **Reverend Jim Jones**, made the news again 18 months later in Guyana when he ordered his followers to kill themselves by drinking poisoned Kool-Aid.

On average, one person leaps from the bridge every two weeks. They almost always jump from the Bay-facing side; it's been theorized that many want the beautiful view of the city as their final tableau. Famous suicides off the bridge include Roy Raymond in 1993, founder of Victoria's Secret, and Duane Garrett in 1995, a Democratic fundraiser and a friend of Al Gore's.

Those who don't die from the 220-foot fall – which once in a very great while happens – usually say that when they are mid-air they suddenly realize they could have gotten past their problems, and some go on to lead what they describe as deeply spiritual lives. Whether this last-moment realization happens to all jumpers, we'll never know.

In 2003, on the day the US launched the Iraq

invasion, an Iraqi-American, Paul Alarab, decided to go to the Golden Gate Bridge and stand on the ledge until TV crews arrived so he could make an anti-war statement. When the Highway Patrol came to the rescue, they recognized him as the man who in 1988 had threatened to jump to publicize the plight of the handicapped and the elderly. This time, the TV crews weren't quick enough for Alarab; he jumped to his death, though by some accounts, he fell accidentally.

In January 2005, the bridge made the news again when Eric Steel explained to the press that he had been using his filming permit on the Golden Gate Bridge to document people jumping off. An ongoing debate on whether anti-suicide barriers should be installed is now back on the table. Proponents say it will save lives; those against the barriers say that a few foolish people shouldn't force new construction that will mar the beauty of the bridge.

The Wild Parrots of Telegraph Hill

In the 1990s, in an effort to learn a little bit about birding while house-sitting on Telegraph Hill, Mark Bittner (then a street musician) put out some seeds and waited for birds to show up. "I was baffled when I saw the wild cherry-head parrots come eat the seeds," he told us.

While most San Franciscans are still trying to guess where the loud flock comes from, Bittner says he knows for a fact that the first birds he saw were pets that had been let free or had escaped because they all had quarantine bracelets.

The birds feed at the bottom of the hill closer to the Bay, but as Bittner says, "The Wild Parrots of Telegraph Hill sounds more romantic than the Wild Parrots of Embarcadero." Another flock of birds can be spotted (or heard) on Dolores St. and in Potrero Hill. "They used to come to Telegraph Hill, but the cherry-head parrots kicked them out," he says. Damn cherry-heads.

PEACE ON THE STREETS
On September 8, 1951, the San Francisco Peace Treaty was signed, marking the end of the occupation in Japan and the hostilities in the Asia-Pacific. Today, even when "yogatestors" are not practicing yoga on Market Street to encourage peace in Iraq, there is the **Gandhi memorial statue** in front of the Ferry Building and the **Martin Luther King, Jr. Memorial Waterfall** at the Yerba Buena Center for the Arts *(701 Mission St., 415-978-2787, yerbabuenaarts.org)*

A FOUNTAIN OF REMEMBRANCE

April 18 marks the anniversary of the 1906 earthquake that destroyed most of San Francisco, and every year at 5:13 am, San Franciscans gather at **Lotta's Fountain** (at the intersection of Market, Geary, and Kearny Sts.) as many families and friends did the day of the quake. The fountain was donated to the city in 1875 by Lotta Crabtree, a popular vaudeville performer. But after almost 100 years, memories get a little hazy; mayor Gavin Newsom mistakenly referred to the "1908 earthquake" at the 2004 reunion.

On a sunny day, nothing beats the view from the 210-foot **Coit Tower** (the tall structure on the left in photo). From here, you can look down to the hilly streets of North Beach, the sailboats of the Marina, and the magnificent Golden Gate Bridge.

Rumor has it, though the architects always denied it, that the tower was designed to resemble a fire hose nozzle in memory of Lillie Coit and her fondness for the local fire department. A San Francisco resident who grew up on Telegraph Hill, Coit lost two of her school friends in a fire. One afternoon, she helped out the short-staffed Knickerbocker Engine Company No. 5. To thank her for her work, they made her their mascot and gave her a gold diamond-studded fireman's badge reading "No. 5" which she wore proudly until she passed away in 1929.

Wearing her honorary uniform, Coit smoked cigars and played poker with the men all night – despite the fact that "ladies" didn't do such things at that time. She donated a large part of her considerable savings "to be expended in an appropriate manner for the purpose of adding to the beauty of the city which I have always loved."

Before you head to the tower, put on a comfortable pair of walking shoes for the steep hike, or catch the #39 Muni bus, which goes to the base of the tower every 20 minutes from Washington Square.
1 Telegraph Hill Blvd., 415-362-0808

A Legendary Building

Built in 1853 by Henry Halleck, **Montgomery Block** was the city's first fire-proof building and the highest one west of the Mississippi. Although the building first attracted lawyers and professionals, the tenants quickly changed to artists and writers.

The building's history is the stuff of legend. In 1856, James King, the owner and editor of the *Evening News Bulletin*, was shot dead on Montgomery Street by Supervisor James P. Casey. By lengthy investigation, the journalist had found out about Casey's shady past in Sing Sing Prison. Shortly thereafter, **Coppa's** restaurant witnessed many a drunken night where it's said that writer Isabel Fraser once got up on a ladder and was christened "Queen of Bohemia." And one day at a Montgomery Block sauna, Mark Twain, a neighborhood regular, met a fireman named Tom Sawyer, whose name he used in his 1876 novel, *The Adventures of Tom Sawyer*. Among the tenants of the building were native San Franciscan Jack London, Bret Harte, Ina Coolbrith, Robert Louis Stevenson, and photographer Arnold Genthe.

The Montgomery Block survived the 1906 earthquake and great fire, but was eventually torn down and replaced by a parking lot in 1959.

APOCALYPSE HERE

Owned by **Francis Ford Coppola**, the **Sentinel** is the only flatiron building in the city. It was built before the 1906 earthquake by Abe Ruef, a corrupt politician who ended up in San Quentin Penitentiary, in part due to the constant criminal accusations published by Fremont Older, editor of the *San Francisco Bulletin*. The building survived the earthquake and fire, but Abe's days were over quickly.

The Sentinel was then home to the Kingston Trio, a band that made folk music a national genre in the 1950s. The building now houses Coppola's studio American Zoetrope. The voice-overs for *Apocalypse Now* were recorded here as was the Grateful Dead's "Anthem of the Sun." Check out the ground floor **Café Niebaum-Coppola** (*916 Kearny St., 415-291-1700*), where it's possible to catch a glimpse of *The Godfather* auteur around lunchtime.

From Sky to Sea

After the Golden Gate Bridge, the most recognizable structure in the city's skyline is the pyramid-shaped **Transamerica Building**. Today, the 48-floor building houses offices and an observation deck that is now closed to the public for security reasons. Cameras on the deck facing the four cardinal points let visitors on the street look into the glass-walled lobby and see the view on four large monitors 24 hours a day.

The area that the pyramid sits on, formerly known as the Montgomery Block or the Monkey Block, is considered the center of the Financial District. Before William Peireira and Associates began building the controversial structure in 1970, the area was the center of **Barbary Coast**, a Bohemian haven. While reading the lobby plaque on the building's history, keep in mind that some people (fictional and real) have claimed that the Transamerica Pyramid is proof that San Franciscans are the reincarnated citizens of the **Lost City of Atlantis**. Supposedly, a pyramid loomed over Atlantis before it fell into the sea, and this is why a certain type of person seems to feel at home in San Francisco – all the denizens of San Francisco/Atlantis are reassembling themselves on the edge of a peninsula before an earthquake dumps it all into the water again.

In 1970, when the construction of the Transamerica Building started, many locals protested what they saw as a disgrace to the city's skyline. John Burton, now a state senator, went so far as to say that the pyramid would "rape the skyline." Today, even though it has become a symbol of the city, residents still love to hate the building, saying that for all its notoriety it is completely out of place and not particularly nice to look at. The fifth floor is the largest: 145 feet per side and 21,025 square feet of space; the smallest floor is only 45 feet per side and 2,025 square feet of space.
600 Montgomery St., tapyramid.com

BEFORE THE TIME OF PYRAMIDS

Across the street from "the pyramid" stands the **original Transamerica Building** where San Francisco's first Jewish religious service took place in 1849. A Star of David can still be seen on the fire escape. The building now houses the Church of Scientology.
4 Columbus Ave.

ANOTHER PYRAMID?

You'd never guess it from the outside, but the John C. Portman-designed **Hyatt Regency San Francisco** *(5 Embarcadero Center, 415-788-1234, sanfranciscoregency. hyatt.com)* is an architectural gem on the inside. Visitors who go up the escalators to the lobby will find themselves in the center of a stunning (and some say, dizzying) pyramid-shaped open-air space.

A 40-foot-tall "Eclipse" sculpture is the centerpiece of the lobby, and is best seen while shooting up or down one of the glass-enclosed elevators. Up on the 20th floor is the city's only revolving rooftop restaurant, the **Equinox** *(415-291-6619)*, reservations recommended.

Grace Chapel was built in the Gold Rush year of 1849 and was yet another landmark to burn down in 1906. The Crocker family, relatives of Charles Crocker the railroad baron/banker, gave their ruined Nob Hill property for a **Grace Cathedral** diocesan building which took its name and founding congregation from the nearby parish.

The Chartres Cathedral-inspired church is a grandiose structure that presides over Nob Hill. Walking up the stairs, visitors can see an outdoor labyrinth on the right where everyone is welcome to walk around and meditate. Another labyrinth is found inside the cathedral. Even for those who don't go to church, the building's murals are worth a look as they depict the history of the city. Grace Cathedral is where actors David Arquette and Courteney Cox got married.

100 California St., 415-749-6300, gracecathedral.org

Maiden Lane and the Barbary Coast may be home to upscale stores, hotels, spas, and the country's first garage under a park, but the dark alleys were first home to the city's most popular brothels, where women hung out their windows bare-chested to entice the rich men walking by. From the **Union Square** area to what is now the **Embarcadero** was where hard-drinking lonely sailors came looking for company. Some unlucky lover-boys were "shanghaied" – drugged, kidnapped, and put on board a ship for compulsory service – and woke up at sea half-way to China; others, such as Calico Jim, made extra money by "shanghaing" others. In the 1890s, Calico Jim was famous for having shanghaied six policemen who had been sent, one by one, to arrest him. He left the city shortly afterwards. At the end of a long search, one of the police officers found the "crimp" in Chile and shot him six times, once for each of the men in blue he sent to China. Today, you'll find classy stores and the biggest names in fashion on Maiden Lane. Worth peeking into is the **Xanadu Gallery** *(140 Maiden Lane, folkartintl.com)*, the only Frank Lloyd Wright building in the city, said to have been his model for the Guggenheim Museum in New York.

HIP IN THE SQUARE

Jackson Square is the center of interior design, über-hip furniture makers, and upscale apartment buildings. This low-key area is so stylin' that even the fire station sign has a funky-cool sign.

In the Jackson Square neighborhood, one can still find **Domingo Ghirardelli's old chocolate factory** standing at 415-417 Jackson St. (somehow it survived the 1906 earthquake). It's currently used as an antique gallery.

Celebrities love San Francisco, so it's no surprise that celebrity hotel stories abound. Perched on top of Nob Hill overlooking the city is the **Fairmont San Francisco**, *(950 Mason St., 415-772-5000, fairmont.com/sanfrancisco)*, one of the most luxurious hotels around. This is the only place where each of the city's cable car lines meet and it was the first hotel to reopen after the 1906 earthquake and fire that destroyed most of the city.

The guests may be well-mannered today, but that didn't stop **Orson Welles** from causing trouble the night of the premiere of *Citizen Kane*, which contained some thinly-veiled stabs at newspaper mogul **William Randolph Hearst**. As Welles put it at the time: "I found myself alone with him [Hearst] in an elevator in the Fairmont

Hotel on the night *Kane* opened in San Francisco. He and my father had been chums, so I introduced myself and asked him if he'd like to come to the opening of the picture. He didn't answer. As he was getting off at his floor, I said, 'Charles Foster Kane would have accepted!'"

For a room closer to Union Square and its shopping, head over to the **Westin St. Francis Hotel** *(335 Powell St., 415-774-0124, westinstfrancis.com)*. A favorite of classy aristocrats, the hotel at one time offered a money-washing service. Guests could leave their coins to be washed and their bills to be ironed while out on the town.

It's here that the corpulent silent movie star **Fatty Arbuckle** enjoyed a wild night with Virginia Rappe and Maude Delmont, two young ladies of questionable character. Rappe died four days later and Delmont spread the rumor that Fatty Arbuckle had raped and

GLIDE ON IN

Bono of U2 fame once told **Time Magazine**, "There's one church that if I was living close by I'd definitely be in the congregation: **Glide Memorial**. Rev. Cecil Williams there looks after the homeless, gays, straights; he marched with Martin Luther King, Jr., he's funny as hell — pardon the pun — and you can get an HIV test during the service. Now that's my kind of church."

For anyone looking for a slice of San Francisco spirit, Glide Memorial Church is the place to get it. Starting in the 1960s, Rev. Williams and his wife, Janice Mirikitani, created a safe place for people of all walks of life. It was here that city residents who came together against the Vietnam War were joined by Bill Cosby, Angela Davis, and Bill Graham. It was here too that Randolph Hearst pleaded for help in securing the release of his daughter Patty who was kidnapped by the Symbionese Liberation Army. And Glide Memorial opened its doors to mourners when the death of gay activist and City Supervisor Harvey Milk was announced.
330 Ellis St., 415-674-6000, glide.org

CIVIC AND GAY PRIDE

City Hall was built by Arthur Brown Jr., who also designed San Francisco's War Memorial Opera House, Veterans Building, Temple Emanuel, Coit Tower, and 50 United Nations Plaza. Famous marriages include: Joe DiMaggio and Marilyn Monroe, Diego Rivera and Frida Kahlo (remarrying), and thousands of gay and lesbian couples who stood in line for hours to get married legally during the "Winter of Love" in 2004, including Rosie O'Donnell and Kelli Carpenter.

crushed Rappe; reports surfaced that Arbuckle, unable to perform, had raped the woman with a Coca-Cola or wine bottle. As a result, the movie star went through several criminal trials that eventually ended his career.

Modern-day celebrity sleuths can spot stars at the **Hotel Triton** (342 Grant Ave., 415-394-0500, hoteltriton.com), or sleep with them, in a way. There are seven suites designed by the celebrities who usually stay there – Jerry Garcia, Red Hot Chili Peppers (see photo of their toilet), and Woody Harrelson, among others. Whether it's the Red Hot Room or Woody's Oasis, hotel guests are in for a treat.

It's also good for the eyes, man. There are pictures of celebrities in all the suites – including one of pot-advocate Harrelson getting arrested, perhaps for the time he chained himself to the Golden Gate Bridge to protest logging.

For a more rough-around-the-edges look, the **Phoenix Hotel** (601 Eddy St., 415-776-1380, jdvhospitality.com/hotels/hotel/12) is a favorite of Sinead O'Connor, Faye Dunaway, and the late Kurt Cobain. A while back, a mix-up in reservations almost had Deborah Harry sleeping in the room John F. Kennedy Jr. had booked for the same night. The Blondie singer admitted to the press that she was a little disappointed it didn't happen.

As an added bonus to staying in this or any other Joie de Vivre hotel, guests can tour the city with a local "Golden Gate Greeter" for free (goldengategreeter.com). Although the name sounds vanilla, we're pretty sure the greeters aren't.

Photo: courtesy of National Park Service

FORGET IT, IT'S CHINATOWN
Today's **Chinatown** has more tourists on the street than local residents, and that's exactly what Look Tin Eli, a Chinese merchant, wanted. The great earthquake of 1906 wiped out the original Chinatown where Chinese immigrants had been living and doing business since the Gold Rush years, and city officials were interested in reclaiming the land. But Eli was able to change their minds by proposing the construction of a new Chinatown, one that would include Victorian buildings with pagodas and other Asian decorations to attract tourists. How did he convince them? By telling city officials that Caucasian architects should do all of the design work.

The Exclusion Act and other discriminatory laws made the "Chinamen" want to stick together. Although the ratio of men to women in the area was 20 to one, Chinatown residents were almost completely self-sufficient. The neighborhood had restaurants, grocery stores, laundry outlets, and even a telephone exchange called the **China 5**.

The operators there, all of whom had to speak five dialects of Chinese, knew residents' phone numbers, addresses, and professions by heart because the Chinese believed it was disrespectful to call people by number.

China 5 operators worked in the building that now houses the **Bank of Canton** (743 Washington St.). To see a switchboard from the China 5, head to the **Pacific Bell Museum** at 140 New Montgomery. The building is worth a look too.

Three of the old telephone booths can still be found today. You'll find one near the corner of Jackson and Stockton, another near the corner of Grant and California (next to Old St. Mary's Church), and another one on Grant between Clay and Washington Streets.

The Mission Was Possible

Famous for its bars and clubs yet virtually ignored by out-of-towners, the **Mission** is home to the city's strongest lesbian and Hispanic communities. Central to it is Mission San Francisco de Asis, commonly called **Mission Dolores**, which could be considered the very first landmark of the city, considering that this town was settled and built around it.

Anza and Father Font, after searching the perfect spot for the mission for days, finally arrived at a lovely creek near an Indian village in June 1776. They named the creek the Arroyo de los Dolores since it was Friday of Sorrows. The resulting church celebrated the first Christian service in the city on June 29, 1776, which now marks the anniversary of the city of San Francisco.

For a chance to meet some of the founders of the city, check out the numerous graves in the back of the church, next to the museum. A visitor to this cemetery is bound to recognize some street names on the tombstones.

The Ohlone and other Native American tribes helped build the mission and decorated it with natural dye paintings. These were eventually covered with an ornate altar and were almost forgotten until recently, when an architect and an artist uncovered some of the paintings and displayed digital photographs of them for the public to see.

3221 16th St., 415-621-8203, missiondolores.org

OPIUM GHOSTS
Chinatown's Spofford and **Ross Alleys** were home to the most popular brothels, bars, and opium dens. Spofford Alley is also where an exiled Dr. Sun Yat-sen wrote the Chinese constitution that would lead to the 1911 revolution which ended the Qing Dynasty. Sun became the first president of the Republic of China in 1912; he died in 1925 and has since become a heroic symbol of modern China.

Opium dens may be a thing of the past, but **Li Po** bar in Ross Alley has kept the atmosphere alive with its dark creepy rooms, stories of the ghosts of opium junkies that still wander the place looking for a fix, and a special herb-laced shot of liquor that is sure to raise the spirits in one way or another.

Photo: San Francisco Convention and Visitors Bureau

The **Castro Theatre** *(429 Castro St., 415-621-6120, castrotheatresf.com)* started as a regular neighborhood theater a few doors down from its present location; it's now bcomes a cult theater for old movie and queer cinema buffs.

Weekend movie-goers can enjoy the live organ music at every show in the grandesque décor. What many people don't know is that according to Rob Epstein, producer of the film *The Celluloid Closet*, some of the ashes of the late Vito Russo (author of the book on which the documentary was based) rest in the theater's walls. With his book, a survey of how LGBT people had been portrayed in Hollywood movies, Russo became a key author in the gay rights movement. He died of AIDS in 1990.

UNDERGROUND SAN FRANCISCO

The 1906 earthquake and fire may have buried the much-talked-about hidden tunnels of Chinatown where opium was supposedly dealt and girls hid to avoid becoming prostitutes, but one can still go underground in San Francisco these days. The **Aquarium of the Bay** *(Pier 39, Embarcadero at Beach Street, 1-888-732-3483, aquariumofthebay.com)* offers visitors a chance to walk underwater through 300 feet of clear tunnels and see more than 23,000 aquatic animals from all over the Bay.

A Triangle to Remember

During the Nazi regime, Jewish prisoners in concentration camps were forced to wear the yellow star, a perversion of the Star of David. Less known were the black triangles worn by lesbians, prostitutes, and women who refused to bear children, and the pink triangles that marked gay men.

The centerpiece of **Pink Triangle Park** is made of 15 granite pylons inlaid with a pink triangle; the pylons join with others to create a large triangle. The base of the monument is oriented toward **Harvey Milk Plaza** *(SW corner of Castro and Market Sts.)* and its rainbow flag. The park is located at the intersection of Market, Castro, and upper 17th Streets *(evpa.org).*

OUR SAVIOR, THE FIRE HYDRANT

At the SW corner of Church and 20th streets is a gold-painted fire hydrant where an annual celebration, which includes a new coat of gold paint, takes place each April. Some may find the ritual odd, but this little fire hydrant saved the neighborhood in 1906 when the huge earthquake and fire flattened many of the nearby neighborhoods. Residents say that a fresh coat of paint and some respect is the least they can do for this local hero.

A Flag for Pride

The **rainbow flag** first appeared in the San Francisco Gay and Lesbian Freedom Day Parade in 1978. Borrowing symbolism from the hippie movement and black civil rights groups, San Francisco artist **Gilbert Baker** designed the rainbow flag in response to a need for a symbol that could be used year after year. Baker and thirty volunteers hand-stitched and hand-dyed two huge prototype flags for the parade.

The flags had eight stripes, each color representing a component of the community: hot pink for sex, red for life, orange for healing, yellow for sun, green for nature, turquoise for art, indigo for harmony, and violet for spirit.

The next year, Baker approached San Francisco Paramount Flag Company to mass-produce rainbow flags for the 1979 parade. Due to production constraints – such as the fact that hot pink was not a commercially-available color – pink and turquoise were removed from the design, and royal blue replaced indigo. This six-color version spread from San Francisco to other cities, and soon became the widely-known symbol of gay pride and diversity it is today. It is officially recognized by the International Congress of Flag Makers.

Still considered a transitioning neighborhood, the **Lower Haight** gets a bad reputation compared to its neighbor, Upper Haight. Nevertheless, **Alamo Square** is the place to go for a picture of the Victorian houses, known as the **Painted Ladies** or "Postcard Row." Chances are, anyone who has bought or received postcards from San Francisco has seen these houses. Some may also remember the area from the TV sitcom *Full House*, starring Bob Saget, John Stamos, and the Olsen twins.

One of the Painted Ladies, The **Shannon-Kavanaugh House**, at 722 Steiner St., can be rented for private parties and special events *(415-563-2727, shannon-kavanaugh.com)*.

Not a landmark per se, but a good example of the importance of community in the city, **908 Page St.** became a meeting place for protesters in the year 2000 when then 83-year-old Grace Wells, a resident since 1989, was told she needed to move out. The landlord claimed that they wanted to start a family and wanted to turn the apartments into one living area. With the help of Dean Preston, a Tenderloin Housing attorney, and the support of neighbors who protested in front of the house or put up posters on their windows that read "Don't Evict My Neighbor Grace," Wells was able to fight back. In April 2004, she moved out of the house, but not without a settlement.

OUR GOD, THE PHALLUS OF SHIVA

Around 1991, a gray concrete structure in the shape of a phallus appeared about 200 feet from John F. Kennedy Drive, across from the Rose Garden in Golden Gate Park. Many Hindus and other religious visitors started making pilgrimages to the city to pray and make offerings to what they believed was a representation of the god Shiva. The stone, an old traffic barrier, was removed in 1994 by Golden Gate Park officials.

Three miles long and a half-mile wide, **Golden Gate Park**, San Francisco's biggest open space, is famous for homeless encampments, the **AIDS Memorial Grove** *(aidsmemorial.org)*, and the Gathering of the Tribes: a Human Be-In concert on the Polo Grounds in 1967 that gelled the Flower Power movement.

Once a barren area full of sand dunes, the park was built in 1870 (designed by William Hammond Hall) to give residents a place to get away from the bustle of city life. Golden Gate Park is larger than Central Park; it has also been said that, as a result of John McLaren's (Hall's successor) correspondence with botanists and gardeners, the park has trees from every country in the world with only one exception: Bolivia (sometimes you don't get everything you want).

One of the most visited areas of the park is the **Japanese Tea Garden** and tea house *(415-752-4227)*, where Makoto Hagiwara invented the fortune cookie served with tea at the house starting in 1914. The tea garden was closed in 1942 when the Hagiwara family was sent to an internment camp.

The park is home to many things, including the **Conservatory of Flowers** *(415-666-7001, conservatoryofflowers.org)*; the **Queen Wilhelmina's Windmill** *(415-751-2766)*; and **Bison Paddock**, which was created after the city began a breeding program in the late 1800s to try to save the continent's largest land mammal from extinction.

MUSEUM MAGIC

For a walk in the park, a day at the **Exploratorium** *(3601 Lyon St., 415-674-2893, exploratorium.edu)* is hard to beat. For the best view of the Golden Gate Bridge, head to the **Palace of Fine Arts Theater** *(3301 Lyon St., 415-563-6504, palaceoffinearts.org)*. Built in 1915 of wood and plaster for the Panama-Pacific International Exposition, the site features a classical Roman rotunda with curved colonnades in a quiet park setting.

Other museums worth visiting include the **MOMA** *(151 Third St., 415-357-4000, sfmoma.org)*, the **Asian Art Museum** *(200 Larkin St., 415-581-3500, asianart.org)*, the **Mexican Museum**, which is currently located at Fort Mason Center, Building D but is in the process of moving *(415-202-9700, mexicanmuseum.org)*, the **Randall Museum** *(199 Museum Way, 415-554-9600, randallmuseum.org)*, and the **Chinese Historical Society of America** *(965 Clay St., 415-391-1188, chsa.org)*.

SAN FRANCISCO'S FRIENDLIEST GHOST

For a friendly ghost encounter, book room 410 at the **Queen Anne Hotel** *(1590 Sutter St., 1-800-227-3970, queenanne.com).* Formerly Ms. Mary Lake's School For Girls, the room is said to be haunted by the school's namesake. Lake was the daughter of James Fair, patriarch of the Fairmont Hotel family, silver baron, and U.S. senator.

When they rent you 410, they don't tell you this room is haunted. Why should they? "What's the worst that's going to happen? You might get tucked in under a cozy blanket," says Jim Fasbinder during his **Ghost Hunt** *(415-922-5590, sfghosthunt.com)* tour.

The Richmond is the "real Chinatown" where many of the newer Asian immigrants live. Now bustling, the Richmond, where the **Columbarium** crematorium is located, was decidedly quieter at one point.

The neighborhood was the final resting place for many San Franciscans until 1901, when housing pressures forced officials to uproot the dead to make more room for the living. When the bodies were moved, it caused a lot of upset – for both the living and the dead, some say.

The Richmond's residents – "long-term" would be a good way to describe them – were taken south of the city, to Colma. A law prohibiting cremations, and another prohibiting burials within the city were passed; and the Columbarium, built in 1898, was closed.

In 1980, the Neptune Society purchased the building and started renovations with the help of Emmit Watson, caretaker and on-site tour guide extraordinaire. Now the Columbarium houses the cremains of many national celebrities, like the Wells Fargo family and the Folgers coffee family, and was the first to accept AIDS patients in the 1980s. It's also the home of lesser-known local favorites such as Bobo the Jamaican bear, and the Tomato King and Queen.

The Tomato King gave Watson a tomato plant before he passed away. The caretaker placed two plastic tomatoes in front of the urns of the "King and Queen," and planted the tomato plant in the yard of the Columbarium.

Watson, with a thick New Orleans accent and warm, friendly demeanor, loves to show people around as long as he knows they're coming. He's especially proud of the tomato plant that's now grown into a small tomato bush. "Don't tell me there's no life at the cemetery," he says.

1 Loraine Court, 415-771-0717, neptune-society.com/index.html

SAN FRANCISCO'S RISING STARS

Sutro Tower is the tallest structure at 981 feet (its base stands 830 feet above sea level).

Transamerica Pyramid is the tallest building at 853 feet.

Mission Dolores is the oldest building in San Francisco.

According to the San Francisco Convention and Visitors Bureau, the celebrity attractions are: **Fisherman's Wharf**, **Chinatown**, **Golden Gate Bridge**, **Union Square**, and **cable cars**.

Japantown Lost – to Internment Camps

Although there is a concentration of "box" karaokes with private rooms and some great Japanese restaurants, **Japantown** was much bigger prior to World War II and the shame of internment camps. Today, "Nihonmachi" is the smallest district in the city, and although plans are underway to make the area more of a tourist destination, many visitors already come for great Japanese food, shopping, and Kabuki Springs spa.

The most recognizable landmark in Japantown is the **Peace Pagoda** at Post and Buchanan Streets, designed by world-renowned Tokyo architect Yoshiro Taniguchi and donated to Japantown in 1968 by San Francisco's sister city, Osaka. The original design was inspired by a set of round pagodas that existed more than 1,200 years ago in Nara, the ancient capital of Japan. The structure featured an eternal flame that was donated by the Sumida Shrine in Osaka and a reflecting fish-pond that encircled the Pagoda. However, due to leaking and other problems, the Pagoda was renovated in 2000 and some features were removed.

Say Cheese!

Although it's lost a lot after the "renovation," the **Cliff House** *(1090 Point Lobos, 415-386-3330, cliffhouse.com)* – a structure anchored on a cliff that hangs over the Pacific Ocean – still houses the only original-location camera obscura (a giant camera) in the country. The camera obscura is based on a 16th-century design by Leonardo da Vinci; several lenses project a 360-degree view of the outside, in this case the shoreline, onto a flat surface inside the giant camera you can stand in. The restaurant is the only structure left of what was once a popular amusement park complex, which included Playland at the Beach, the Sutro Baths, and the Musée Mécanique.

Sutro Baths and the Cliff House were built by **Adolph Sutro**, the first Jewish mayor of San Francisco. Complete with fountains, gardens, sculptures, and historical pieces from around the world, these "Tropical Winter Gardens" featured 100,000 feet of stained glass covering more than three acres of sculpted pools filled with fresh and salt water. But the success of the baths was short-lived and only ruins remain. Sutro also gave his name to the **Sutro Tower TV antenna** overlooking the city.

The original carousel that was once at the Playland can be seen today at **Yerba Buena Center for the Arts** *(701 Mission St. at 3rd St., 415-978-2787, yerbabuenaarts.org)*. As for the **Musée Mécanique**, it's now on the other side of town, at Pier 45. Look at the rocks and plants on the hill across the street from the Cliff House. If the scene looks eerily lifeless, that's because all those rocks and plants are made of plastic.

While in the nearby upscale Sea Cliff neighborhood, be sure to keep an eye out for celebrities. Robin Williams is probably the most famous resident.

AKA

To visitors, San Francisco is also known as:

7 by 7

Baghdad by the Bay

Fog City

Frisco

Gay by the Bay

Quake City

Shaky Town

The Golden Gate City

The only nicknames that won't annoy locals are: The City and SF.

Duboce Street – du-BOHSE

BART – bart (not B-A-R-T)

Bernal Heights – BUR-nel

Cesar Chavez Street – ceesar SHAH-vez

Clement Street – Cle-MENT

Haight Street – hate

Noe – NO-ee

Geary Street – GEEry

Gough Street – goff

The Name Game

San Francisco was first known as **Yerba Buena**, after a plant that grew in the area. As people settled in Yerba Buena cove, a group of settlers realized that the eastern shore of the bay would be a better location to start a city. They named the settlement Francisca after the name of the bay, while at the same time honoring one of the settler's wives whose name was Francisca. Yerba Buena residents soon wanted to be linked to Francisca. The two settlements joined forces and named their new town San Francisco.

homes, sweet homes

Although the style isn't from the area, San Francisco is known for its intricate and colorful Victorian homes. These houses were popular when the city was built because they were mostly made of redwood, a local material that was cheap and plentiful; redwood resists rot, termites, and fire, and is easily worked into different shapes. Here are some houses worth looking at:

Bregers Art House: *80 Brontë*, Gaudi-inspired house that is made to look like it's melting into the ground.

Defenestration Building: Art Howard and Sixth Streets (defenestration.org).

Haas-Lilienthal House: *2007 Franklin St.*, between Washington and Jackson.

Hallidie Building: *130-150 Sutter St.*

Malloch Apartments: *1360 Montgomery St.*

Nightingale House: *201 Buchanan St.*

Octagon House Museum: *2645 Gough St.*

Spreckels Mansion: *2080 Washington St.*, home of romance novelist Danielle Steele.

TV's *Party of Five* House: *2311 Broadway*, between Fillmore and Steiner.

Vollmer House: *1735-1737 Webster St.*, between Sutter and Bush.

Former Headquarters of the Vedanta Society: *2963 Webster St.*

Transportation

With two airports, a world-famous bridge, and the top-rated regional transit system in America, getting into or out of "The City," as locals call it, is a snap. The neighborhoods are made for walking, and when the hills start to get too much, public transportation is cheap and convenient. Cable cars, light rail, buses, and bicycles are all available for the visitor.

The "power to the people" character of the city is written into its transportation system – how cars, bicycles, and pedestrians get along, or don't, is a touchy and important subject.

Using a Car

Don't. If visitors can at all help it, they should not use a car in San Francisco. The **parking** situation is atrocious. If parking headaches are not enough, once mobile, a driver has to share the narrow, crowded road with every imaginable form of public transportation, angry bike messengers, and homeless residents who feel perfectly justified strolling into moving traffic. The pedestrian rules in this city, so it's probably best to stay one and leave the driving to others.

For those who insist, beware the constant four-way stops. The city tried to install a roundabout system, much to the dismay of residents and safety advocates. Although it's good in theory, the roundabouts were so small, and people so unfamiliar with them, that at many intersections there were near-accidents and people going the wrong direction on a daily basis.

Protesters took to holding picnics and get-togethers in the traffic circles before they were finally removed. Now, look alive – a rolling "California Stop" is not only an expression, but a way of what can only charitably be called driving.

Many of the downtown streets are one-way, and it's important to pay attention to the lane-markings; some lanes are reserved for buses and other forms of public transportation. Other lanes are left-turn/right-turn only, and there's very little given to out for people who want to change their minds.

Although **freeways** might make getting across town easier, San Francisco has seen many emotional "freeway revolts" by citizen's groups that did not want a highway-scarred city. When the 1989 earthquake crumbled the freeway that ran along the Embarcadero and hid the Ferry Building, few tears were shed for the symbol and agent of urban sprawl.

We Won't Get Burned Again

Keen-eyed travelers might notice that at some intersections of San Francisco, there are **circles outlined in brick**. According the San Francisco Fire Department (SFFD), in 1909 city officials wisely decided that there would always be enough water to fight fires. Due to the Great Quake of 1906 and the fires that started because of broken gas lines, fire fighters were forced to scrounge sewer water to try to stop the blazes.

Those circles at 100-plus intersections mark underground cisterns, most with a 75,000 gallon capacity. The Auxiliary Water Supply System (AWSS) is fed from a ten million gallon reservoir on top of Twin Peaks, along with some subsidiary tanks. Pumping stations and SFFD fire boats can suck water from the Bay into the AWSS in emergencies. One station is at the foot of Van Ness Avenue, the other at 2nd and Townsend Streets, the location of the SFFD Headquarters.

All AWSS hydrants have caps that are painted green.

STREETS OF SAN FRANCISCO: MILES OF ROAD

Freeways (including ramps and exchanges) 59

Streets 946

Park Streets (Golden Gate Park, McLaren Park, Presidio & Lincoln Parks) 65

Military Streets (Hunters Pt. Shipyard, Ft. Mason) 12

Private Streets 6

Total Miles 1088

Paved Street Area 195,000,000 sq ft

credit: www.bicycle.sfgov.org/ site/dpt_index.asp?id=13454#peds

Drugs and Cars

According to the most recent report from the San Francisco-based **Trauma Foundation** (tf.org), in the United States, motor vehicle accidents are the most common cause of injuries that lead to death. Not so in the City by the Bay. Our number one killer is drugs and other "poisonings," as they're officially classified. Here, death by car – as a passenger, driver, pedestrian, or bicyclist – is the number two cause of accidental death.

Parking (Dis)Services

Parking of the parallel variety makes up the vast majority of the scarce parking opportunities in the city – nerves of steel and a pro athlete's depth perception are required to back a car into a space that is barely big enough while cars and bicycles impatiently whiz by.

GET TO WORK!

How San Franciscans start their 9-to-5 grind:

Percent

Drive Alone 40.5

Public Transportation 31.1

Carpool 10.8

Walk 9.4

Work at Home 4.6

Bicycle 2.1

Motorcycle 0.9

Other 0.7

credit: www.bicycle.sfgov.org/ site/dpt_index.asp?id=13454#peds

Depending on the neighborhood, expect to either pay for parking (at least $20 per-day downtown on weekdays, less on weekends) or search for a long time for it.

Many downtown businesses will validate for parking, which can considerably cut down the expense. Most hotels have guest-only parking lots, and the better ones offer free spaces.

The closer to the ocean, the more parking spots there usually are. In a popular neighborhood on a Friday night, expect to keep circling, and circling, and circling some more – some residents have given up after 45 minutes and then parked so far away they took public transportation to their final destination. It is common to see cars make unexpected u-turns or suddenly drive down the street in reverse to nab a spot that's about to open up.

The Department of Parking and Traffic *(sfgov.org/site/dpt_index.asp)* has a wealth of information online for finding city-owned garages and the lowdown on parking in different neighborhoods. The "DPT" constantly roams the city looking for violations. Late on a Saturday night someone might be able to get away with bending the rules, but there are already too many DPT horror stories that start with, "I was just parked there

for two minutes when...."

Be sure to look long and hard at the signs, and never park in a bus zone. If you don't see a sign right away, it doesn't mean it isn't there. It often takes some looking to find the grimy, behind-a-tree, looks-like-a-crumpled-can-on-a-pole parking signs here. The cash-strapped city is more than happy to dole out tickets, boot a car, or, in a bus zone, tow it away and charge hundreds of dollars in fees to get it back. And because the city is so broke, putting up easy-to-spot signs hasn't been a priority.

Many streets downtown have truck-only and special tow-away zones during commute hours. Depending on the neighborhood, the street cleaners come by once or twice a week, and many locals circle the block a few times to get their spot back as soon as the street cleaning truck, escorted by a squad of DPT agents in little electric carts, move on.

Watch for colored curbs. Yellow and black curbs are for commercial vehicles or trucks only. Bus zones and wheelchair-friendly curb ramps are marked in red. Parking on or obstructing a sidewalk is a definite no-no and carries a $100 fine. Locals do it sometimes, but they also usually have a good sense of what they can get away with and for how long.

Most metered spaces have a 30- or 60-minute time limit to encourage parking turnover. It's necessary to pay the parking meters even on Saturdays here. According to the DPT, feeding the meter is illegal, but this rule doesn't seem too strictly enforced. If the meter is broken, the parking time limit still applies.

When parking on even the slightest hill, be sure to curb the wheels of the car inwards. Not doing so is a ticketable offense. Out-of-towners sometimes curb their wheels the wrong way; look at everyone else and remember that the purpose for this is so that if the emergency brake fails, the car rolls into the curb and (hopefully) stops there. Every year, a few cars roll away without their owners.

For anyone who thinks they can visit San Francisco, rack up the parking tickets, and just leave, be sure never to come back to the city with the same car. As the DPT website explains, those who don't pay their tickets risk getting their car booted at the next infraction: "In 1991,

STREETS AND AVENUES
The east side of San Francisco has numbered streets, the west side has numbered avenues.

STREET WISE

Steepest:
31.5 percent grade, Filbert Street between Leavenworth and Hyde Streets and 22nd Street between Church and Vicksburg Streets

Longest:
Mission Street, 7.29 miles

Widest:
Sloat Boulevard, 135 feet

Narrowest:
De Forest Way, 4.5 feet

First street constructed:
Grant Avenue, formerly known as "Calle De La Fundacion"

a year after Parking & Traffic was created by the voters, we began a traffic boot program to encourage individuals with multiple citations to pay their outstanding tickets."

A yellow chunk of metal locked to the wheel of your car definitely qualifies as encouragement.

Here are the hard numbers on parking tickets the city handed out in the fiscal year of 2002-2003.

Parking citations issued:
2,214,198 (yes, that's 2.2 million)

Number of parking control officers:
279

Number of vehicles towed for various parking violations:
60,399

Number of vehicles towed for non-payment of parking citations:
8,846

Number of vehicles booted:
5,520

Number of illegal disabled placards (fake handicap signs) confiscated:
936

Total parking ticket revenue:
$69,264,942

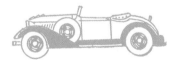

A LONG & WINDING ROAD

Winding along some of the most scenic coastline in Northern California, the **Pacific Coast Highway** is not for those afraid of heights or the impatient. But the visual payoff is spectacular. Depending on how you count it, Route 1, or the PCH as they say in Southern California, is between 120 and 139 miles long.

Cab Stories

An anonymous cabbie wrote a column in the *San Francisco Chronicle* entitled "**Night Cabbie**" for eight years, finally retiring in December 2004. In his farewell column he said he'd received mail from cabbies all over the world thanking him for chronicling a life roaming the streets. Some cabbies loved him, others hated him.

A few questioned whether he was even a real cabbie, noting that he would talk about making turns onto one-way streets that had him going the wrong direction. Whether it was jealousy or knowledge speaking, many people had a theory on who the night cabbie really was; a friend of a friend who knew somebody at "the Chron," a cabbie who used to be an English professor, a one-time dot-com millionaire. We've questioned many a cab driver on this, and we've heard a lot of ideas. Regardless who he really was, many people looked forward to his columns on Mondays, chronicling the sexy, bizarre, and just plain mean fares he'd pick up.

Another San Francisco writer who also drives a cab is **Brad Newsham**. He's written a few well-received travel books, including *Take Me With You*, detailing the 100-day journey that led to what is probably the longest cab ride in history. When world-wandering Newsham was 22, he made a note to himself that when he was "rich" one day, he'd give someone the chance to take a vacation in his country, much like he was able to take a vacation in theirs. When he was a little older and more financially stable, he spent 100 days traveling through Africa, Asia, and South America to find someone to

WIRED TO RIDE

Luxor Cabs and **Yellow Cab Cooperative** are giving their riders something to do while in their cabs. The two companies recently added free touch-screen terminals in their cars to allow passengers to check out information on local restaurants and entertainment.

And for those who choose Yellow Cab, having cash beforehand is no longer an issue; customers can purchase a prepaid Yellow Travel Card online and add money to it when necessary.
(*yellowcabsf.com*)

invite to the US for a one-month visit. He finally found Tony Tocdaan (a rice farmer and tour guide from the Philippines who had never left his country before).

When word of his project got out, another taxi driver lent him a cab and Newsham spent the next few months driving his friend from San Francisco to Washington, DC, with the meter running. They were received at foreign embassies, interviewed on national radio from the cab, and given a VIP White House tour.

When Newsham clicked off the meter at the end of his journey, the grand total was $20,644.90.

An account of the trip and of Newsham's current Backpack Nation project is at *backpacknation.org and bradnewsham.com.*

THREE NUMBERS, FREE INFO

No matter what kind of transportation information a traveler is looking for, **511** *(511.org)* is a toll-free way to get bus and train schedules, traffic updates, bridge toll information, etc. Most major cell phone providers allow callers to dial this number without additional charges.

Damn Electric-Guzzlers

San Francisco has another unique mode of transportation: **electric-gas hybrid SUV taxis**. "San Francisco is proud to be the first city in the United States using hybrid SUVs as taxis. Our city and county take great pride in being socially responsible, and adding these Escape Hybrids, the most fuel-efficient SUV available, is a big step toward making our civic transportation cleaner and more environmentally friendly," said Mayor Gavin Newsom at a ceremony outside City Hall in 2005. **Yellow Cab Cooperative** *(yellowcabsf.com)*, the city's biggest cab outfit, has ten of the environmentally-friendly SUVs to cart people around. **Luxor Cab** *(luxorcab.com)* has five.

The Mystery Jitney

Jess Losa, who runs **Jess LOSA Jitney 97** *(415-928-8016)* doesn't like to talk about his one-of-a-kind **jitney service**. Losa's jitney is the only one registered in the city of San Francisco.

Jitneys are typically private vehicles that go along a fixed route, like a cross between a bus and a taxi. But the word means different things in different places. We were eager to find out what a jitney is, exactly, but Losa was not forthcoming.

"What do I get? I've been in all the papers and I get nothing. If you want to talk to me, I take time to answer your questions, I must get something," says Losa, ever the entrepreneur.

We decided to save our money for a ride — all one really needs to know is that his jitney runs every ten minutes from in front of the Old Navy at 4th and Market Streets, between 4-7 p.m. on Fridays only.

GET BUSSED

For those who don't feel like talking to anyone, visit *nextbus.com* for up-to-the-minute information on buses around town.

On the Bus

If tolerance for drama is low, consider using the extensive light rail system supplemented by the occasional short hike. The **bus system** in San Francisco is used by all types of people, which is a mixed blessing. Unlike other US cities where taking the bus might be an iffy proposition in terms of personal safety, the bus in San Francisco is fairly safe, but can range anywhere from enjoyable to downright unpleasant. Even on a mellow bus ride, some character can step on and change the whole dynamic.

Here's a short laundry list of scenes from the bus: a man who asked for money and then put a live chicken on his head when refused; a woman who told the bus driver to stop and threw a trouble-maker out the door while other passengers cheered; a man adorned with a train of drying marijuana leaves who joyfully discussed the Second Coming and the ninety-nine-cent burger that was on sale at a nearby fast-food joint; and a woman who had a whole loaf of bread thrown at her from a few seats ahead, one slice at a time.

That said, one can also expect a sing-along, a date, or almost anything else to happen on the bus. The drivers might be a little curt at times, but they are amazingly helpful. For those who don't know where they're going (and haven't called the Muni information line, detailed on page 53), step up and tell the driver your destination and you'll either be told to get inside, or what bus you need and where to catch it. Also, most locals would prefer to help out while everyone is waiting at the bus stop instead of seeing one person hold up the whole production. People here are usually more than happy to help.

A PLEASANT REVOLUTIONARY

Born into slavery, **Mary Ellen Pleasant** made and lost a fortune, challenged the powerful, and was either vilified or loved by the public. At the end of her life, there were rumors of strange happenings at her house – the secret orgy kind. She's known as the Mother of Civil Rights in California because she won a lawsuit that allowed black people to ride the streetcars of San Francisco. She also established the Western terminus of the Underground Railroad, the loose network of abolitionists who helped slaves escape to free states. A memorial plaque is located at the site of her former home on the southwest corner of Bush and Octavia Streets.

The Cable Guy

Invented by an English immigrant who witnessed a gory horse-car accident, **cable cars** are synonymous with the city, and tourists and locals alike hang off of these historic contraptions at all hours. **Andrew Smith Hallidie**'s father was an inventor who had a patent in Great Britain for "wire rope" cable, and the junior Hallidie came to San Francisco in 1852, during the Gold Rush.

Hallidie's story is typically Californian. He spent much time trying to make a name for himself without much luck – a failed restaurant, career as a gold miner, and a couple of disagreements that almost cost him his life rank on the short-list of near misses – but finally hit it big once he stopped going on half-baked adventures and applied himself. He saw passengers on the Clay Street Hill Railroad riding his invention on August 1, 1873.

He now has a plaza named after him near Powell Street Station (see photo on previous page), next to one of the three remaining cable car lines. Hallidie would be proud if he saw what an attraction his cable car turnarounds have become – cable cars go up a hill and then down it, but can't turn around. This means that at their end points there are big wooden platters. To turn a cable car the right direction, a group of workers spin the car by hand. Imagine a lazy Susan or record player.

In 1947 the mayor of San Francisco wanted to axe the cable cars, saying that they were too expensive and that electric cars were much more efficient. The Citizens' Committee to Save the Cable Cars, spearheaded by Friedel Klussmann, successfully campaigned to save the car. After all, Klussmann asked, who comes to San Francisco to ride the buses?

These days, the cable cars are as popular as ever. Because it runs through the Financial District, the California Street line is the one most used by locals. The California line is not as popular as the Powell-Hyde cable car or the Powell-Mason cable car, both of which run from Powell and Market streets to the Fisherman's Wharf area, but because it goes through Chinatown and up Nob Hill, it's a great way to experience cable cars and avoid the extremely long lines of the other two routes.

Although the fare is as steep as the hills these cars climb, it's not cheap to keep Muni's 26 cable cars operational. But people are willing to pay the price – on an average weekday, more than 21,000 people ride the cars.

NO SLEEPING ON THE BUS

According to Muni officials, some tips to avoid being pickpocketed:

Stay awake. A pickpocket's easiest victim is a sleeping passenger.

Beware of loud arguments or commotion. Incidents can be staged to distract while a pocket is being picked.

Never wear your backpack on your back.

Carry wallets inside coat or front pants pocket – never in a backpack.

Close all handbags and carry them securely in front of you.

Avoid displaying large amounts of money in public.

If you're the victim of a pickpocket, note what bus you were on, the direction you were heading, and time of day. Then, contact Muni or the police right away – they might be able to pull the videotape from the bus and get a picture of the thief.

Clang-Clang-Clang Goes the Trolley

The group that saved the cable cars in the 1940s were right. Tourists just can't get enough of mechanical, fun-to-ride anachronisms. Taking various forms since the first contest in 1955, including an ill-advised swimsuit competition where contestants had to bare it all in the freezing cold, the modern form of the **Annual Cable Car Bell-Ringing Contest** took shape in 1995 to raise money for charities. There's also a professional cable carman-only section of the contest. The contest usually takes place in July or October on an authentic cable car that's transported into Union Square.

YEARLY HAUL

Pick pocketing incidents on Muni by fiscal year:

2001: 611
2002: 687
2003: 691
2004: 755
2005 (first six months): 670

A Bargain After the Ride

For more cable car fun at a great price – free – be sure to visit the **San Francisco Cable Car Museum** *(1201 Mason St., 415-474-1887, cablecarmuseum.org)*. Located in the historic Washington/Mason cable car barn and powerhouse, the museum deck overlooks the huge engines and winding wheels that pull the cables.

Downstairs is a viewing area of the large sheaves and cable line entering the building through the channel under the street. There also are historical displays on San Francisco's cable cars, as well as actual cable cars that operated in 19th-century San Francisco, including one that ran on Hallidie's Clay Street Hill Cable Railroad.

It comes as a surprise to many that San Francisco has a **light rail system**. In downtown, the trains run below Market Street and stop at the major intersections. Outside of downtown, most of the trains exit their tunnels to run on surface tracks. When catching a train above ground without a transfer or a pass, enter the very first door of the first car. There, a machine accepts the $1.25 fare as cash or tokens.

The light rail lines, usually referred to as "trains" or "the Muni," are designated by letters. Currently, there are the J, K, L, M and N lines. The very first Muni line was the A line, which has since been put out of service. Same with the B, C, D, etc. The exception to this is the F line.

When taking the light rail lines, notice the wall murals; they usually have a story to tell. At the Castro Muni station, for example, a plaque explains why the rainbow flag was installed in the Castro – to commemorate the 20th anniversary of the election of the openly gay City Supervisor Harvey Milk, who was later assassinated.

Light rail is the quickest way to travel east-west across the city. A ride on the N-line takes 40 minutes from Embarcadero Station to the terminus, one block from the Pacific Ocean. Also, because of tighter control over passengers entering and exiting the station, light rail tends to have more hygenic, (i.e., less-smelly) commuters.

Destination Muni Lines

Asian Art Museum
5, 19; short walk from 6, 7, 9, 21, 26, 66, 71, F-Market & Wharves, and J-K-L-M-N Metro (Civic Center Station)

Cable Car Museum
Powell-Hyde or Powell-Mason cable car

Cable car terminals: California cable car
1, 2, 7, 9, 14, 19, 21, 31, 47, 49, 71, F-Market & Wharves; short walk from 10, 12

Cable car terminals: Powell-Hyde and Powell-Mason cable car
5, 6, 7, 9, 10, 19, 21, 31, 47, 71, F-Market & Wharves; short walk from 14, 15, 26, 49

Candlestick Park
29 (also special 9X, 28X, 47X express buses on 49ers game days only)

The Castro
24, 33, 35, 37, K-L-M Metro (Castro Street Station), F-Market & Wharves

tickets to ride

San Francisco Municipal Railway, or "Muni" (415-673-6864, sfmuni.com), is the organization that runs about 1,000 vehicles that transport nearly one million people in San Francisco on a daily basis.

It's not the only public transit authority in the city, but it's by far the biggest and most important one for getting around within city borders. Most people associate San Francisco with its world famous cable cars – the agency runs those, as well as buses, the light rail system, and the historic street cars.

The $1.25 fares are scheduled to go up to $1.50 as of this writing. These fares are payable in cash or Muni tokens, for any Muni vehicle except cable cars, which cost $3, and may soon go up to $5. Transfers are good for 90 minutes and can be used between every Muni vehicle except for cable cars, which don't give out or accept transfers. Exact change is required, and the turnstiles to enter an underground light rail station don't take dollar bills like the buses or above-ground light rail.

To save money and the hassle of always having exact change, here are some other fare options. If the controversial fare hike goes through, tack another dollar or two on to all of these prices.

Muni Passport:

Good for unlimited travel on all Muni services and is available for one, three, or seven consecutive days, at $9, $15, or $20 respectively.

Chinatown

1, 9X, 12, 15, 30, 45, cable cars

Civic Center, City Hall

5, 21, 47, 49; short walk from 6, 7, 9, 31, 71, J-K-L-M-N Metro (Civic Center Station)

Coit Tower

39

Crissy Field

29

Fillmore Jazz Preservation District

22, 31, 38, 38L

Fisherman's Wharf, Alcatraz, and Angel Island ferry

10, 15, 19, 30, 39, 47, F-Market & Wharves, and Powell-Hyde or Powell-Mason cable car

Fort Mason

28; short walk from 22, 30, 43

Golden Gate Bridge

28 (daily); 76 (Sundays and Sunday-service holidays only) or any Golden Gate Transit buses from downtown San Francisco

The San Francisco CityPass:

$42 for adults and $34 for children is good as a pass for seven consecutive days on all Muni services, including cable cars, and is also good for admission to several attractions in the city. It's available at those attractions and at the Visitor Information Center at Powell & Market Streets, or can be ordered in advance online at *citypass.com*.

Adult Fast Pass:

$45, good for one calendar month (with a three-day grace period) for all forms of Muni transportation.

Weekly Pass:

$12 Monday-Sunday, with a $1 surcharge for cable cars.

There are discounts for seniors and children on almost all of these options.

Although not the first publicly-owned transportation system in the country, Muni officials proudly note that theirs is the first public transportation system in the US that offered a viable alternative to private vehicle ownership.

Half of the vehicles that Muni runs are electric – which is why many San Francisco streets have an urban jungle canopy of electric wires. When a bus comes off its wires, there's usually a loud pop from the electrical spark. But not to fear, all bus drivers carry leather gloves; when it happens, they stop the bus and put the connector between the bus and the overhead wires back on themselves.

Golden Gate Park
5, 21, 28, 29, 44, 71,
N-Judah Metro

The Haight (Haight-Ashbury)
6, 7, 33, 37, 43, 71

Japantown
2, 3, 4, 22, 38, 38L

Legion of Honor
18

Marin Headlands
76 (Sundays and Sunday-service holidays only)

Mission District
14, 18, 22, 24, 33, 48,
J-Church Metro

Moscone Convention Center
12, 30, 45; short walk from 5, 6, 7, 9, 14, 15, 21, 31, 38, 38L, 71, J-K-L-M-N Metro (Powell Street Station)

Mount Davidson
36; short walk from 43, 48

North Beach
9X, 12, 15, 30, 38, 45

Ocean Beach
5, 18, 23, 31, 38, 71,
N-Judah Metro

Palace of Fine Arts, Exploratorium

28; 76 (Sundays and Sunday-service holidays only); short walk from 30, 43

Piers 39 & 41, Alcatraz & Angel Island ferry

10, 15, 19, 30, 39, 47, F-Market & Wharves, and Powell-Hyde or Powell-Mason cable car

SBC Park

N-Judah Metro; short walk from 10, 15, 30, 45, 47

San Francisco Museum of Modern Art

14, 15, 30, 45; short walk from 5, 6, 7, 9, 21, 31, 38, 38L, 71, F-Market & Wharves, and J-K-L-M-N Metro (Montgomery Street Station)

San Francisco Zoo

23, L-Taraval Metro

Twin Peaks

37 (take stairway from Crestline Drive)

Union Square shopping district

38, 38L, Powell-Hyde or Powell-Mason cable car; short walk from 5, 6, 7, 9, 21, 31, 66, 71, J-K-L-M-N Metro (Powell Street Station)

Union Street shopping district

22, 45

Muni Station

The original Muni trains ran under Market Street, with the **Embarcadero** as the terminal station. **Montgomery** is the busiest of the Muni stations, in the heart of the Financial District.

Popular Muni Routes

The easiest way to figure out how to get around on Muni is to call their main number *(415-673-6864)* Mon.-Fri. 6 a.m.-8 p.m., weekends and holidays 8 a.m.-6 p.m.

The friendly operators will tell travelers how to get where they want to go, how to get back, and anything else they'd like to know about getting around inside the city. Many San Franciscans have the Muni information number stored in their cell phones — no matter where you end up in the city or how, figuring out how to get home is only a phone call away.

Online, the convenient *transit.511.org* allows users to type in an address or destination they want to start from and where they want to go, and the trip planner does the rest. The "next best trip" button cycles through the different ways to get someplace.

A Streetcar Named Desire

Cable cars aren't the only vintage forms of transportation in San Francisco. The F-Market line, which started in 1995, uses classic trolleys that ran in San Francisco at one time and other trolleys purchased from cities around the world.

Although the F-line is operated by Muni, a 1,200-member non-profit volunteer organization, **Market Street Railway** (415-956-0472, streetcar.org), helps acquire vintage trolleys from all over the world, finds volunteers to clean the cars and serve the trolleymen cold drinks on their breaks, and educates the public about this environmentally-friendly form of transportation.

Market Street Railway helped Muni raise money to restore the streetcars that served the city for more than 30 years and now make up the bulk of the fleet, with 11 more coming online in 2005. Market Street Railway members have also helped the city score the open-top Boat Tram from Blackpool, England, and the authentic "Streetcar Named Desire" from New Orleans.

In the near future, the organization will finish overhauling a 1912 Russian tram from Moscow, and a circa-1924 San Francisco car from the organization's namesake and Muni's now-defunct competitor, Market Street Railway Co.

The group is always looking for helpers – people can volunteer for just a few hours per afternoon, once a week, at the F-line terminal at 17th and Castro Streets and give the streetcars a quick cleaning while the operators enjoy their break.

CROWDED HOUSE
Muni lines with at least 20,000 weekday boardings:

38 Geary/38L Limited: 50,893
14 Mission/14L Limited: 43,069
N Judah: 41,628
L Taraval: 31,692
M Ocean View: 31,227
49 Van Ness-Mission: 28,946
1 California: 28,080
15 Third Street: 26,534
30 Stockton: 26,002
22 Fillmore: 22,017
F Market & Wharves: 20,057

The group is especially proud of playing a big role in adding a new trolley line to the city, set to debut in late 2005. The Embarcadero, or E-line, will initially share track with the F-line north of the Ferry Building and the N-line south of Hills Plaza. Market Street Railway members advocate extending the E-line to the south and the north along the coast of the Bay. Also in 2005, the Market Street Railway will open a museum and retail shop in the new Hotel Vitale, at the F-line's Steuart Street stop near the Ferry Building.

20,000 LIGHT YEARS FROM HOME

The longest Muni route is the 91-Owl at 24.1 miles one way.

The longest daytime route is the 29-Sunset at 17.4 miles.

The longest train line is the M-Oceanview at 9.0 miles.

The longest trolley bus route is the 14-Mission at 7.8 miles.

The longest cable car route is the Powell-Hyde at 2.1 miles.

The shortest route is the 89-Laguna Honda at 0.6 miles.

For Night Owls and Drunkards

There's a pleasant all-night route, the **AC Transbay N Line/MacArthur Owl** (510-891-4700, actransit.org), that's just the thing for getting back to San Francisco after a night of checking out Oakland's lively nightlife and eclectic music scene.

The route starts at 12th Street and Broadway in Oakland, and ends at the transportation hub of the Transbay Terminal at Mission and 1st Streets (which might be housed in a much spiffier building come 2008).

The buses that leave San Francisco after the bars close at two a.m. are parties on wheels. The long buses are in two parts, which makes for some creative driving when the city streets are empty.

"The best time was when the bus driver missed this woman's stop," says Jason Poyner, an Oakland resident. "It was about three a.m. and she was in a wheelchair, so he couldn't just stop anywhere. Without saying anything he made a u-turn in the street, which I didn't think was physically possible. Everyone started cheering, but the driver was completely dead-pan. After he dropped the woman off, he made another u-turn, and people started cheering again, but he just kept driving his route like it was no big thing."

The first bus starts its run at 12:40 a.m., and the last bus arrives in San Francisco at 5:55 a.m. This three-dollar ride has saved many an inebriated San Franciscan a night of sobering up at a coffee shop waiting for BART (see next page) to start.

BART is Best

Photo: used with permission of Bay Area Rapid Transit

Thanks to a 3.7-mile tube that lays on the floor of the San Francisco Bay some 135 feet under water, **Bay Area Rapid Transit** *(415-989-2278, bart.gov)*, or BART, links San Francisco to the East Bay cities of Oakland, Berkeley, and beyond. Recently voted the number one transit system in the US by the American Public Transportation Association, BART is quick, safe, and the best way to cover long distances in the Bay Area.

Descending into the tube can be a scary experience the first time. The trains go deep enough underwater where those with sensitive sinuses will have to yawn to pop their ears. Impressive to this day, when the Transbay Tube was completed in August 1969 it rewrote civil engineering history. Although it only took three years to build, six years were spent conducting seismic studies so that the tube would be as safe as possible during an earthquake. During the 1989 Loma Prieta quake, the tube held up well and passengers crossing the bay were unaware that a major quake was rocking the city.

In 1969, before the tube was closed to the public for the installation of train tracks, thousands of people walked, ran, and poked around in the tunnel. The train tunnel under the water captured the world's imagination in much the same way that the underwater tunnel

PULLING A FAST (PASS) ONE
On an average weekday, there are over 37,000 boardings by passengers using Muni Fast Passes to ride BART within San Francisco.

Illustration: Daniel Martinez

Photo: used with permission of Bay Area Rapid Transit

GET THE MESSAGE

Like in other big cities, **bike messengering** is a lifestyle more than an occupation. The San Francisco-based International Federation of Bike Messenger Associations (*www.messengers.org*) gives the following statistics on the usually tattooed, full-of-attitude bike messengers here:

Number of messengers: 350-400
Number of companies: 40
Price for downtown client: $4-$4.50
Commission to messenger: 50%
Cost of inner tube: $4
Cost of pint of beer: $3-$4
Where to find messengers by day: "The Wall" near Montgomery BART/Muni Station.
Where to find messengers by night: Zeitgeist bar, at Valencia and Duboce Streets.

between England and France became a modern marvel two decades later.

Today, BART stations can be found along Market Street, with Civic Center Station set in the heart of the central city before the BART lines veer south and connects the Mission District and the cities south of San Francisco to the recently opened SFO Station. Trains run 4 a.m.-midnight Monday-Friday, 6 a.m.-midnight on Saturday, and 8 a.m.-midnight on Sunday. The minimum fare is $1.25, the maximum is $7.45 for one-way trips.

Bikes are Beautiful

Critical Mass, the international group that promotes bicycles as the transportation mode of choice, started on September 25, 1992, in San Francisco. Years later, it's still going strong and has spread to more than 300 cities.

Chris Carlsson and his friends were avid bicycle enthusiasts who came up with the idea of "Commute Clog," where a group of bicyclists would seize the road. "I've been a bicyclist on the streets of San Francisco since the 1970s," says Carlsson. "And I found it frustrating how little recognition and space there was on the street for bicycling, and it's still generally treated as a toy in the United States. So I thought, if a bunch of us get together once a month and ride home together we can displace cars and actually have the streets to ourselves for a change, instead of the other way around. Surprisingly, that worked."

Critical Mass rides occur on the last Friday of every month at 5:30 p.m. at Justin Herman Plaza, between Embarcadero BART and the Ferry Building. All are welcome; there is no "Critical Mass" organization, membership, or dues. Critical Mass is more of a planned get-together with nobody in particular in charge. There is no official Critical Mass website because there is no official Critical Mass.

This fact has irked some police departments – with no organizers, there's no one to apply for permits to take over the road. In San Francisco, the police now react with "benign neglect," after failing at attempts to harass the bicyclists and stop the monthly rides.

"In the beginning, there were about 50 people," says Carlsson. "The cops didn't even notice it for six months, but by then it was several hundred people big. Then, some motorist plowed into it, broke somebody's bike, and got into a little fist fight. That's what led to police intervention. When people get stuck in traffic and have no idea what's going on, they get a little freaked out, for sure. So you do have to make some effort to talk to people and let them know what's happening and say that you're sorry you're holding them up, and invite them along next time."

Carlsson says that Critical Mass has definitely had an impact on bicycling in San Francisco. "I would guess that Critical Mass got some people to ride their bicycle, they saw that it was pretty fun, so they started riding their bikes more – there used to be only one or two bicycles on Market Street during the morning commute. Now, you have anywhere from 5-20 bikes stopped at every light in the morning. I think that Critical Mass has a lot to do with that."

The Long Haul

The **Green Tortoise Adventure Travel** *(494 Broadway St., 415-956-7500, greentortoise.com)* company doesn't just operate a funky hostel in North Beach, it also runs a number of bus tours around the country that those with big spirits and small budgets rave about:

Alaskan Expedition:
28 days

Baja (Mexico) Daze:
9 or 15 days

Burning Man Festival:
3 or 5 days

Canyons of the West:
8 or 9 days

Costa Rica Loop:
14 days

Cross-Country:

12 or 14 days

Death Valley National Park:

3 days

Mardi Gras:

16 days

Maya Trail:

14 days

National Parks Loop:

16 days

Northern Pioneer:

8 days (National Parks in the west)

Pacific Trek:

9 days

Pyramids and Playas:

14 days

Southern Migration:

28 days

Western Trail:

5 days

Yosemite National Park:

3 days

For the skinny on where to rent bicycles, tips for safely navigating the city, or to download the "SF Bike Map & Walking Guide," the **San Francisco Bicycle Coalition** *(415-431-bike, sfbike.org)* is a great resource. Their bike and walking guide shows bike routes, paths, bike lanes, and indicates the grade of a street so the faint of heart can avoid steep hills.

"San Francisco has seen a significant increase in bicyclists from 1990 to 2000," says Josh Hart, the coalition's former program director. "That's attributable to the citywide bicycle route network and the expansions of bike lanes, though there's still much work to be done." Hart says that there are nearly 30,000 San Franciscans who use their bicycle on a daily basis.

For visitors looking for that one sweet ride, Hart recommends the "Wiggle Route," which starts at the Duboce Bikeway (Market and Duboce Street), heads through Duboce Park, jags up to Fell Street's bike lane, goes through the Golden Gate Park, and then heads across the Golden Gate Bridge into the hilly paths of the Marin Headlands.

A city law makes it a requirement that all major outdoor events with more than 2,000 people have "bike valets." At SBC Park, bicyclists can park their bikes for free in guarded areas. As with valets who park cars, tips are appreciated.

When you're surrounded on three sides by water, bridges become important. There are five in the Greater Bay Area, but only two are connected to San Francisco proper. The one good time to have a car is to get out of San Francisco and drive across the **Golden Gate Bridge**.

The Golden Gate Bridge is 1.7 miles long and links San Francisco to Marin County. A $5 toll is only charged one direction, heading into the city. The fee is used to pay the 17 iron workers and 38 painters who maintain the bridge and continuously touch up the paint job. It's a popular myth that crews constantly repaint the bridge from one end to the other.

The name of the bridge doesn't come from its color, but because the Golden Gate Strait is the entrance to the San Francisco Bay from the Pacific Ocean. In any case, the bridge is not golden, but "international orange."

Bridge authorities say that if the Navy had their way, the bridge would have been painted black with yellow stripes to make it visible to passing ships. Somehow, we think it might not have become the icon of San Francisco if the bridge looked like a bumble bee.

Ironically, the bridge that has become the biggest suicide magnet in the world (see Landmarks & Destinations) has an impressive construction safety record. Eleven men died during its four-year construction – 11 men too many, but that was a feat during that time. Safety nets saved many a man from falling to his death, and hard hats were used. As a matter of fact, hard hats became *de rigueur* in the construction world thanks to the safety record of the Golden Gate Bridge.

The best way to savor the bridge, though, is on foot or bicycle; more than nine million people cross the bridge

CRUISE THE PARK
The Golden Gate Park Shuttle
(goldengateparkconcourse.org) is a free service that makes the massive Golden Gate Park more manageable. Service usually runs from late May or early June through October, with the shuttle operating on weekends and holidays every 15 minutes. 10 a.m.-6 p.m.

without a car every year. The 28/Fort Mason bus stops at the parking lot at the base of the bridge, and the walk from one side to the other takes a good 40 minutes for a fast walker. On Sundays and holidays, only the little-known 76 bus crosses the bridge between San Francisco and the Marin Headlands. The bus is nearly deserted, and the ride is the same price as any other bus ride in the city.

Bay Bridge Characters

A VINE TIME

Oenophiles can take a three-hour, 36-mile round-trip on the **train** between the towns of Napa and St. Helena and enjoy the fruit of the vine in world-famous Napa Valley. *707-253-2111, winetrain.com*

The two-level **San Francisco-Oakland Bay Bridge** is not nearly as scenic as the Golden Gate Bridge, but does have its charms — each level is dedicated to one-way traffic, and the view from the top deck coming into San Francisco, especially at night, is well worth the $2 toll collected in Oakland for west-bound traffic.

The most famous depiction of the bridge is the scene from *The Graduate* in which Dustin Hoffman's character races across it in his car; the shot shows Hoffman driving on the bridge's top road. In the movie, he's supposed to be driving to Berkeley, but in reality, the top road only goes to San Francisco.

Pedestrians are forbidden on the Bay Bridge, though it is possible to come up close and personal with the behemoth by either stopping on Yerba Buena Island — traffic bores right through the island in a tunnel — or renting a kayak and paddling under the bridge.

The current Bay Bridge may be the Emperor Norton Bridge soon. The most valuable natural resource in San Francisco is definitely its people, and Emperor Norton, the man behind the "don't call it Frisco" fetish in this city, was one of the richest, in his self-minted currency and personality, at least. He declared himself "Emperor of the United States and Protector of Mexico," and made it illegal to call the city "Frisco," among other things.

Who would have thought the two-level bridge that's pleasant at a distance but nothing special up close could have so much character?

Ferries are a cheap, scenic way to travel to the cities that ring the San Francisco Bay or to simply sightsee from the water. There are two main ferry operators you should know: **Golden Gate Ferry** *(415-923-2000, goldengateferry.org)*, which has vessels that make the 30-minute run between the Marin County city of Sausalito and the Ferry Building once an hour; every hour, seven days a week (roughly 7 a.m.-7 p.m. on the weekdays, 10 a.m.-6 p.m. on the weekends), and the **Blue and Gold Fleet** *(415-705-5555, blueandgoldfleet.com)*.

The Blue and Gold Fleet offers ferries to Angel Island, Alcatraz, Tiburon, Sausalito, and around-the-bay cruises. The company has bus tours to Muir Woods, Yosemite, wine country, and Monterey/Carmel.

The funkiest offering is the twice-yearly trip to Alcatraz Island for special **Sunrise Ceremonies**. The island was seized by Native American activists in 1969 and held for two years, in part to make a statement about how the federal government took over Native peoples' land. One Sunrise Ceremony is to commemorate the Indigenous Peoples Day of Solidarity (formerly Un-Columbus Day) in September, and one for a Day of Thanksgiving (formerly Un-Thanksgiving Day) in November. Boarding starts at 5 a.m., and the events sell out quickly.

SEGUE INTO SEGWAYS

Even though the city made it illegal to ride Segways on the sidewalk, it is possible to rent them as part of a guided waterfront tour in the Fisherman's Wharf area from the **San Francisco Electric Tour Company** *(415-474-3130, sfelectrictour.com)*.

Also available at Fisherman's Wharf is **Go Car** *(1-800-GOCar, gocarsf.com)*, a small gasoline-powered two-person "talking" car. A GPS in the car signals to the pre-recorded virtual tour guide, so when the vehicle passes a point of interest, the in-car voice pipes up.

Mean Streets

The city's most dangerous streets for pedestrians, according to Walk San Francisco *(walksf.org)*, a pedestrian advocacy group:

19th Avenue at Holloway

Geary Boulevard

Market Street, from Van Ness Avenue east

Mission Street, particularly at 16th Street

Van Ness Avenue

The City by Sea (Part Two)

For baseball fans who also like to kayak, **City Kayak** *(Embarcadero at Townsend, 415-357-1010, citykayak.com)* is right next to SBC Park. Owner Ted Choi says that on game days, many kayakers, including himself, are bobbing in McCovey Cove (formerly known as China Basin) with baseball gloves on their hands waiting to catch a home-run ball.

During the 2002 World Series, when the hometown San Francisco Giants battled it out with the much-despised Anaheim Angels, McCovey's Cove was carpeted with boats, kayaks, people on surfboards, and pretty much anything that floated. Media reports told of a few fans, not content with just baseball, on an artificial floating green, smacking golf balls into the Bay between innings.

For those who don't love America's favorite past-time, Choi offers a guided tour that's perfect for first-time kayakers or anyone who wants to see a different side of the city.

After getting close to the Bay Bridge and having lunch in McCovey Cove, kayakers pass under the Fourth Street Drawbridge (while cars cross the bridge a few feet above their head) to a hidden area of the city where the only residences on watery "streets" are house boats, complete with mail boxes, kids' toys on the porch, and other trappings of domesticity.

Over The Top

A great way to see the Golden Gate Bridge, Alcatraz Island and other sights is via helicopter. One company is **San Francisco Helicopter Tours** *(800-400-2404, sfhelicoptertours.com)*, which also offers tours in wine country. Prices start at around $130 per adult, $95 for children.

A Two-Airport Town

Both **Oakland International Airport** *(501-563-3300, flyoakland.com)* and **San Francisco International Airport** *(650-821-8211, flysfo.com)* are easy to get to and from. Oakland tends to have cheaper domestic fares, thanks to discount carriers JetBlue Airways and Southwest Airlines.

BART serves both airports, although from Oakland it's necessary to buy a $2 ticket for the AirBART Shuttle that runs between the airport terminals and the Coliseum/Oakland Airport station.

For those hauling lots of luggage, it's best to get a door-to-door airporter shuttle, especially from Oakland, as carrying luggage on and off the shuttle bus and into the BART station can be a hassle. And, it can take a lot of time (an hour to an hour-and-a-half) to get into the city from Oakland airport.

At Oakland International Airport, expect to pay around $25 for the first person and an additional $15-$20 for each additional person (negotiation seems to work, especially at Oakland airport). In San Francisco, because there is no bridge to cross and it's a straight shot up the peninsula, two people can get into the city for as little as $30 total, not including tip. It depends on time of day and season.

BAD YEAR FOR WALKING

Since the Department of Parking and Traffic has been keeping statistics, 1963 was the worst year for pedestrian fatalities in the city, with 48 deaths. The best year (if you could call it that) was 2001, with 16 fatalities.

More Walking Tours

Comedian-led tours:

foottours.com

Ghost tours:

sfghosthunt.com

Haunted Haight:

hauntedhaight.com

True Crime Tour:

sfcrime.com

Vampire haunts:

sfvampiretour.com

Walking City

A great place to walk, there are a number of self-guided and city-run walking tours. Be careful, though; San Francisco has the fourth-highest pedestrian fatality rate in the United States.

It's so high, in fact, that the police department started a "safe streets" program in 2005 where undercover officers pose as pedestrians at dangerous intersections to catch reckless drivers. Be sure that a driver sees you and comes to a complete stop before you cross the street.

Some parts of the city are made for aimless wandering – the Financial District is filled with plaques commemorating this or that (notice how many horse-whipping stories there are), and in Chinatown a person may find the best dim sum of their life, never to find it again. Other neighborhoods might not be so obvious, but there are little gems everywhere for those with sturdy shoes and patience.

Even in the more touristy areas like North Beach, getting off of the main streets is the best way to soak up local color. Almost every neighborhood in the city is safe, with the exception of the Bayview/Hunter's Point neighborhood, parts of the Mission District, and parts of the Western Addition. The Tenderloin at night isn't where lone visitors want to find themselves, either. A good rule of thumb is that if there are other people who look like they are walking through the area and not just hanging out, it's probably safe.

The San Francisco Public Library offers a **City Guide** service that offers walking tours for free, guided by residents who want to share their love of San Francisco.

About 30 different itineraries are posted every month, and tours are offered every week of the year, with an expanded schedule in May and October. No reservations are required – just find out when and where a tour starts and show up. Walks last from one-and-a-half to two hours, and take place rain or shine.
100 Larkin Street, 415-557-4266, sfcityguides.org

Photo: Mats Lund

San Francisco is a green city, even if sometimes that greenery is hidden behind a gritty urban façade. The Bay Area boasts one of the largest urban parks in the world spread along 59 miles of waterfront, secret rooftop gardens accessible to all but known by very few, and local sports teams populated by homegrown characters that range from colorful to downright dangerous.

Oddest Sport Invented in San Francisco

There are weird activities that have found some fringe popularity here – **dolphin rodeos**, for instance, where participants jump on top of an inflatable, lubed-up dolphin in a pool or lake and are timed for how long they can stay on. But **Ride & Tie**, invented in 1971 by a marketing executive at jeans manufacturer Levi Strauss & Co., has gained legitimacy, although the first event was a publicity stunt for Levi's.

Ride & Tie is an endurance race featuring two people and one horse. The first person on the horse rides ahead, ties the horse up to a tree or a post for the second person, and runs ahead. The second person then rides the horse past the first person, ties up the horse, and so on; the leapfrogging continues to the finish line. The goal is to let the horse do most of the work without tiring it out. Horsemanship and running endurance play a part in success, but strategy is important as well. In San Francisco, the sport seems to attract the moneyed class, as most equine sports do.

Levi's must have a creative marketing department – at one time there was an urban myth that everyone who survived a jump from the Golden Gate Bridge was wearing Levi's. Talk about tough jeans.

rideandtie.org

Catching Crabs (and No, Not the Tenderloin)

All types of fishing are possible in the Bay and along the coast, but with a $20 crab net and a pier, you can catch large, succulent crabs. If you know where to go, the best **crabbing** spots become parties where people barbecue their catches and share beers with other crabbers.

It helps that crabbing takes very little skill: tie some old meat to a crab net, drop it in the water, and pull it up 10 minutes later. Those who do this say it's best to keep the crabs alive in a bucket of water and cook them at home within hours. No permit is needed to fish from a pier in California, but crabs must be a certain size (6.25 inches across at the time of this writing), male, and, in the Bay, it's illegal to keep Dungeness crabs, partly because they use the area to breed.

Berkeley Marina Pier (ci.berkeley.ca.us/marina) is a good place to see the San Francisco skyline from the other side of the Bay, although during the search for Scott Peterson's missing wife it was the noisiest place in Northern California to go crabbing because of all the news copters overhead. Peterson was eventually convicted of murdering his wife and unborn son and dumping their bodies in the Bay.

The best place to crab in the city is at **Fort Mason** (photo above) at the intersection of Marina Blvd. and Buchanan St., in the Marina district, off the piers at the back of the fort, behind the old military buildings that now host many special events (including the Crab and Wine Marketplace).

Outside the city, the main pier in the coastal town of **Pacifica**, 15 miles south of San Francisco, is another good place for crabbing. Here, it's legal to keep Dungeness crabs during the season.

Regulations can be found at ca.gov, and at the California Department of Fish and Game's site, dfg.ca.gov/mrd.

DIVING IN

Abalone diving is a big sport north of San Francisco along the coast. But almost every year during abalone season, at least one person dies on the quest for the expensive, delicious mollusk. By law, abalone divers can't use any scuba equipment, so they need to hold their breath in murky, swift waters as they pry abalone loose with a special knife shaped like a sharpened, flat crowbar.

Additionally, the best abalone are often found in kelp forests, meaning that if divers get tangled up and can't get loose before their single gulp of air runs out, they're not going to breathe air ever again.

Divers who want every piece of technological help they can get are advised to go on a guided dive in Monterey. The kelp forests are otherworldly and well worth having to suit up in a thick, armor-like wetsuit to withstand the cold waters. In San Francisco, a good place to get oriented with the diving scene is with the **San Francisco Reef Divers**. They also encourage their members to get involved with marine conservation.

San Francisco Reef Divers, sfreefdivers.org. Meets the 3rd Wednesday of every month at Sinbad's Pier 2 Restaurant, Pier 2, Embarcadero, 415-781-2555.

After touring Alcatraz Island, we've overheard children asking their parents if anyone besides escaping prisoners swim in the San Francisco Bay. The answer is yes, and the proof is at **Aquatic Park**, located between Fisherman's Wharf and Ghirardelli Square. Almost every day of the year, some hearty, cold-water-loving soul is paddling away at the park.

Any member of the public brave enough to swim the cold waters is allowed in Aquatic Park, though many of the swimmers there are members of the non-profit, open-to-all **Dolphin Club** *(502 Jefferson St., 415-441-9329, dolphinclub.org)*, established in 1877. Dolphin Club members can be distinguished by their swimsuit-only attire – "Dolphins never use wetsuits or wear fins," the club proclaims. A line of buoys in the water is a quarter-mile long, and a member in good standing who swims at least 40 miles between December 21 and March 21 qualifies as a Dolphin Club Polar Bear.

The club also organizes the yearly **Escape from Alcatraz triathlon**. Swimmers jump off a boat at Alcatraz Island and swim to Aquatic Park; from there, a 14-mile bike ride across the Golden Gate Bridge and into Marin County is topped off by a 13-mile run. The members-only event culminates in a celebration dinner – anyone who crosses the finish line gets an Escape from Alcatraz triathlon belt buckle. The buckle's not exactly pretty, but neither are most participants by the end of the race.

There used to be an old riverboat named Fort Sutter docked in Aquatic Park near the headquarters of the Dolphin Club and South End Rowing Club, but in 1959, South End Rowing Club members – who apparently didn't care for the boat – allegedly burned it down. One year later, the first Escape From Alcatraz swim took place – did the boat burners want some practice escaping the law?

Sweatin' with the Stars

The single best place to see celebrities working out is the **Sport Club/LA** *(thesportsclubla.com)*, at the **Four Seasons San Francisco** *(757 Market St., 415-633-3000, fourseasons.com)*. The membership is steep – we were quoted an initiation fee of $550 (prices change all the time at health clubs), but with a swimming pool, indoor soccer area, social events, and beautiful people, it's probably worth every penny for those who can pony up. For those who prefer their workouts to consist only of lifting drinks to their lips, check out **Seasons Bar** inside the hotel – nothing extraordinary as far as hotel bars in San Francisco go, but this particular property is blessed with staff that have the knack of making everyone feel like a star, even if you can't afford to sweat with them.

Muay Thai Warriors

Muay Thai, the national sport of Thailand, is alive and well in San Francisco thanks in part to the large Asian population. It doesn't hurt that many of Thailand's champions, including Bunkerd Faphimai, "the people's champion," call the Bay Area home. Muay Thai is similar to western boxing, except the boxers are allowed to kick, knee, and elbow their opponents.

The local boxing and kickboxing community was stunned when on August 1, 2003 world champion **Alex Gong** was murdered. On that day he was training at the Fairtex gym he owned – which was world-renowned, with only one location outside of Thailand – when boxers heard a crash and told him that his car had been hit. He chased the driver down, and when he became stuck in traffic Gong tried to force him out of the car. The man, who was wanted for parole violations, shot Gong in the chest. The 32-year-old Gong, who had

ORGAN-IC TUNES

For a free, bayside concerto courtesy of Mother Nature, check out the **Wave Organ**, on a small jetty in the Marina district of San Francisco, within walking distance of the **Exploratorium** *(3601 Lyon St., 415-561-0360, exploratorium.com)*. The Wave Organ is a type of sculpture designed to create music from the impact of the waves and the movement of water in and out of the 25 "organ pipes" made out of PVC and concrete.

The jetty itself was constructed with material taken from a demolished cemetery. Visitors need to listen closely to the sound produced by the Wave Organ – creators. Peter Richards and George Gonzales have noted that the subtle sounds of the organ force visitors to become attuned to the bayside environment.

"It is a wonderful place to get away from it all," says Richards, now a senior artist at the Exploratorium. "Early mornings are great because the sun warms up the masonry and it seems more peaceful. My favorite time, though, is to go out there on a full moon and high tide. The sounds are at their best and the light is wonderful. Many people, upon finding the place by accident, are delighted by this weird ruin that makes music."

won 27 out of his 29 professional fights, died almost instantly a few blocks from his gym.

Within a few days, police tracked Rodger Chastain, 23, to a small motel near a freeway. After a twelve-hour standoff, Chastain broke through one wall of his hotel room and, police surmise, seeing that there was no way out of the motel which had been evacuated and cordoned off, crawled under a mattress and shot himself in the head.

After a dark period of confusion and sadness, the Muay Thai scene re-emerged with two gyms: **Fight and Fitness** *(734 Bryant St., at 5th St., 415-495-2211, fightandfitness.com)*, led by Bunkerd Faphimai and recently turned pro

fighter Chris Cariaso, and **Fairtex Muay Thai Sports Camp** *(132-140 Hawthorne St., 888-324-7839, fairtex.com)*, a new incarnation of Gong's gym.

Faphimai is known as the "people's champion" in Thailand because of his warm, playful ways outside the ring, and ferocity and dedication inside of it. He started fighting at the age of 13 to make extra money and earned one dollar for his very first fight. Eventually he worked his way up the ranks, and after some 350 fights became a star in Thailand – and accomplished the almost unheard of by winning the title belts of *both* of the main Muay Thai stadiums in Bangkok. Today, he trains fighters at all levels, from beginners to pros.

Cariaso, a BMX champ before a broken jaw ended his promising career, is one of those single-minded individuals who excel at whatever they do. He also stages spectacular fights.

Fight and Fitness hosts "smokers" (fight events that got their names from the cigar-smoke-filled rooms the events took place in at one time) almost every other month that are free and open to all; the barbecue and after-fight party sometimes stretches into the evening. When there, check out the impressive collection of title belts accumulated by the two owners.

Photo: Jack Hollingsworth, San Francisco Convention and Visitors Bureau

Locals' love of baseball was reaffirmed when, during the 1989 World Series, the streets were empty and all eyes were on the game. Luckily, this meant that most people were off the bridges and roads when the Loma Prieta quake hit.

One of the city's most popular baseball legends is SF-born **Lefty O'Doul**. He played for a number of teams, including the San Francisco Giants, during the 1920s and 1930s. He also managed the San Francisco Seals baseball team for a time, and was a goodwill baseball ambassador to Japan. He loved the ardent baseball fans in the Land of the Rising Sun, and they loved him in return – he's known there as Japan's Father of Baseball.

O'Doul was deeply troubled by the December 7, 1941 surprise attack on Pearl Harbor, but returned throughout his life to Tokyo, where he suggested the name of Japan's first professional team be changed to the "Tokyo Giants," which it was, though now the team is known as the "Yomiuri Giants." O'Doul did many good deeds for the war-torn citizens and the sport of baseball in Japan. Ironically, he died on December 7, 1969, exactly 28 years after the Pearl Harbor attack.

Today, the bar and restaurant called **Lefty O'Doul's** (333 Geary St., 415-982-8900), near Union Square, is a shrine to San Francisco sports and is one of the top places to watch a game or catch up on SF sports history. There's also a working drawbridge, the 3rd Street Bridge near the new Pac Bell Ballpark, that bears Lefty's full name: Francis Lefty O'Doul.

Joe DiMaggio, another hometown-born baseball hero, was encouraged by Lefty O'Doul early in his career. Lefty is on record saying that the best thing he ever did for DiMaggio was not to change a thing. "Elegant" is the word that many old-timers who knew DiMaggio, born "Giuseppe," used to describe him.

SWING FOR THE FENCES
The San Francisco Gay Softball League has men's and women's divisions and is committed to giving all participants, regardless of orientation, an LGBT-friendly place to enjoy softball. Those who don't even play softball say the games and related events at local gay bars are a riot. With team names like "Bernal Babes" and "Scared Hitless," the emphasis seems to be on having a good time. LGBT amateur athletes who want to play other sports in the Bay should check out *outsports.com* for local teams. SFGSL game hotline: 415-436-0707, *sfgsl.org*

Both of DiMaggio's marriages took place in San Francisco. The first, to **Dorothy Arnold**, was described as a near riot in film reel reports – a crowd of 30,000 San Franciscans swamped the **Sts. Peter and Paul Church** (660 Filbert St., 415-421-5219) in the North Beach area, where DiMaggio grew up. The streets were so crowded that Arnold was late to her own wedding.

His second marriage, to **Marilyn Monroe**, didn't last long but it's said that they reconciled toward the end of her life, and he apparently carried a flame for her long after her death by barbiturate overdose at the age of 36. It's said that they were planning to remarry. DiMaggio claimed Monroe's body and arranged her funeral, and had a dozen red roses sent to her crypt three times a week, every week, for 20 years. A classy gentleman to the end, he never breathed a word in public about her or their relationship. DiMaggio is buried in Colma, just south of San Francisco.

Bad-boy **Barry Bonds** hails from the Silicon Valley city of San Mateo, and at over 40 years of age, is still going strong as one of the greatest home run kings of all time. Born into a baseball family – Bobby Bonds is his father and Reggie Jackson is his cousin – he started his

career with the Pittsburgh Pirates; in 1993 he moved to the San Francisco Giants and has been with the hometown team ever since.

Locals have mixed emotions about Bonds – he's not exactly the warmest guy, and doesn't feel the need to play nice with the media, or fans for that matter. He's also given some conflicting statements on steroid use – many are incredulous that when most people retire as their bodies break down, Bonds is just naturally getting bigger and stronger. One of his trainers was linked to BALCO, the Bay Area Laboratory Cooperative, which became newsworthy by admitting it manufactured designer steroids. Bonds claims he may have been given some muscle cream by his trainer, but he didn't know steroids might be involved.

Bonds also features in *Up for Grabs*, a documentary that shows two men's descent into what could charitably be called madness as they fought for the right to hold on to Bonds' record-setting 73rd home run ball, a "million-dollar ball" that fetched $450,000 at auction.

FREE BEER

Not really, but free baseball – one-half of the recipe for a baseball fan's happiness – is available to the enterprising fan who doesn't mind some stiff bayside breezes. For those who aren't able to secure a ticket, head to the **Portwalk** located beyond the outfield wall, and soak up the expansive views of the Bay and a free peek at the ballgame. Fans are encouraged to circulate a little bit and not hog the best spots. On big game days or on opening day, things can get quite festive. No chairs allowed.

Photo: Jason Blalock

Ex-Oakland Raiders have a bad habit of getting into trouble, and thuggish behavior by fans is not unknown either. Most fans, however, are just good-natured and boisterous, and are glad to have the 45-year-old franchise back in the Bay after a 12-year relocation to Los Angeles, a city much-despised in the long-running sports rivalry between North and South.

Back in the 1950s, the American Football League's eighth franchise was forced to look for another home when a deal with Minnesota fell through. After briefly flirting with Atlanta, it was decided to put the new team in the Bay Area. The Oakland Raiders played their first game ever at San Francisco's Kezar Stadium on September 11, 1960, where they lost to the Houston Oilers by a score of 37-22.

Since then, the Raiders have become the bad boys of football, rivaled only by the Pittsburgh Steelers for "baditude." Most football observers agree that the fans, however, are rivaled by no other team in the National Football League – a Raiders game in Oakland feels more like stepping into a *Mad Max* movie than a sporting event.

The team's signature colors, black and silver, lend themselves well to the studded leather outfits that partying fans seem to favor (imagine a death metal Halloween). The fans call themselves "**Raider Nation**," although they should really be called "Raider Planet," because they're quite out of this world. Some might look intimidating, but they're surprisingly nice to visitors – as long as they're rooting for the Raiders – who can join them in the parking lot that's open five hours before game time for tailgate parties. Out-of-towners who wear the opposing teams' colors are strongly advised to rethink their decision.

The Raiders arguably have more fans around the world than any other American football team. Their website is available in Spanish, German, and most recently, Chinese (raiders.com/newsroom/chinese.jsp). "The Raider Nation transcends languages, borders, and

HAI! HAI! HIKE!

The NFL's **San Francisco 49ers**, named for the year of the Gold Rush that made the city what it is today, is a team of firsts. On August 3, 2002, the 49ers played the Washington Redskins in the 11th American Bowl in Osaka, Japan – a city of three million people that is the "sister city" of San Francisco and a hotbed for American football. For many fans in the US, it was just another game (the 49ers lost, 38-7), but for the two cities by the bay, it marked the 45th anniversary of their affectionate relationship.

From 1964-1967, **Dave Kopay** played for the 49ers, and after his retirement from the NFL became the first major sports figure to publicly declare his homosexuality. He was interested in coaching for the NFL, but was turned down because of what was euphemistically called his "lifestyle."

The first football player to achieve worldwide infamy, **O.J. Simpson** was born in San Francisco and grew up in the Potrero Hill neighborhood housing projects. He finished his career with the 49ers during the 1978-79 season. Before he was accused of murdering his ex-wife and her friend, some people who knew Simpson said that if he hadn't become a star football player he would have probably been a criminal. After his trial and the infamous not guilty decision, a mural at the **Potrero Hill Recreation Center** *(at the intersection of Connecticut at 17th Sts.)* that used to be a tribute to the local hero was defaced.

When it comes to football, though, the San Francisco 49ers are clearly winners: they've won all five of the Super Bowls they've played in.

cultures," says Raiders chief executive Amy Trask.

Although the Raiders have had some impressive seasons (they've made it to five Super Bowls and won three of them), the past few years have not been good to former players:

Former lineman **Barret Robbins** assaulted a security guard at the **Sir Francis Drake Hotel** *(450 Powell St., 415-392-7755, sirfrancisdrake.com)* near downtown's Union Square in December 2004. Less than a month later, Robbins was shot by police in what they say was a robbery attempt at a Miami Beach pub. The 380-pound man beat three police officers and was taken down by two bullets to the chest – they didn't kill him, but he was hospitalized for months afterwards. In football history, Robbins is known as the man who went AWOL in the days prior to the Super Bowl in 2003 and showed up the night before, incoherent. Robbins has said he suffers from alcoholism and bipolar disorder.

In November 2004, former kicker **Cole Ford** drove by the Las Vegas home of Siegfried & Roy, the duo famous for white tigers and magic tricks, and fired off a few shotgun blasts. Psychiatric evaluations after his arrest determined that Ford saw the pair as a threat – he thought there was a dangerous sexual intimacy between the performers and their animals, and saw their illusionist tricks as malevolent manipulations of reality itself.

On a (slightly) less psychotic note, in March 2005, a jury ordered **Bill Romanowski** to pay former teammate **Marcus Williams** $340,000 in damages for tearing off his helmet and punching him in the face. Romanowski played in the NFL for 16 years and had an infamously bad temper: he had spit at other players on national TV before and was fined nearly $100,000 for bad behavior during his career.

The last time the Raiders played in a Super Bowl was in 2003, losing to the Tampa Bay Buccaneers 48-21. Some sports fans in Oakland were none too happy: at least ten private vehicles were set on fire, a McDonald's was looted and burned, and almost 20 police and fire vehicles were damaged. We happened to be in Oakland that night, and let's just say that the sight of burning cars blocking intersections is not a reassuring one.

Anyone who wants to know more about "Raider Nation" without actually visiting it should find the *Raider Nation* documentary, released in 2003.

My Secret Garden

Rick Evans loves to explore the secret parks and public spaces of San Francisco. As the occasional tour guide for *sfcityguides.com* explains, "You have to poke around places where you don't think you belong to find these hidden spots." A San Francisco ordinance dictates that new or newly renovated buildings have to dedicate a percentage of their total square footage to open space accessible to the public. "Now, just because they do it doesn't mean they advertise it or make an effort to let people know where to find it," Evans says.

Here's a rundown on the hidden spaces of San Francisco, courtesy of Evans and our own poking around:

• At the Wells Fargo Bank known as **The Crocker Office** *(1 Montgomery St.)*, walk inside and make an immediate left to find a hallway just past the elevators. Keep going up until you find the rooftop garden that's visible from the street below.

• Attached to the Crocker Office is the **Crocker Galleria** *(50 Post St.)*. Take escalators to the second floor of the indoor mall and go to the very end of the mall to find a door that marks the rooftop garden.

• At the **E*Trade Building** *(532 Market St., at Sansome St.)*, go down some steps to find a little, none-too-welcoming public area with no benches. Evans said that only once has he seen people down here. Look across the street to 150 Bush Street where you will see **"The Pencil Building"** named for its extremely tall, narrow design (see photo).

• For a full-length view of the Transamerica Building to the west, check out the **Sun Terrace** on the 15th floor of the original **Crown Zellerbach Building** *(1 Bush St.)*. "The Spooks" statues of three apocalyptic figures on top of 501 California Street are visible from here as well. Evans says they are firmly anchored and made of very lightweight material.

Go for Pro

BASEBALL:

Oakland Athletics
oaklandathletics.com

San Francisco Giants
sfgiants.com

BASKETBALL:

Golden State Warriors
nba.com/warriors

FOOTBALL:

Oakland Raiders
raiders.com

San Francisco 49ers
sf49ers.com

HOCKEY:

San Jose Sharks
sj-sharks.com

SOCCER:

San Jose Earthquakes
sjearthquakes.com

• On the rooftop garden on the second floor of the **Delta Tower** building *(100 1st St.)* is Waterwall, a water sculpture of reflection pools containing wavy sheets of glass created by sculptor John Luebton.

• At Pine and Sansome streets is the former **Pacific Coast Stock Exchange**, recognizable by the statues guarding either side of the steps. It was the site of a lot of street theatre during the lead-up to the Iraq War, and now houses an upscale fitness club – talk about banking on your looks. Evans told us that when it was still a stock exchange, he was able to go on a private tour: "All I can say is it was one of the most dismal spaces I've seen in my life. It was like a casino."

RUNNING GAGS

Every party is an excuse to dress up or take it all off here, and **Bay to Breakers** *(baytobreakers.com)*, a 7.5-mile run from the San Francisco Bay to the Pacific Ocean, features serious joggers, drunken spectators, and participants gunning to win the costume contest. (The best is usually the group of guys, dressed as salmon, who run in the wrong direction – i.e. upstream.)

The event has made the record books for the greatest number of participants in a footrace – 110,000 in 1986. It's also been held for more consecutive years in a row than any other foot race in history; started in 1912, it was designed to give San Franciscans a fun, healthy event to boost their spirits and bring them together after the turmoil of the 1906 quake.

• Across from the E*Trade Building is the **Citicorp Center** *(1 Sansome St.)*. It used to be the site of the Paris/London National Bank, but it's now an open-air atrium where many downtown workers enjoy lunch. Walk inside the Citicorp building to see a preserved façade of the old bank suspended on the wall.

• Although Yerba Buena Gardens *(between Mission and Folsom Sts., 3rd and 4th Sts., yerbabuenagardens.com)* are known as the premier outdoor oasis in downtown San Francisco, not everyone knows about the **Butterfly Garden**, our personal favorite of the many interesting gardens in the 2.5-acre outdoor space. Reiko Goto, with the help of an entomologist and a botanist, designed the garden with plants and landscape features to lure native San Francisco butterflies into the middle of the city. She succeeded, but it might take a little patience to see a butterfly, depending on time of day and weather.

• At the **Fairmont San Francisco** *(950 Mason St., 415-772-5000, fairmont.com)*, a short but steep walk from the downtown core up Nob Hill, there is a roof garden that's open to the public, guest or not. From the main lobby, veer right and turn left at the elevators. Walk past the gift shops to the end of the ramp and look for the sign – the garden is on the left.

- In North Beach, the **San Francisco Art Institute Café** *(800 Chestnut St., 415-771-7020, sanfranciscoart.edu)* serves up well-priced meals and fantastic views of Alcatraz and Angel Island, Coit Tower, and Telegraph Hill. The art-littered trip up to the café includes views of a Diego Rivera mural.

- On the 9th floor of the **Shih Yu-Lang Central YMCA** *(220 Golden Gate Ave., 415-345-6700, centralymcasf.org)* is one of the best rooftop gardens in the city. Once open to the public, it is now only accessible to YMCA members. But if you stay at the budget hotel, the garden is definitely worth a look.

This is just a small sampling of hidden public spaces. The best thing to do as you wander the streets is to look up – most residents of San Francisco are under the mistaken impression that the rooftop gardens that they stare at dreamily while working are only for upper management. This is sometimes true, but usually not. If there's an interesting garden, don't hesitate to walk inside a building and ask about it.

alleys of the financial district

Alley where you're likely to see European tourists with outdated guidebooks looking for the now-defunct Spanish restaurant and dance club Barcelona: **Spring Street**.

Alley that dead-ends into a youth hostel most locals don't know about: **Derby Street**, with the **Union Square Backpacker's Hostel** *(70 Derby Lane, 415-775-7506)* as a terminus.

Alley with the most cool people: **Minna Street**, thanks mainly to **111 Minna Gallery** *(111 Minna St., 415-974-1719, 111minnagallery.com)*, a bar/art gallery that hosts some of the hippest events of the city.

TALK AND WALK

People who aren't vision-impaired might not know that when walking around downtown San Francisco, there are **Talking Signs** (*talkingsigns.com*, see list of installations). The talking sign system works with a receiver that a person points in a certain direction, and then hears "Powell Muni Station" or "public bathroom," depending on what they're pointing at.

Photo: Phillip H. Coblentz courtesy of the SF Convention and Visitors Bureau

PARK WAYS

Golden Gate Park has almost everything a park could have – bocce ball, a Japanese tea garden, the tranquil AIDS Memorial Grove, a bison paddock – but some of the more interesting features are the windmills at the very end of the park, right across the street from where Ocean Beach meets the Pacific Ocean. During the day, the photogenic windmills and tulip garden are full of photographers and families. At night, however, the windmills are probably the city's cruisiest spot (tied with **Buena Vista Park** in the Haight). *Between Great Highway and Stanyan St. (west-east), and Fulton St. and Lincoln Way (north-south)*

Alley with most well-dressed people:
Cosmo Place, thanks to **Ryoko's** *(619 Taylor St., 415-775-1028)*, one of the most authentic Japanese food places in town with always-stylish Japanese clientele (the bottles of hard liquor behind the bar have their patrons' name written on them in Japanese, just like bars in Japan), and **Le Colonial** *(20 Cosmo Pl., 415-931-3600)*, an upscale restaurant with mid-scale bar that recreates French Indochine through décor and dining.

Best alley to get a haircut and watch fortune cookies being made:
Ross Alley, which has the **"Famous Operator"** Barbershop (one of many names the shop has; has also been known as Jun Yu Barbershop) at 32 Ross Alley, which has seen many celebrities pass through since it opened in 1963. Jun Yu, the owner, has shorn the locks of Clint Eastwood and Michael Douglas, among others. Yu can sometimes be seen playing his Chinese violin as he waits for customers. Next door is the **Golden Gate Fortune Cookie Factory** where a big bag of still-warm fortune cookies costs $10.

Best-smelling alley:
Belden Place, sometimes referred to as the French Quarter of San Francisco, where six bistros feature outdoor seating for lunch and dinner.

Poshest alley:
Maiden Lane, home to a number of upscale spas and chic pedestrian mall.

Worst-smelling alley:
Commercial Street at **Front Street**. Although the McDonald's is one of the nicest in the city thanks to its Financial District location – the place is decorated with interesting aerial photographs of different parts of the city – the alley outside reeks of spent fat and garbage.

It's not Central Park, nor is it Golden Gate Park – the **Golden Gate National Recreation Area** (GGNRA) is two-and-a-half times the size of the city of San Francisco and encompasses Alcatraz and Angel Islands, the Presidio, Marin Headlands, Fort Funston, Fort Point, and a slew of other places of interest along 59 miles of coastline.

It's partly thanks to the Cold War, and partly because of the "Parks to the People" program (launched by President Richard Nixon, of all people), that resulted in the 1972 congressional funding for GGNRA that this huge park exists. The United States Army wanted to make sure the San Francisco Peninsula and Bay were impenetrable by invading countries – there are seven former military installations in the GGNRA, some that date before the Civil War.

Former missile installations are scattered along the Pacific Coast, with most of them in the **Marin Headlands** (nps.gov/goga/mahe), on the Marin County side of the Golden Gate Bridge. All of the missile batteries are now empty, except for one: SF-88, a restored (but not "live") Nike missile that's the centerpiece of the **Cold War museum** in the heart of the Marin Headlands (415-331-1453, nps.gov/goga/nike).

While visiting the Marin Headlands, the **Point Bonita Lighthouse** (nps.gov/goga/mahe/pobo) is worth a visit.

Photo: Mats Lund

Operated by the US Coast Guard, the lighthouse is still active and is the only one in the United States that's accessible by suspension bridge only. The pedestrian bridge is not for those afraid of heights – we were so nervous crossing it the first few times that we didn't notice it is a small copy of the Golden Gate Bridge.

Inside the lighthouse is a map of all the old ships that sank trying to get through the "Golden Gate," the entrance to San Francisco Bay. Volunteers at the lighthouse will happily point out that the Marin

Great Views, History, & Green Thumbs

• **Clipper Community Garden**, on Clipper Street at Cesar Chavez in Noe Valley, was converted from a farm into the first community garden in the city. This garden boasts spectacular views of downtown.

• The Mission **Dearborn Community Garden** on Dearborn Alley between 17th and 18th Streets and Valencia and Guerrero Streets is a slice of pastoral serenity in a bustling neighborhood.

• Overlooking the Bay is the **Fort Mason Community Garden**, at Bay and Franklin Streets, the city's largest community garden, with 125 plots, a greenhouse providing seedlings for members, and a beautiful Zen garden on a hill.

Headlands sits very near the **San Andreas Fault**, where the Pacific and the North American tectonic plates meet and cause major damage to life and property when they butt against each other.

This is not something to think about when walking to the lighthouse – there's a short tunnel which was dug by hand through a mountain – or when crossing the suspension bridge that park rangers watch to make sure only five people cross at any one time. The lighthouse is only open to the public on Sat.-Mon. 12:30-3:30 p.m.

Fort Funston, just north or Lake Merced, is a great place to hike along the beach and watch hang gliders use a former Nike Hercules missile site on the edge of a steep cliff as their launch pad to glide over the ocean. **Golden Gate National Recreation Area**, *415-561-4700, nps.gov/goga*

• **Potrero Hill Community Garden** *(San Bruno at 20th St.)* is a 25-year-old open organic garden sanctuary with expansive views clear to the Golden Gate Bridge and Marin.

• The **Sunset Community Garden** at 37th Avenue and Pacheco Street was the first WWII "victory garden" in San Francisco and has nice ocean views. Victory gardens were encouraged during the war because rationing was in effect, and nutritional self-reliance was expected so that every extra scrap of food could be sent to the soldiers overseas.

Last Shot

Visitors to **Lake Merced** – really a group of four interconnected lakes in the southwest corner of the city – might notice two small granite posts and a nearby plaque referring to a famous duel. On September 13, 1859, US Senator **David C. Broderick** and **David S. Terry**, formerly Associate Chief Justice of the Supreme Court of California, dueled over the issue of slavery; Broderick was shot and died three days later. The Terry-Broderick duel is often referred to as the **duel that ended dueling** in California.

The American Civil War started two years later, and the pro-slavery Terry fought for the losing side. In 1889, Terry, famous for his bad temper, attacked a judge (and former friend) at a train station in Stockton, California. It seems the judge had ruled against Terry in a bizarre case that looked like a scheme to cash in on a silver baron's fortune. As it turns out, this judge had a bodyguard, a former federal marshal, who handily shot Terry dead. The bodyguard, ironically, was from Tombstone, Arizona.

These days, Lake Merced is the best place in the city for bird-watching, and also has hiking and biking trails, a fishing pier with boat rentals, an 18-hole golf course, and a gun club with a skeet and trap range. There's also a pistol range, appropriately enough, but it's only open to San Francisco police officers.

sailing, takes me away...

The Bay sports some of the best-year round sailing in the US. It's always windy, which makes it a great place to unfurl a jib and get all hands on deck. Below are a few areas that each have something special, but there are many more sailing clubs in the greater Bay Area. See *sailors.org* for a full list.

Cal Sailing Club

Cal Sailing Club *(124 University Ave., Berkeley, cal-sailing.org)*, in the Berkeley Marina, is a non-profit co-operative that hosts an open house every month where they give anyone who shows up a no-pressure orientation and free sailboat rides. The civic-minded club also has windsurfing packages and some of the best membership prices in the Bay. The club doesn't have a phone, and members plan to keep it that way.

OCSC

OCSC *(1 Spinnaker Way, 510-843-4200, ocscsailing.com)*, also in the Berkeley Marina, offers an Intro to Sailing course every Saturday. It's a good time and the views are phenomenal. Even those who don't know a thing will be at the wheel and raising and dropping sail by the end of the day thanks to the friendly, laid-back staff on board the boat.

MAVERICKS: THE BIG KAHUNA OF BIG WAVES

Cold water, world-class waves, and a shark attack or two every year: Surf's up in the city, but you better have a full-length wet suit or the mental equivalent to bull-sized cojones. Most beginning surfers are advised to head south towards the more forgiving waves in Pacifica or even further south towards Santa Cruz, which boasts the **Santa Cruz Surfing Museum** for those who want to enjoy waves outside of the water *(701 West Cliff Dr., Santa Cruz, 831-420-6289, santacruzsurfingmuseum.org)*.

Treasure Island Sailing Center

Treasure Island Sailing Center *(698 1st St., Treasure Island #112, 415-421-2225, tisailing.org)* is a sailing club that tries to do good for the community and provide affordable sailing for its members. The center has an adaptive sailing program for disabled people who want to get out on the water, and youth sailing classes where low-income kids can get full or partial scholarships. The non-profit center encourages volunteerism among its members, and has the stated mission to make sailing possible for all people, regardless of socioeconomic background, skill level, or physical ability.

Surfing

Windsurfing and kite surfing lessons are available at **Cityfront Boardsports** *(2936 Lyon St., 415-929-7873, boardsports.com)* which has locations in Berkeley and San Francisco.

Kayaking

For those who prefer paddle power to wind power, or don't have a whole day to spend on the water, kayaking is an option. **City Kayak** *(Embarcadero at Townsend, 415-357-1010, citykayak.com)* on the Embarcadero, offers guided tours along the downtown waterfront. On game days at **SBC Ball Park**, City Kayak has outings to nearby McCovey Cove. Bring a glove, because this is where balls sometimes splash down.

Bay Area resident Jeff Clark is the surfing legend credited with finding and showing to the surf world the holy grail of Nor Cal surfing: **Mavericks**. Clark organizes an invite-only surf contest that draws the biggest names from around the world to ride the awesome swells there. These waves can break into walls of water up to 30 feet in height, and are known in the surf world as *the* most dangerous waves on the planet.

The gnarliness of this area near Half Moon Bay, 20 miles south of San Francisco, is no joke: in 1994, Mark Foo, a champion surfer from Hawaii, died at Mavericks. His death was caught on film in the 2004 documentary, *Riding Giants*, on big-wave surfing. *surfline.com; mavericks.bolt.com; mavsurver.com*

Letting It All Hang Out

Wearing clothes – so passé. The fashion is decidedly minimalist at the **nude beaches** of San Francisco. **North Baker Beach** and **Golden Gate Bridge Beach** (the latter is the cruisiest, we're told, and has many nicknames in the gay community, but "Nasty Boy Beach" has the most pizazz) are just a few of the many clothing-optional beaches that extend both directions on the San Francisco shores. The plucky independent weekly, *San Francisco Bay Guardian*, proves why it's so much better than its corporate counterparts once again by providing a guide to all of them updated on an annual basis: *sfbg.com*.

The place that locals go to get in touch with *warm water* in their birthday suits is **Harbin Hot Springs** (*18424 Harbin Springs Rd., Middletown, 707-987-2477, harbin.org*), about 90 miles northeast of San Francisco. Some people say it's a little New-Agey, but everyone is nice and there's a positive vibe. There's a rideshare board to get there from San Francisco, reasonably priced accommodations, and camping. No reservations are needed for camping or day trips, but reservations are necessary to secure a dorm bed or private room. To experience Harbin, you must become a member of their "church," which hosts a lot of optional outdoor workshops and New-Age-type events. It's an innocent environment where people are welcome to keep their clothes on if they like. The only part that freaks some out is when couples "float" each other in the warm pool. It's not uncommon to hear, "Would you like me to float you?"

MUSIC IN THE WOODS

During the summer months, free performances of world music, symphony, and ballet fill up **Sigmund Stern Grove**, a 33-acre valley in the Sunset district. It's also one of the best places to get away from it all and lounge under the towering eucalyptus and redwood trees. A lake, hiking trails, and a picnic area are all available to the public.
19th Ave. and Sloat Blvd., sterngrove.org

Funky Sculpture Garden Park

A little off the beaten path and unknown by most San Franciscans, the **Cayuga Playground** features a sculpture "sanctuary" of sorts where wood animal carvings seemingly melt into the trees and you sometimes don't notice them until you're about to trip over them.

Demetrio Braceros, a gardener with the City of San Francisco, was instructed in 1986 to fix up the rather drab park in a not-so-pretty part of town. He went above the call of duty and created a mini-wonderland. There are three different pathways along the edge of the park; one is called the "Garden of Eden," where Braceros has crafted biblical scenes into trees. In other parts of the park, there's a 9/11 memorial and totems of local celebrities like Herb Caen, Barry Bonds, and former mayor Willie Brown. Braceros isn't able to say how many sculptures he has made, since so many of them are hidden between branches and undergrowth. "They hide from me," he's said.

One of the most recent sculptures is a memorial to **Jo-Carol Davidson** (née Block), a musician who toured with disco legend Sylvester and was one of the founding artists of Megatone Records. Davidson lived nearby and spearheaded neighborhood efforts to make the park a safe and fun place for children. She succeeded, and a memorial wake was held for her at the rejuvenated park after her untimely passing away in 2003. Look for the sculpture with a colorful musical note under the name "Jo."

To get to the park via public transportation, take BART to the Balboa Park stop, find Geneva Street right outside the station, and walk three blocks downhill, then make a right on Cayuga Street. The playground is about a 10-minute walk from there, at the end of the street.

CAMPING IN THE CITY

It's not really in the city proper, but reservations for a camping spot and a quick ferry to **Angel Island** (one of the 12 islands within city limits) add up to a virtually deserted island for the night and great views of nearby San Francisco. Trails leading to campsites are unmarked, and rangers make sure that the campers are really supposed to be there. It's the coolest, most unusual camping experience most people will ever have. For those who *really* want seclusion, there is also a site accessible only by kayak. *Angel Island, 800-444-7275, angelisland.org*

John Muir and Yosemite: the Heart of the World

John Muir, naturalist extraordinaire, co-founded the **Sierra Club** (sierraclub.org) in San Francisco in 1892. Muir was also an early champion of **Yosemite** (nps.gov/yose).

Muir had long been enchanted with Yosemite through reading about it and had set off for the majestic mountains soon after arriving in San Francisco in 1868. He was planning later on heading to the Amazon to study botany, but had what can only be described as a spiritual experience at Yosemite: "As long as I live, I'll hear waterfalls and birds and winds sing. I'll interpret the rocks, learn the language of flood, storm, and the avalanche. I'll acquaint myself with the glaciers and wild gardens, and get as near the heart of the world as I can." In 1870 he complained that tourists were ruining Yosemite's natural beauty, a favorite subject of hometown photo bug Ansel Adams.

Muir was ahead of his time in many ways – he called hunting "the murder business," and his theories on how vast glaciers carved up Yosemite Valley were later found to be accurate. He also contributed greatly to the modern concept of an ecosystem, observing that everything in nature is interconnected and that changing one minor part of the landscape can ripple into unforeseen catastrophes.

Muir wasn't just an observer of nature, but a protector of it as well – he's largely responsible for giving Yosemite national park status and is credited with making the US national park system what it is today. Muir and President Theodore Roosevelt spent a few days tramping around Yosemite largely on their own, and Muir was able to convince the outdoorsman president of the importance of federal oversight for national treasures.

EMBASSY OF PARKS

Located far from the Bay Area, **Camp Mather**, 15 miles from the entrance of Yosemite, is run by the city of San Francisco as a place for weary city dwellers to get away from it all. Long ago, it was the home of a group of Miwok Indians (artifacts still occasionally turn up) and occasionally used by prospectors; the area didn't become heavily populated until a sawmill opened up on the banks of Birch Lake. In the mid-1920s, the City of San Francisco designated the property as a family recreation area, a use the camp has been serving ever since. Located approximately 180 miles east of San Francisco, Mather is situated on the rim of the Tuolumne River gorge at an elevation of 4,520 feet.
209-379-2284, parks.sfgov.org

Back in San Francisco, the half-acre **Transamerica Redwood Park** is one of the best places to see Muir's beloved redwoods. These 80 trees were transported here from Santa Cruz in 1972. Note the plaque to Emperor Norton's dogs, Bummer and Lazarus.

Outside the city, Muir Woods (nps.gov/muwo) is, in the words of Muir himself, "the best tree-lovers monument that could possibly be found in all the forests of the world." Muir Woods was featured in the *Star Wars* film *Return of the Jedi*.

IF QUAKES MAKE YOU TREMBLE

A venue with a fantastic view, the **Randall Museum** is the place to go for nature and science lovers – it's geared mainly to kids, but adults with an unhealthy fascination with Mother Nature's tectonic writhing might enjoy the seismometer in the museum's lobby that records local tremblers. Jumping up and down on the floor will register on the seismograph, and a full-sized replica of an earthquake cottage, typical of shelters which displaced residents constructed all over San Francisco after the 1906 earthquake, is also on the grounds. Permanent areas of the experiential museum include a live animal exhibit, woodshop, arts and ceramics studios, theater, darkroom, lapidary workshop, greenhouse, and gardens. *415-554-9600, randallmuseum.org*

Mountain Highs

San Francisco has 42 hills ranging from 200 to 938 feet. **Mt. Davidson** is the highest point in the city, and is set in the geographic center of the town, topped by the tallest cross in the United States. Even though Mt. Davidson is a city-owned park, the area surrounding the cross is technically private property. In 1997, the city sold a portion of the park to an Armenian religious group as a result of legal pressure – a number of atheist and religious groups had accused the city of using tax dollars to maintain a religious symbol. Clint Eastwood fans will recognize the large concrete cross from its appearance in *Dirty Harry*. The state of California, by the way, has more Armenians than anywhere outside of Armenia.

Hiking fanatics who enjoy the summer wildflowers of **Mt. Diablo**, about 30 miles outside the city in Clayton, proclaim that besides Tanzania's Mt. Kilimanjaro, its peak has the farthest view, in the most directions, of any mountain in the world. For great views within San Francisco, nothing beats a wind-whipped hike up to the top of **Twin Peaks**, just a little bit north of Mt. Davidson. It's the only place in the city where a view of the San Francisco Bay and the Pacific Ocean at the same time is a certainty. Although it can be beautiful during the day, most Twin Peaks fans say night time is the right time to see the city lights spread out below.

Dining

Specials

Open chicken Burger
w̄ Sweet Chilli, yoghurt
Dressing & Fries $16⁵⁰

Smoked Salmon Orzo
w̄ Spinach & a Caper
Salsa $16

2004
PINOT GRIS

$8 glass $36 bottle

Photo: Linda & Colin McKie

From cheap eats to the most refined cuisine, San Franciscans take food seriously and it shows. Whatever type of food you're in the mood for, you're bound to find it here at a decent price. You'll also probably find a great bottle of wine to go with it; with more than 100 wineries in the Bay Area producing some of the world's best wine — which yes, even the French drink — San Francisco has got the goods, so sit down and eat your supper.

Photo: Bob Ecker

Not So Frank

According to a recent survey done by the People for the Ethical Treatment of Animals, an activist animal-rights organization, **SBC Park** *(24 Willie Mays Plaza, 415-972-1800, sbcpark.com)*, home of the San Francisco Giants, is the number one vegetarian-friendly stadium in the nation. The vegetarian selection includes veggie dogs and burgers, vegetarian sushi, fruit platters, edamame, and portabella mushroom sandwiches.

In second place was Oakland's **McAfee Coliseum** *(7000 Coliseum Way, 510-569-2121, coliseum.com)*, home to the A's, where you can order veggie burgers and dogs, bean pies, tofu burgers, baked potatoes, fruit cups, and salads.

eat your veggies

Japanese Jewels

A list of vegetarian restaurants around town:

Ananda Fuara

Although the food gets mixed reviews, everyone loves the friendly sari-clad waitresses, the wide selection of vegan fare, and the otherwordly surroundings. Meaning "Fountain of Delight," the name Ananda Fuara was given to the restaurant by Sri Chinmoy, a spiritual leader. The restaurant is run by the Bay Area chapter of India's Sri Chinmoy religious sect, which guests are reminded of everywhere they look: there are pictures of him with the Pope and lifting weights, and a video of him plays on a TV screen in the back. Additionally, some of his poetry is printed on cards at each table and his books are available for anyone who wants to read during dinner.
1298 Market St., 415-621-1994, anandafuara.com

The oldest Japanese restaurant in the US opened here in 1946. Although J.T. Nakahara's establishment has since closed, San Francisco has a great selection of Japanese restaurants.

Izumiya

Office workers in Japan spend almost every evening with co-workers over beer, sake, and small plates of food that everyone shares in *izakaya* (Japanese pub-style) restaurants. Unfortunately, *izakayas* haven't made their way to the city yet, so Izumiya is the closest you'll get, where friends can enjoy chilled plum wine, seaweed salad, and *okonomiyaki* (Japan's version of the crêpe). It's a great place to get the evening started before heading to the karaoke box.
1581 Webster St., Suite 270 (at Geary), 415-441-6867

Kappa Restaurant

Located above Denny's in Japantown, this restaurant has no outdoor sign, making it easy to miss. The windowless restaurant with a sliding door is as authentic as it gets — let the friendly Japanese couple who run this place recommend dishes as you sample some of their 15 types of sake.
1700 Post St., Suite K,
415-673-6004

Ryoko's

A little-known restaurant in the Theater District that has only a sign in Japanese out front and the authenticity to match. Regulars can buy a bottle of sake, put their names on it, and leave it for the next time they come. This custom already mentioned in previous chapter.
619 Taylor St., 415-775-1028

Geranium

Housed in what used to be the All American Meat Market, this is a cozy restaurant known for its veggie comfort foods — meatless meatloaf, stews, pastas, and greens.
615 Cortland Ave., 415-647-0118

Green's

Opened by Zen Buddhists in 1979, this restaurant has a great view of the Bay and the Golden Gate Bridge, and some of the tastiest vegetarian dishes in the city. Most produce served here is grown organically at a Buddhist meditation center near Stinson Beach, just outside of the city.
204 Bay St., 415-771-6222

Herbivore

This modern vegan restaurant describes itself as an "earthly grill." They serve excellent seitan *shawarmas* and the chocolate cake is to die for.
983 Valencia St., 415-526-5657; 531 Divisadero, 415-885-7133, herbivoresf.com

Millennium Restaurant

For a classy vegetarian-friendly evening, head to this place in the Theater District. With appetizing dishes such as the truffled white bean *cassoulet* and organic wines, you'll have plenty to choose from.
580 Geary St., 415-345-3900,
millenniumrestaurant.com

Minako

Judy and her mother run this slow-paced organic Japanese restaurant. Not all dishes are vegetarian, but there is a wide selection. The pair often makes their own tofu, and guests rave about the mixed rice grains and the freshness of the vegetables.
2154 Mission St., 415-864-1888

The Fong-Torres family is a great San Francisco success story. **Shirley** and **Ben Fong-Torres**, son and daughter of immigrants to the Bay Area, were raised in Oakland and later made it big in San Francisco.

While Ben Fong-Torres was the news editor of *Rolling Stone* from 1969 to 1981 (he was featured in the 2000 film *Almost Famous*), his sister Shirley took to the streets of Chinatown and established **Wok Wiz Tours** *(654 Commercial St., 650-355-9657, wokwiz.com)*. Her "Eat Your Way Through Chinatown" tour is exactly what you think it is. After a morning of grazing at a number of legendary spots, you and your growing belly will stop for lunch. Tours are available seven days a week and prices range from $40 to $85.

One of the stops on the tour is **Sam Wo's** *(813 Washington St., 415-982-0596)*. Customers walk

BAD BOYS OF CHINATOWN
The Golden Dragon *(816 Washington St., 415-398-3920)* is a low-key Chinese restaurant, so it's hard to imagine that this was where of one of the city's biggest shootings took place. In 1977, the Joe Boys gang located the Wah Ching gang members who were having a late dinner there. The Joe Boys, most of them in their late teens, took out their guns and started shooting everyone in the restaurant. Five people died, including two tourists, and 11 were injured. The shootings prompted the formation of a Gang Task Force by city police.

through the kitchen and up narrow stairs to the second floor in what used to be **Edsel Ford Fong**'s room. Fong, a waiter legendary for his rudeness, started working in the restaurant in the 1940s and continued until he passed away in the 1980s. He would throw chopsticks on tables as customers arrived, make fun of customers' weight and choice in food, and often ask them to write their own orders down. People who didn't know about him often left the restaurant upset, but most San Franciscans loved his quirky ways. **Edsel Ford Fong's** restaurant at SBC Park was named after him. (Legend also has it that Gary Snyder taught Jack Kerouac how to use chopsticks at Sam Wo's).

Not on the tour but also part of Chinatown's history is **Johnny Kan**, a successful restaurateur who helped out many eateries in the neighborhood by giving them free utensils and tips. In 1939, he opened the Chinese Kitchen, the first authentic Chinese delivery service in the US. Later, he opened **New Kan's Restaurant** *(708 Grant Ave., 415-362-5267)*.

Other Chinatown classics include the **Empress of China** *(838 Grant, bet. Washington and Clay, 415-434-1345, empressofchinasf.com)*, the only high-rise Chinese roof garden restaurant in town. The Empress boasts one of the most impressive collections of celebrity photos on the walls; beneath many of the photos, you can read what the star had for dinner.

If you're still a little hungry, head to **Hang Ah Tea Room** *(1 Pagoda Pl., bet. Stockton and Grant Sts., 415-982-5686)*, the oldest Chinese restaurant in the city, opened in 1920.

VIETNAMESE TREAT

Watch out, Rice-A-Roni: **Tu Lan** *(8 Sixth St., 415-626-0927)* could very well be the real San Francisco treat. Ask any San Franciscan and he or she will agree that Tu Lan offers the best and possibly the cheapest Vietnamese food this side of the Bay. Since given the thumbs up for spring rolls, crispy noodles, and ginger fried fish by Julia Child in the 1970s, the restaurant has achieved cult status for foodies despite the greasy tables and run-down location.

A Slice of the Boot

Bits of North Beach history and a list of places for good Italian food:

Capp's Corner *(1600 Powell, 415-989-2589)* was a favorite of Joe DiMaggio and Marilyn Monroe, and looking at the walls covered with black-and-white photos of boxers, baseball players, and performers, they weren't alone. Families enjoy minestrone and pasta at tables covered with checkered tablecloths; every other Thursday, cast members from the stage show *Beach Blanket Babylon* and other local entertainers meet here.

Since its opening in 1886, **Fior d'Italia** *(601 Union St., 415-986-1886, fior.com)* has survived several earthquakes and fires, most recently in early 2005. It's the oldest Italian restaurant in the city and although the food hasn't changed much, the clientele certainly has. At its first location, the staff served meals for clients of a bordello next door *(492 Broadway St.)*; nowadays, you'll see sports figures (in photos, or in person) like Tour de France champion Lance Armstrong and 49ers quarterback Jeff Garcia.

The **Gold Spike** *(527 Columbus Ave., 415-421-4591)* opened in 1920 as a candy store, but during Prohibition, the Mechetti family sold homemade wine in the back room. People who lived in the building couldn't resist the aromas of Natalina Mechetti's homemade pasta and would peek in every day at dinner time. She offered to have the tenants over for meals if they paid 25 cents a day. Soon, passersby were joining the family at the dinner table and the candy store turned into a restaurant. Today, the restaurant's walls are covered with business cards and old dollar bills. The tradition started in the early 1960s when fitness guru Jack Lalaine started giving a customer a hard time for drinking and smoking. Lalaine licked a cigarette and flicked it to the ceiling, where it stuck. The man paid the restaurant owner a dollar to stick his business card next to the cigarette, and other customers' cards followed.

HI-TECH HUNGER

Next time you're dining in town, ask restaurant owners and servers to tell you their dot-com stories. It's San Francisco and people love to talk. Besides, almost everyone here was a virtual stock millionaire at one point. Sajjad Baig, co-owner of **Naan N' Chutney** *(525 Haight St., 415-255-1625)* was an engineer for Microsoft, but luckily for our palates, he agreed to open this Indian-Pakistani restaurant with his brother, Tariq Baig.

Since 1998, Lorenzo Petroni, co-owner of **North Beach Restaurant** *(1512 Stockton, 415-392-1700, northbeachrestaurant.com)*, has made his own wine in Sonoma Valley, as well as his Petroni extra virgin olive oil *(petronivineyards.com)*. The restaurant specializes in Tuscan cuisine, and customers can choose to dine in the Prosciutto room under hanging cured hams, in the Wine Cellar, or in the regular dining room.

You'd think **Original U.S. Restaurant** *(515 Columbus Ave., 415-397-5200)* might specialize in American cuisine, but U.S. in this instance stands for *Unione Sportiva*, the Italian name for the San Francisco Italian Athletic club nearby. The location and owners have changed a few times over the years, but the stewed rabbit, *osso bucco*, and pasta is as good as it's always been.

Dog of a Restaurant

P. Allarme and A. B. Blanco opened San Francisco's first French restaurant, **Le Poulet d'Or**, meaning "Gold Chicken"; it was nicknamed the "Poodle Dog" by gold diggers because the French name was too difficult to pronounce. The owners were two Frenchmen who were asked to move to San Francisco, as many others would, to improve the quality of food in restaurants here. Le Poulet d'Or, which stood at 445 Bush Street, was the best dinner in town you could get for a dollar until it burned down in the 1906 fire.

Many French restaurants have opened up nearby including **Café Claude** *(7 Claude Lane, 415-392-3505, cafeclaude.com)*, an authentic Parisian bistro. The owner was able to achieve a perfect Parisian look by shipping every piece of furniture, including the zinc bar, from a defunct bistro in Paris.

CALIFORNIA EATIN'

Alice Waters is the mother of California cuisine, which we think is French cuisine with Californian ingredients, but who are we to say? Having studied in Paris in the 1950s, Waters quickly became a fan of farmers' markets here and couldn't resist buying food even though she had no place to cook. In 1971, she opened the now-legendary **Chez Panisse**, a small Berkeley restaurant that began with little fanfare. But word spread and soon customers were making reservations months in advance to sample what everyone was talking about the secret to her cuisine is using fresh and local produce and organic meats: they're driven or flown in every day from farmers throughout California. *1517 Shattuck Ave., Berkeley, 510-548-5525, chezpanisse.com*

A Popular Moose

Ed Moose, a former newspaper employee, opened the **Washington Square Bar & Grill** *(1707 Powell St., 415-982-8123)*, nicknamed "the Washbag," in 1973. He has since sold it, but still runs **Moose's** *(1652 Stockton St., on Washington Square, 415-989-7800)*, a North Beach spot that fills up quickly at lunch time when Moose greets customers by name at the door.

Regulars here include politicians, media people, and celebs like Walter Cronkite and Danielle Steele. Herb Caen, the town's beloved columnist, ate here regularly. Besides the great food and star-studded crowd, the best thing about this restaurant is that cell phones are to be turned off at all times.

Tips du Jour

Check out restaurant menus before you go with the *San Francisco Bay Guardian*'s list of online menus at *sfbg.com/menus/index.html*. Also read Dan Leone's Cheap Eats column for dining suggestions.

If it's restaurant reservations you're looking for, visit *opentable.com*, a San Francisco company that lets you reserve a table without a credit card (this service started here, but is now available in most US cities). You can even send special requests to the maitre d'.

ON TOP OF THE WORLD
Julius Castle Restaurant *(1541 Montgomery at Union St., 415-392-2222)* has been serving fancy dinners on top of Telegraph Hill (just below Coit Tower) since 1922. In the 1920s, a turntable similar to the ones used for cable cars was installed at the top of steep Montgomery street because cars didn't have enough room to turn around. The turntable has been taken out, but valet parking and public transportation should take care of parking problems.

San Francisco Vice

DINNER AND A MOVIE

Foreign Cinema is the perfect first date destination where you can watch a movie as you enjoy a Californian/Mediterranean dinner prepared by chefs John Clark and Gayle Pirie, who got their start at **Zuni Cafe** *(1658 Market St., 415-552-2522)* and **Chez Panisse** (see page 97). Chelsea Clinton, Charlize Theron, and Madonna have been spotted here. *2534 Mission St., 415-378-7600, foreigncinema.com*

In the mid-1990s, *Miami Vice* star **Don Johnson** was back on television screens starring in the locally filmed show *Nash Bridges*, in which Johnson played a smartass cop who fought crime in the Bay Area with his costar Cheech Marin (of Cheech and Chong fame).

The two were often seen around town and the local press frequently had juicy gossip to report. The piece most people remember is one that appeared in the *San Francisco Chronicle* by Phillip Matier and Andrew Ross; the article which claimed that Don Johnson got drunk while having dinner at **Mas Sake** (2030 Lombard St., 415-440-1505, massake.com) and hit on a woman who filed charges against Johnson, claiming that he touched her breasts and asked, "They're real, aren't they?" Johnson denied the story and threatened to sue the *Chronicle*. No one is sure who was telling the truth, but the story suggests that someone could use a little help with pick-up lines.

Come for Dinner

"Dine-About-Town" is an annual month-long event organized by the San Francisco Convention & Visitors Bureau during which customers can enjoy three-course lunches for $21.95 and dinners for $31.95. In 2005, 108 restaurants participated and 21,159 meals were served. Dine-About-Town started in late 2001 in an effort to motivate residents and visitors to return to restaurant dining after September 11. A list of participating restaurants can be found at *sfvisitor.org*.

Amy Sherman started thinking about food when she was sharing an office with a friend a few years ago. The lack of work allowed them to discuss recipes, plan dinners and lunches, and chat about the best places to shop. "When I left the company, I really missed it. Every morning, I started asking my husband what he wanted to eat for dinner that night," Sherman told us. Her husband suggested that she start a food blog and that's how **Cooking With Amy** (cookingwithamy.blogspot.com) was born. Sherman is now one of the well-known food bloggers in the Bay Area and writes for several publications. "I'm not sure whether the blog has fed my obsession with food or if it has given me an outlet," Sherman said.

Sherman goes out to eat regularly and tries new places all the time, but she has some all-time favorites. When in the **Ferry Building Marketplace** (ferrybuildingmarketplace.com), there's no need to spend lots of money in pricey restaurants, she told us. Check out the to-go counters like the **Slanted Door**'s (415-861-8032, slanteddoor.com), **Out the Door** counter, where you can have the same meal as Bill Clinton without the big bill. For a cheap but delicious Vietnamese meal, she goes to **Bodega Bistro** (607 Larkin St., 415-921-1218) in the heart of the Tenderloin.

Plouf (40 Belden Place, 415-986-6491) and **Baker Street Bistro** (2953 Baker St., 415-931-1475) are her favorite French restaurants and the **Helmand** (430 Broadway St. at Montgomery, 415-362-0641) is where she goes when in the mood for Afghani food.

Local Food Blogs

To find out the best and most current food offerings in the Bay Area, check out the many local food blogs, and if you're inspired to start to your own, visit foodblogscool.blogspot.com for tips and tricks.

101 Cookbooks

Recipes and stories.
101cookbooks.com

Becks & Posh

Recipes and restaurant reviews.
becksposhnosh.blogspot.com

Chez Pim

Recipes and restaurant reviews.
chezpim.typepad.com

Gastronomie

Recipes, food stories, and wines.
gastronomie-sf.com

Monday Night Dinner Party

Photo: Jay Ober

Two brothers, a private home, and great food is what the **Ghetto Gourmet** is all about. One brother has since moved on, but every Monday night, at a cost of about $30 per person, customers can still gather together in the host's living room, where they are served an ever-changing gourmet meal – a true example of home-style cooking
ghetto-gourmet.com

Photo: Jay Ober

Meathenge

Meat recipes and descriptions of ingredients and *cooking techniques.*
cyberbilly.com/meathenge

An Obsession With Food

Recipes, cooking techniques, and food stories.
obsessionwithfood.com

Saute Wednesday

Food and wine news.
sautewednesday.com

Tomatilla!

Recipes.
tomatilla.com

Vinography

Wine and restaurant reviews and winemaker profiles.
vinography.com

Happy Meals

The oldest US chapter of the **Slow Food Movement** (*slowfoodsanfrancisco.com*), dedicated to protecting our eating experience from the perils of modern fast food and life, is the one here in San Francisco. Alice Waters of Chez Panisse is on the board of directors and food events are scheduled throughout the year.

Every second Saturday of the month, people get together for the **San Francisco Vegetarian Society Monthly Potluck**; the San Francisco Vegetarian Society (415-273-5481, *sfvs.org*) also organizes Dining Out events, picnics, and lectures.

The San Francisco Living Foods Enthusiasts (415-751-2806, *living-foods.com*) provides information and support to people who follow a fruitarian diet and for those who eat only living and raw foods.

the quest for the perfect burrito

Burritos are to San Francisco what pizza is to New York, and everyone here knows where the perfect burrito is. Now, if San Francisco residents could only agree on its location, the world would be a happier place.

El Castillito

Bad cooks on a budget can be seen ordering a burrito every night of the week. At $3 or $4 each including chips and all sorts of salsa, who can blame them? 136 Church St., 415-621-3428; 2092 Mission St., 415-621-6971

Cucos

Serves possibly the best burritos outside of the Mission district with lots of fresh herbs and homemade salsa. 488 Haight St., 415-863-4906

Doña Tere

For those looking for something beyond burritos, try the *flautas* and *tortas*. 21st and Alabama Sts.

Mariachi's

Although it doesn't look like much on the outside, Mariachi's cooks up the freshest ingredients right before your eyes and makes some of the lightest burritos and tacos out there. 508 Valencia St., 415-621-4358

PARK BITES

Nothing beats a hot coffee or cocoa after a cold day on the Bay and there's no better place than the **Crissy Field Center Café**, which overlooks the Crissy Field Marsh. Visitors can choose from a wide selection of organic recipes inspired by Chez Panisse's Alice Waters and peruse the bookstore. All waste is recycled and used as compost in the Golden Gate National Parks and all proceeds support the Golden Gate National Parks Conservancy. 415-561-7756, crissyfield.org

Naughty Treats

If you're in the mood for some Asian fusion delights, check out **Asia SF** *(201 Ninth St., 415-255-2742, asiasf.com)*, the hip restaurant/club where waitresses are really waiters and customers go for the food. No, really. Got a sweet tooth? How about some erotic baked goods?:

The Cake Gallery

With free delivery service, who could resist the X-rated cakes the staff can bake for you? Show your friends some love on a cake. *290 9th St., 415-861-2253, thecakegallerysf.com*

Hot Cookie

Penis-shaped cookies in all sizes and colors with white frosting on top. *407 Castro St., 415-621-2350*

Pancho Villa Taqueria

If people here were to agree on one place to get a great burrito, this would probably be it. Every evening, especially late on weekend nights, this Mission spot is packed with people having a bite before partying or filling up on a high-carb meal to soak up the alcohol before going home. *3071 16th St., 415-864-8840*

La Taqueria

For a more low-carb-friendly burrito, try La Taqueria's rice-less wraps. *2889 Mission St., 415-285-7117*

Taqueria Cancun

Some of our office worker friends are willing to take the bus from the Financial District down to this Market Street location just to bring tasty burritos back to their cubicles. That's how good they are. *2288 Mission St., 415-252-9560; 1003 Market St., 415-864-6773*

El Tonayense

Cheap but delicious and authentic Mexican dishes for half the price of most places. *3150 24th St., 415-550-9192*

For more locations, check *citysearch.com, sfweekly.com,* and *sfbg.com.* Each year they publish a Best of the Bay list which often includes the Best Burrito list.

Chocolate Does a Body Good

 **Scharffen Berger** is the tastiest thing that's happened to chocolate since Ghiradelli, and once again, the magic happened in San Francisco. In the 1990s, two friends, **Robert Steinberg** and **John Scharffenberger**, decided to get together and make chocolate. Steinberg, a physician by trade, was diagnosed with a rare disease and decided to close up shop and focus on things he really liked, such as cooking and fine dining. A friend of his showed him a book on how to make chocolate, which got Steinberg interested. He decided to go to the Bernachon factory in Lyon, France to intern for a couple of weeks and came back with the intention of offering great quality chocolate to the US market.

Scharffenberger, a local wine producer, decided to help his friend out and together they made their first batch of chocolate in 1996. They quickly won over local foodies, and when Steinberg's South San Francisco home became too small for the business, they moved to Berkeley where they now have a factory. Free tours are given there every day.

Robert Steinberg still lives in San Francisco and practices medicine part-time at the San Francisco Free Clinic.
Scharffen Berger, 914 Heinz Ave., Berkeley, 510-981-4050; San Francisco Ferry Building Store, 415-981-9150, scharffenberger.com

Emmy's Spaghetti Shack

This Outer Mission spot is a great place for spaghetti and meatballs, which happens to be the best deal on the menu. What's even better is that the portion could probably feed two people. Bring your own bottle of wine for an even cheaper date. Put your name down on the list and grab a few drinks at the bar next door, because there's always a long line here. Trust us, it's worth the wait; you'll love the clothes pinned to clotheslines around the room, the DJ spinning, and the cozy atmosphere.
3355 Mission St., 415-206-2086

Slurp It

Temperatures can drop at any time here, which makes any day a great noodle soup day.

Hotei
Japanese noodle house specializing in soba, udon, gyoza, and ramen.
1290 9th Ave., 415-753-6045

Iroha
A quiet ramen noodle house without the long lines often seen in Japantown.
1728 Buchanan St., 415-922-0321

King of Thai Noodle House
The name says it all; noodle soups and pad thai are excellent and cheap.
*639 Clement St., 415-752-5198;
346 Clement St., 415-831-9953;
156 Powell St., 415-397-2199*

Mifune

The sign on the window says it's okay to slurp your noodles, so just do it.

1737 Post St., 415-922-0337

Osha Thai Noodle Café

Meaning "delicious" in Thai, this place not only has great noodles, they serve awesome seafood and beef dishes. Their Geary location is the cheaper one.

696 Geary St., 415-673-2368; 819 Valencia St., 415-826-7738, oshathai.com

Sapporo-ya

Casual Japanese restaurant that specializes in steaming bowls of ramen noodles.

1581 Webster St., 415-563-7400

Established in 1849, **Boudin Bakery** (*boudinbakery.com*) is the oldest business in town; Isidore Boudin, the French immigrant who started the company, can thank his wife for that. During the 1906 earthquake and fire, as their bakery was burning down, Louise Boudin was able to quickly grab a bucket of dough and save the business.

The sourdough bread sold today is still made with the 1849 "mother dough," a starter dough made of flour, water, and yeast that keeps expanding. The Bay Area is home to a unique bacteria called lactobacillus San Francisco; when mixed with yeast, called candida milleri, it becomes the "mother dough."

Although Boudin didn't come up with the recipe – it came from local mining families – he did bring his French-style baking skills and made the bakery one of the most successful in town. In 1941, Boudin Bakery was purchased by Steven Giraudo and is now run by his son Lou. The company bakes 25,000 loaves of bread a day, in 20 varieties.

Smart Cookies

Photo: Mee Mee Bakery

In 1964, **Edward Louie** of San Francisco's Lotus Fortune Cookie Company built a machine that folded dough and slipped in a fortune. Today, the world's largest fortune cookie manufacturer, Wonton Food Inc. of Long Island City, Queens, ships out 60 million cookies a month.

The oldest fortune cookie company here is **Mee Mee Bakery** (1328 Stockton St., 415-362-3204, meemeebakery.com) where fortune cookies, big and small (giant ones can be ordered for special occasions), continue to be produced on site. They are sold under the Shangri-La Brand and are still served at the Japanese Garden Tea House.

Golden Gate Fortune Cookie Factory (56 Ross Alley, 415-781-3956) may not be the oldest, but it's the only place in town where fortune cookies are still made by hand. Hidden in a dark building on narrow Ross Alley, two women make some 20,000 fortune cookies a day.

What Is It?

In 1928, **George Whitney** scooped out some vanilla ice cream, put it between two large oatmeal cookies, and dipped the sandwich into dark chocolate — the **It's It Ice Cream Sandwich** (itsiticecream.com) was born. For over 40 years, Whitney sold the ice cream sandwich at Playland-at-the-Beach by the Cliff House.

When Playland closed in the early 1970s, Whitney also closed up shop, ending the sales of the favorite local treat. But San Franciscans demanded their It's It back and Whitney started selling them to small independent stores in 1974.

By 1978, the facility he worked in became too small, so he moved the company to a factory near the San Francisco Airport. Nowadays, Whitney sells his It's It in more than 15 states. The ice cream sandwich is now known by many as "the official food of San Francisco."

Mixin' It Up

Fusion is the Haight's signature cuisine, where prices are reasonable and portions are huge.

Cha Cha Cha

Santeria altars, small plates of hot Caribbean dishes, and a tangy sangria make this spot a great place to meet friends for a fun dinner with a Cuban flair. Plan on spending some time at the bar, as the restaurant doesn't accept reservations and the line is always long. Did we mention that the sangria is really good?
1801 Haight St., 415-386-7670;
2327 Mission St. bet. 19th & 20th,
415-648-0504

Citrus Club

A hip noodle house where you can enjoy Asian beer, sake, and all sorts of noodles. Some of our favorites include garlic edamame, fresh spring rolls, and tofu coconut soup, but be careful, portions here are so big, you could feed an entire family (or one very hungry person).
1790 Haight St., 415-387-6366

We All Scream for Ice Cream

Indian restaurants are plentiful here, but not many places serve Indian ice cream, and that's why owners Suresh and Bharti Parmar, who immigrated from Gujarat, India in the mid-1970s, opened **Bombay Ice Creamery and Chaat** *(552 Valencia St. at 16th St., 415-431-1103)*. Saffron-pistachio, cardamom, *chicku* (a tropical fruit that looks like a potato), rose, ginger, chai, green tea, fig, cashew, raisin, lychee, and mango are only some of the flavors available.

Ice cream too fattening for you? Try the lighter green tea, ginger, and mango gelato at **Yoogo Gelato** *(601 Broadway, 415-398-2996)*.

For more fresh gelato, try **Ciao Bella Café's** *(1 Ferry Plaza, Ste. 8, Market and Embarcadero, 415-834-9330, ciaobellagelato.com)* family recipe out of Torino, Italy, or walk in **Gelato Classico** *(576 Union St., 415-391-6667)*, a small North Beach shop.

Vegan ice cream lovers and Internet surfers finally have a place they can share. **Maggie Mudd** *(903 Cortland Ave., 415-641-5291, maggiemudd.com)* sells dairy-free ices and offers Wifi Internet.

Since 1953, locals have been enjoying the rich and tropical flavors at **Mitchell's Ice Cream** *(688 San Jose Ave., 415-648-2300, mitchellsicecream.com)*. With names like Deep Dish Apple Pie, French Custard Vanilla, or New York Cherry, ice cream here is certainly not low-fat, which is why it's so good. The Mitchell family imports *buko* (young coconut), *ube* (purple yam), and avocado from the Philippines and makes their ice creams and sorbets fresh daily.

Want restaurant-like dessert creations without the upscale restaurant bill? Head to **Sketch** *(1809 Fourth St., Berkeley, 510-665-5650)*, where former pastry chefs Eric Shelton and Ruthie Planas make ice creams in small batches as well as cookies, brioches, waffles, and crêpes. Flavors change regularly, and the friendly staff is always happy to recommend the flavor of the day.

Sophie's Crepes *(1581 Webster St., 415-929-7732)* is a good place to sample the Japanese take on French crêpes and ice cream.

SWENSEN'S

America's favorite ice cream parlor got its start here. Earle Swensen opened his first parlor on Russian Hill in 1948 and to this day, ice cream fans come to enjoy old-fashioned flavors like Peppermint Stick, Lemon Burst, and Wild Mountain Blackberry.
1999 Hyde at Union St.,
415-775-6818

Who said Seattle was the city for coffee lovers? Good coffee's been around for a lot longer here. As early as 1849, three Croatian immigrants set up a canvas coffee stand on the waterfront. **Tadich Grill** *(now located at 240 California St., 415-391-1849)* is the oldest restaurant in the city and one of the only places where you can sit in curtained booths. It also serves more seafood and cocktails than coffee these days.

Just a year later, in 1850, William Bovee opened the city's first coffee-roasting plant; one of his early employees was J.A. Folger. In 1865, Folger bought out Bovee and changed the name to **J.A. Folger & Co**.

In 1878, brothers Austin and Reuben Hills opened a small dairy stall at Bay City Market, and a few years later, they purchased Arabian Coffee & Spice, which became **Hills Brothers Coffee**.

In 1899, **Freed, Teller & Freed** *(1-800-370-7371, freedscoffeetea.com)* began selling their coffees and teas downtown. Although the company's Polk Street store has closed, it still roasts its own beans and sells them online. We heard that if you peeked in the company's database, you'd still find the special blends made for Tina Turner and Harvey Milk.

There are so many places to get a great shot of espresso here that the hardest thing isn't finding a spot but choosing among the many local favorites:

Caffe Trieste *(609 Vallejo St., 415-392-6739, caffetrieste.com)* was the first espresso coffee house on the West Coast, opening in 1956. It quickly became a favorite of Jack Kerouac and other Beat writers. The Giotta family still runs the place and roasts coffee beans next door.

Another favorite of the Beat generation was **Vesuvio** *(255 Columbus Ave., at Jack Kerouac Alley, 415-362-3370, vesuvio.com)*. Legend has it that in 1960, Henry Miller wrote Kerouac and told him that he enjoyed reading *The Dharma Bums* and invited him to come visit in Big Sur. The evening they were supposed to meet, Kerouac headed to Vesuvio to have a few drinks. Vesuvio must be a difficult place to leave because even

Morning Glories

Breakfast is the most important meal of the day, so indulge.

All You Knead

A good place to go on a lazy Sunday, this Upper Haight restaurant is right next to shoe and clothing stores, so you can walk off the calories from the huge breakfast you just ate. *1466 Haight St., 415-552-4550*

Beach Chalet Brewery & Restaurant

Even on foggy days, you'll enjoy the ocean view from the restaurant. Micro-brewed beers, great mussels and French fries, and smoked salmon and capers — everything you'd want for a brunch that's a tad fancier than usual. *1000 Great Hwy., 415-386-843, beachchalet.com*

Boogaloos

A Mission District favorite where breakfast is made all day and the staff is nice enough to serve free coffee to people in line for seats. *3296 22nd St., 415-824-4088*

Eddie's Café

No two mugs are the same
and tables aren't always clean,
but the coffee is always fresh
and the staff friendly.

800 Divisadero St., 415-563-9780

The Grind

We're not sure how they do it, but no
matter how packed this place is, you
never have to wait too long. Their
hearty omelettes and potatoes are a
great way to start the day.

783 Haight St., 415-864-0955

Kate's Kitchen

This friendly neighborhood place
serves large pancakes and other
breakfast classics.

471 Haight St., 415-626-3984

though Kerouac called Miller every hour to tell him he
would be delayed a little longer, he never did make it to
Big Sur.

The **Graffeo Coffee Roasting Company** *(735
Columbus Ave., 415-986-2420, graffeo.com)* has been
delivering quality beans since 1935.

We don't like chains here except if it's a local one –
Peet's *(2124 Vine St., Berkeley, 510-841-0564,
peets.com)* has been filling tea and coffee cups in the
Bay Area since 1966. Its first location on Vine Street in
Berkeley brought in some serious coffee drinkers who got
hooked after the first few sips. A Berkeley police officer
nicknamed the loyal customers the "Peetniks" after the
word "beatnik." The group proudly wore coffee brown T-
shirts with the term printed on them. Starbucks founders
Jerry Baldwin, Zev Siegl, and Gordon Bowker spent the
1970 Christmas season working at Peet's before starting
their own coffee business in Seattle in 1971. For the first
21 months, Starbucks used Peet's beans.

In addition to coffee, **Tosca** *(242 Columbus Ave.,
bet. Broadway and Pacific, 415-986-9651)* also serves
great cocktails, and they have the oldest espresso
machine in town.

If all this coffee talk has inspired you to get your
own espresso machine, head to **Thomas E. Cara's**
shop *(517 Pacific Ave., 415-781-0383)* in the hip
Jackson Square area. While stationed in Europe in the
1940s, Cara bought a gas-fired, chrome-plated Pavoni
espresso machine in Milan. He brought it home and was
inspired to open a store that would carry espresso
machines and other kitchen tools; today, the store sells
only espresso machines. The Cara family still has the
original Pavoni machine.

food firsts

Fishy Tales

Rumor has it that the fish stew known as **Cioppino** was invented at **Fisherman's Wharf** in 1900. Fishermen who wanted to eat fish stew once they returned from a hard day out at sea would contribute or "chip in" fish for the meal and cook it in a communal pot. The name is said to have come from "chip-in-o" which, over time, became Cioppino.

Catching Crabs

In 1914, San Francisco added a new local specialty, the **Crab Louis**, which was invented at **Solari's** restaurant. Nowadays, locals head to **Swan Oyster Depot** *(1517 Polk St., 415-673-1101)* during Dungeness crab season (Nov. to June). The seafood is always fresh and half the price of most places in town.

Oysters Kirkpatrick were first baked at **The Palace Hotel** *(2 New Montgomery St., 415-512-1111, sfpalace.com)* by Chef Ernest Arbogast in 1900. These oysters, dipped in a mix of ketchup and butter, covered with bacon and some Parmesan cheese and then baked, were named after the hotel manager, Colonel John C. Kirkpatrick.

St. Francis Fountain

Sure, regulars say come here for the ice cream sundaes made with Mitchell's ice cream, but what they really come for is the retro décor, something you rarely see in the city. *2801 24th St., 415-826-4200*

Sears Fine Food

Ben Sears, then a circus clown, decided to go into the restaurant business with his brother Hilbur Sears and in 1938, they opened Sears Fine Food. To this day, people still line up on the sidewalk for the "Sear's World Famous Swedish Pancakes." Make sure you're hungry; they serve them in stacks of 18. *439 Powell St. at Sutter, 415-986-0700, searsfinefood.com*

Squat & Gobble Cafe

Inexpensive omelettes, crêpes, and other breakfast favorites served in an often packed venue. *237 Fillmore St., 415-487-0551*

Midnight Snacks

Unlike most US cities, San Francisco doesn't have a lot of restaurants that stay open 24 hours. But here is a list for the night owls who still enjoy a good hearty meal even at three in the morning:

Café Mason
320 Mason St., 415-544-0320

King Diner
1390 Mission St., 415-552-2707

Orphan Andy's
3991A 17th St., 415-864-9795

Silver Restaurant
737 Washington St., 415-434-4998

Sparky's Diner
242 Church St., 415-626-8666

Video Cafe
5700 Geary St., 415-387-3999

All Dressed Up

Green Goddess salad dressing (made with blended anchovies, green onions, parsley, tarragon, vinegar, chives, and mayonnaise) was invented in the **Palace Hotel** for actor George Arliss in 1920. Arliss was in town to appear in William Archer's play, *Green Goddess*, which later became one of the earliest "talkie" movies.

Hoity Toity Celery

Union Square's **Westin St. Francis Hotel's** *(335 Powell St., 415-397-7000, westinstfrancis.com)* claim to food fame is the **Celery Victor** – celery stalks boiled in chicken, veal, and vegetable stock and topped with salt, black pepper, chervil, tarragon vinegar, and olive oil. It was invented by chef Victor Hertler in 1910.

Chicken Pasta for the Soul

Chicken Tetrazzini was invented here in 1908 for **Luisa Tetrazzini**, a beloved Italian opera diva, remembered for her amazing voice as well as a free outdoor concert she gave in 1910. She sang before an estimated quarter of a million people in front of the *San Francisco Chronicle* building.

Food on a Stick

Oakland resident **Frank Epperson** invented the **Popsicle** in 1905. The then-11-year-old left his cup of fruit soda on the porch with a stirring stick in it overnight; the drink froze to the stick and Epperson decided to name his tasty invention the Eppsicle ice pop. He patented his creation much later, in 1923, and changed its name to Popsicle after his children started calling it that. In 1925, he sold his Popsicle to the Joe Lowe Company of New York.

A Very Rice Story

In 1890, Italian-born **Domenico DeDomenico** came to America via Ellis Island. After spending a few years in New York, he was tempted by business opportunities in California and decided to move out West. Once in San Francisco, he opened a fresh produce store.

As was done in Italian families at that time, he was sent a photo of Maria Ferrigno, a young lady in Italy, through his best friend. He courted Ferrigno, married her, and persuaded her to move here. In 1912, she convinced him to open a pasta factory, Gragnano Products, in the Mission district. The DeDomenico family started selling boxes of pasta to Italian stores and restaurants in the area.

One of their neighbors, an Armenian immigrant, shared a rice pilaf recipe with DeDomenico's wife which she cooked for dinner. The family loved it and the recipe became a regular meal.

Inspired by the neighbor's recipe, Vince, one of the DeDomenico sons, combined a dry chicken soup mix made at the plant with rice and vermicelli – and named it **Rice-A-Roni**. With the help of a legendary television commercial naming it "the San Francisco Treat," Rice-A-Roni became a staple on dinner tables across the country.

Despite its status as "the San Francisco Treat," Rice-A-Roni is now mass-produced in Illinois.

Comfort and Soul

San Franciscans may rally against fast food places, but they still like their burgers and soul food.

Blue Jay Cafe
Southern-style breakfast, lunch, and dinner.
919 Divisadero, 415-447-6066

Burger Joint
A retro burger restaurant serving Niman Ranch beef.
700 Haight St., 415-864-3833; 807 Valencia St., bet. 18th and 19th Sts., 415-824-3494

J's Pots of Soul
Southern-style home cooking.
203 Octavia St., 415-861-3230

Memphis Minnie's Barbecue Joint

Slow-smoked meats and plenty of mashed potatoes and macaroni and cheese.
576 Haight St., 415-864-PORK, memphisminnies.com

Powell's Place

Sweet corn bread, fried chicken, and other soul food favorites are served at this place owned by Emmitt Powell, a gospel radio and television broadcaster who formed the Gospel Elites in 1977.
1521 Eddy St., 415-409-1388

The 700-pound, seven-foot fiberglass dachshund head at the median strip on Sloat Boulevard at 45th Avenue has reason to smile. Thanks to Diana Scott and Joel Schechter of the Ocean Beach Historical Society and other concerned citizens, the Doggie Diner head, nicknamed **DD**, is back on its pole after going through repairs and a paint job following a hard fall during an April 2001 storm.

Doggie Diner was a local hamburger and hot dog chain that opened in 1949. To the regret of many locals, the chain closed in 1986, but the legend lived on. Nostalgic San Francisco residents visit DD regularly and tell their children (dogs and their owners are also often seen there) about the good old days at the burger joint, which was originally located at Sloat Boulevard at 46th Avenue.

Illustrator Harold Bachman designed the doggie head in the 1960s and says he is still surprised that people are so enamored with DD. He designed it simply because he thought it would help sell hamburgers. Although DD is officially known to be the last doggie standing, rumor has it that doggie siblings are spotted around the Bay Area from time to time.
doggiediner.com

Literature & the Arts

From the acidic essayists who came to San Francisco after the Gold Rush to the Beat poets to modern playwrights and street mural artists, the arts here are not a luxury but a necessity, a tragicomic salute to the forgotten, the broken, and the just plain weird. Artists wrestle with their angels and demons in the public eye, and in fine literary tradition, nobody is afraid to throw back a few drinks while sharing the best of the city's culture.

Photo: courtesy of Karlyn Lotney

Sex Positive

Although most artists here, and most artists in general, are more open-minded about sexuality and orientation than your average – er, average guy or girl (say "bear" here and people will think you're talking about a big burly gay man), there are some who turn open-mindedness into an art.

Carol Queen (carolqueen.com), who made the video *Bend Over Boyfriend: An Adventurous Couple's Guide to Male Anal Pleasure*, and the follow-up *Bend Over Boyfriend 2: Less Talkin', More Rockin'*, is a lecturer, educator, one-time sex worker, advice columnist, and prolific writer. She's been featured in a number of books, and is the author of *Real Live Nude Girl: Chronicles of Sex-Positive Culture* and *Exhibitionism for the Shy*, among others. Queen, who made the *Bend Over Boyfriend* videos with her partner, Robert, says that the first one was a surprise hit – it topped the Good Vibrations best-selling video list for years.

The Fairy Butch Dynasty (fairybutch.com), headed by none other than **Fairy Butch** (aka Karlyn Lotney, see photo), is a burgeoning media juggernaut that includes books such as *The Ultimate Guide to Strap-On Sex*, sex education classes that include "Dyke Sex Tips for Straight Men," and advice columns. Its real claim to fame, though, is the In Bed With Fairy Butch live shows, that range from amateur stripping (for and by lovely ladies) to campy cabaret.

Susie Bright (susiebright.com) has written eight books and edited 15 anthologies, all having to do with the many-flavored joys of sex. In the early 1980s, soon after moving to San Francisco, she wrote a play called *Girls Gone Bad*, and became involved with the queer arts group Mainstream Exiles. She lives a few hours south of the Bay Area, in Santa Cruz.

Lawrence Ferlinghetti, Gary Snyder, Michael McClure, and Philip Lamantia are the main writers associated with the Beats who called San Francisco home – Lamantia recently passed away, but the other three are still kicking. Most of the better known Beats, like **Jack Kerouac**, **Allen Ginsberg** (see above photo), and **William S. Burroughs**, met in New York and came west pursuing freedom from conformity and the East Coast literary establishment. Kerouac, in *On the Road*, is heading towards "Frisco."

The San Francisco Renaissance, as the West Coast face of the Beat movement is called, began at the famous **Six Gallery** poetry reading in 1955 where Allen Ginsberg first read *Howl*. Gary Snyder was there as well, as were Kenneth Rexroth, Jack Kerouac, Michael McClure, Philip Lamantia, and Phil Whalen. The Six Gallery, once at 3119 Fillmore St., is now an Oriental rug shop.

City Lights *(261 Columbus Ave., 415-362-8193, citylights.com)* was ground zero for the nascent movement, serving as publishing house, hangout spot, and reading space. It is still the matriarch of

WHERE MANY ARTS MEET
The Intersection for the Arts
(446 Valencia St., 415-626-3311, theintersection.org) is the city's oldest independent art space, and has a long history of presenting new and experimental work in the fields of literature, theater, music, and the visual arts. The organization has something for everyone, from jazz concerts to the art-in-process series, where the audience can watch a production take shape. There are performances and exhibitions almost every day of the week, and the space is known most recently for hosting standout jazz concerts and the monthly Hybrid Project, a fusion of hip-hop beats, dance, poetry, and live music.

The Corner of Memory Lane

Photo: Stacey Lewis

Writers, dancers, and artists who have called San Francisco home and whose names are immortalized with streets and plazas around the city:

Ambrose Bierce

Beniamino Bufano

Herb Caen

Richard Henry Dana

Isadora Duncan

Lawrence Ferlinghetti

Dashiell Hammett

Bob Kaufman

Jack Kerouac

Jack London

Frank Norris

Kenneth Rexroth

William Saroyan

Mark Twain

independent bookstores in San Francisco. In 1956, City Lights published *Howl*. The bookstore manager, "Shig" as he was known, was arrested by two vice cops, as was Lawrence Ferlinghetti (see above photo), the publisher. A highly publicized obscenity trial that eventually cleared all involved put City Lights on the map for the rest of America.

City Lights was the country's first all-paperback bookstore, and is named after the Charlie Chaplin movie. Legend has it that Chaplin created the hapless everyman character while he was in San Francisco. Apparently, the silent movie star perfected the loveable tramp after spending some time with one of the city's down-and-out residents.

Ferlinghetti, still the co-owner of City Lights, was christened San Francisco's first poet laureate in 2001. In his laureate speech, he decried that the artistic spirit here is being strangled by the high cost of living and nature is buried under cars and parking lots.

Green Tortoise Hostel *(494 Broadway St., 415-956-7500, greentortoise.com)*, a few blocks away from City Lights, is now a cool place to meet budget travelers from around the world, but it used to be a residence hotel. Allen Ginsberg lived there for awhile before moving to an apartment a few blocks away.

By far, the most important literary festival in San Francisco is **Litquake** *(litquake.org)*, started in 2002 by a group of writers and local journalists who wondered why San Francisco, of all places, did not yet have a festival for literature.

A typical Litquake festival is a nine-day affair, taking place at hotels and watering holes throughout the city. Highlights include a Litcrawl in the Mission or some other bar-filled neighborhood, where writers and their fans accumulate blood alcohol levels and literary lore as they visit bars and bookstores in the space of three hours: Loudmouths of Lit, featuring spoken word performers; and Kidquake, for pint-sized bookworms.

The founders wanted to bring literature out of its ivory tower and into the places where most writers and readers really spend their time. "Bookstore readings are deathly boring, for the most part," says author and organizer **Jack Boulware**. "We want to bring some excitement back to the connection between writers and readers – make it sexier."

One of the highlights from Litquake 2004 was a William S. Burroughs night where people got to try a "dream machine," a favorite contraption of Burroughs that supposedly resets the frequency of brain waves. **David Woodard** *(davidwoodard.com)*, a one-time San Francisco resident and accomplished classical musician who composed music for Timothy McVeigh's final hours at the convicted killer's request, manufactures and sells the machines. "This city has always been for thinkers and dreamers, unbound by the mad dash of New York and the lowest common denominator cash allure of Los Angeles," says Boulware.

LITERARY WALKING TOURS

The one walking tour dedicated to literature in San Francisco starts at **City Lights** bookstore and only covers a few square blocks. But in these blocks, you'll see where **Lenny Bruce** fell out of a window and broke his arm, hear *Howl* read at near-screaming level (as it was originally read) below **Allen Ginsberg**'s old apartment, observe where **Mark Twain** held his first job in the city, and have a drink in the Chinatown bar **Li Po**, named after the famous Chinese Tang Dynasty poet. The Beats used to hang out at Li Po, and there was reportedly an opium den in the basement at one time. "This area has so much literary history packed into just a few blocks, but San Francisco makes you seek it out. It's not like New York where there are plaques everywhere," says tour guide **Scott Lettieri**, himself the author of *Sinner's Paradise*, set mainly in San Francisco.

sfliterarytours.com, 415-441-0140

Photo: Winni Wintermeyer

CENTER OF THE WORLD

We'd confidently wager that per square mile there are more travel writers and travel publishers here than anywhere else in the western world. Travel guide publishers **Lonely Planet**, **Avalon Travel Publishing** (of Rick Steves and Moon Guides fame), and **Travelers' Tales** all call the Bay Area home.

The woman who bridges the world of travel and the world of books in the Bay is **Jen Leo**, who writes the blog at *writtenroad.com*. Her site lists travel-related author events locally and nationally, travel writer news, and gives a lot of useful advice for people who want to break into the business.

Laurie King, of *laurieking.com*, is also dialed into the travel writing community. Her site has an online calendar useful for anyone who needs to plan their literary travel fix ahead of time.

For sometimes half-baked, sometimes incisive political commentary outside the mainstream mega-media, the **Annual Bay Area Anarchist Bookfair** (*bayareaanarchistbookfair.org*) is the place to go. This one-day annual event brings together hippies, yippies, conspiracy theorists, and anti-WTO activists from all over North America.

Porchlight, A Story Telling Series (*porchlightsf.com*), is storytime for adults, with drinks. The literary event happens the third Monday of the month, at the Castro's Café du Nord or upstairs at the Swedish American Hall (*2170 Market St., 415-861-5016, cafedunord.com*). It may look like open mic, but it's not. The stories revolve around a theme and storytellers are screened beforehand. The events feature a range of San Francisco characters, from local politicians to bus drivers to senior citizen mushroom hunters. Anyone who has a good story to tell can participate. **Arline Klatte**, who co-founded the series in 2002 with **Beth Lisick** (see photo), said that normal people with a good story usually do better than professional writers. "It's the people who are just themselves who really shine on stage. All we have to do is listen to them beforehand, give them some feedback, and they do great," she said.

Although there are readings throughout the city almost every night of the week, Porchlight events often come up in literary conversation – a recurring thread in the tapestry of literary culture.

As the organizers of the **Writers with Drinks Variety Show** (*writerswithdrinks.com*) say, "[Variety is] more than just having sex dressed up as Alan Greenspan once in a while." Regretfully, we'd have to agree. The monthly show takes place at the **Make-Out Room** (*3225 22nd St., 415-647-2888, makeoutroom.com*), and features writers of all stripes, but with a strong comedy contingent, talking about whatever the hell they want to. Oh, and when we say comedy writers, we're talking about writers and stand-up comics good enough for Comedy Central and Jay Leno.

Caen was Able

"Baghdad by the Bay" might not sound like much of a compliment these days, but to literary icon **Herb Caen**, who wrote impish observations and commentary on his favorite city, "Baghdad" had connotations of otherworldliness and the apex of a civilization.

Caen said that it was no surprise he fell in love with San Francisco. He claims his parents conceived him during the 1915 Panama Pacific International Exhibition world's fair – the domed Palace of Fine Arts building was built especially for the occasion.

The list of Caen's quotable lines about the city that first appeared in his long-running *San Francisco Chronicle* column are long; in addition to the "Baghdad by the Bay" moniker, he popularized the term "beatnik" in 1958 after overhearing it at a literary hangout.

He loved the city, and the city loved him. He wrote six columns a week for nearly 60 years. Speaking in front of a crowd towards the end of his career, he said, "When it's time, if I get to heaven, I'm going to say what every San Franciscan says when they get to heaven: 'It ain't bad, but it ain't San Francisco.'"

A three-mile stretch of the Embarcadero was renamed Herb Caen Way... in 1996, with the signature ellipses at the end of the name. It was going to be called Herb Caen Promenade, but Caen, a francophile who first visited Paris during his time in the military in World War II, said "promenade" sounded too French, "like something you spread on toast."

During the dedication ceremony of the street, bike messengers, whose manic energy Caen had a fondness for, slowly rode by and saluted him with full vodka martinis, his favorite drink. When the city came together to commemorate Caen in 2002, five years after his death to cancer, martinis went on sale everywhere and many people raised a glass to the man who best articulated what makes the city Baghdad by the Bay.

His son, **Chris Caen**, started writing a newspaper column in 2004. Although it's apostasy to say it, the younger Caen might not have the one-liners of his father, but his writing is arguably better. He focuses on issues large and small, and like Caen Sr., is highly recommended for anyone who wants an enjoyable peek into the machinations of San Francisco.

GONZO BOUNCER

Hunter S. Thompson spent a lot of time in the Bay Area when he was writing the book that put him on the map, *Hell's Angels*, and for a time lived in the Upper Haight neighborhood, at 318 Parnassus Ave., to be exact. After he made it big, the brothers who owned the infamous O'Farrell Theatre strip joint hired him as night manager.

As Susie Bright, a friend of the late Thompson, wrote in her blog (*susiebright.blogs.com*), the night manager position was a "job description that didn't exist before or since his tenure…. The gonzo muscle machine? I never saw him lift anything besides a glass and a card."

There are exceptions to every rule, but in San Francisco, gritty, sexy, and semi-autobiographical portraits dominate the city's literary landscape.

Armistead Maupin's multi-book series *Tales of the City* is a soap-operatic account of the city's social scene, gay and otherwise, before, during, and after AIDS. Most of the stories first appeared as a newspaper serial in the *San Francisco Chronicle* newspaper. Never has one writer peered into so many facets of the city, or spent so long on one group of local characters. We've read (in *mistersf.com*, a modern chronicler of the city's mud-puddle wonderful side) about parties where people try to take a hit of pot whenever the main character in *Tales of the City* (Mary Ann Singleton, a naïve Ohio girl who grows up in the big city) does the same. (The landlord, Mrs. Madrigal, is a major stoner, and most people probably couldn't keep up with her.) Maupin's seven-novel series was made into a TV miniseries by PBS, but the casual drug use and depictions of homosexual affection led to complaints. The heads of public television caved and pulled the series. Showtime picked it up a few years later where the original series left off. Besides some jolting changes to the lineup of actors, the second series, *More Tales of the City*, is arguably better than the first.

Dave Eggers of **McSweeney's** fame is best known for his breakout book, *A Heartbreaking Work of Staggering Genius*, published in 2000. It's officially fiction, but is largely based on the move Eggers and his younger brother make to Berkeley after the death of their parents. Eggers headed the independent humor magazine, *Might*, and auditioned for MTV's *The Real World*. The book captures, among many other things, the oh-so-self-referential Gen-X of San Francisco in the 1990s. Eggers now runs the city's "only independent pirate supply store" **826 Valencia** *(826 Valencia St., 826valencia.org, 415-642-5905)*, a writing workshop for kids and adults that really does sell pirate paraphernalia.

The peace-loving city has a dark side, and nobody

GOOD GRAMMAR, ANYONE?
The Grammar Queen

(thegrammarqueen.com), known less royally as Sandra Stewart, a writing and editing consultant, makes official proclamations on common grammar questions to her newsletter readers. This might not sound like a dangerous endeavor, but when grammar is on the line for the large community of Bay Area residents who make their living putting words on a page, every comma, and comment about commas, counts.

"She is pleased," the Grammar Queen tells us in her royal third-person voice, "and frankly, astonished that so many people care about writing well and correctly. This gives her hope that clarity and grace may not vanish from written expression. The Grammar Queen may be tart, but she is not a pessimist."

captured it better than the pioneering author of hard-boiled detective fiction **Dashiell Hammett** (see photo). The hard-drinking, fast-living Hammett worked for a detective agency in the city before giving up the gumshoe life for health reasons – one of his last cases was trying to find evidence to bolster the defense in the Fatty Arbuckle rape and murder case. There's a plaque in a downtown alley that marks the death of a fictional character in one of the Sam Spade books – don't read the plaque before you finish *The Maltese Falcon* is all we can say. And Hammett fans can grab chops, a baked potato, and sliced tomatoes at **John's Grill** *(63 Ellis St., 415-986-3274, johnsgrill.com)* where Sam Spade had a quick meal in *The Maltese Falcon*. Today, John's Grill is a fine dining establishment where Hillary Rodham Clinton and Olympia Dukakis (star of the TV version of *Tales of the City*) are known to sup.

A talented young writer, **J.T. Leroy** turned his time as a street prostitute and drug addict into disturbing, cathartic short stories. Due to his extreme shyness and fondness for sending famous people in his place to do readings for him, there were rumors at one time that LeRoy was himself a fictional character. His band Thistle LLC has put an end to that speculations. (Besides, we spoke to him on the phone and he, or someone who goes by his name, sounded alive and well.) It's in San Francisco that LeRoy started writing; as a teenager he wound up at a child crisis center and his therapist encouraged him to

ANARCHY, ANYONE?

AK Press is a worker-owned and run anarchist collective based right here in the Bay Area, publishing and distributing anarchist books and other media (including some titles by Noam Chomsky). They're also known for their great book parties and events at their base camp in Oakland.
674-A 23rd St, Oakland; akpress.org

write his experiences down. LeRoy says that many of the stories that wound up in *Sarah* (about his drug-addled mother who got him into prostitution) and *The Heart is Deceitful Above All Things* were written originally as a form of therapy. LeRoy wrote the screenplay for the Gus Van Sant film *Elephant*, inspired by the Columbine High School massacre, and collaborated with Asia Argento on the film version of *The Heart is Deceitful Above All Things*.

Oakland-born **Amy Tan** is most famous for *The Joy Luck Club* and is said to have taken up writing after her therapist fell asleep – for the third time. Writing and Zoloft, she says in interviews, have helped her keep the depression that plagues her family (her grandmother committed suicide) at bay. Tan is also the lead singer for the Rock Bottom Remainders, a rock band made up of fellow writers Stephen King and Dave Barry.

Mission resident, lesbian luminary, and author of books, the young, hip **Michelle Tea** most recently published *Rent Girl*, an illustrated memoir about her time as a call girl in Boston and San Francisco; her previous book *Valencia* is a witty commentary on the lesbian scene in the Mission. She keeps the San Francisco satirist tradition alive with her (mostly) loving caricatures of locals.

Although not as well known as many other San Francisco writers (yet), **John Mulligan**'s first book has won wide critical acclaim and seems destined to enter the pantheon of important novels set in San Francisco. *Shopping Cart Soldiers* is based on Mulligan's life; his family moved here from Scotland, and days after turning 18, the young Mulligan was drafted into Vietnam. He came back a broken man and eventually found himself on the streets for more than 10 years. The book, which chronicles the protagonist's alcoholic humiliations and eventual recovery in "Paranoid Park" (based on North Beach's Washington Square Park), was born in a writing workshop for veterans led by Maxine Hong Kingston.

THE TART SUCCESS OF LEMONY SNICKET

Those who need a breather from the adult pleasures of San Francisco can read the children's 11-book oeuvre *A Series of Unfortunate Events*, by Lemony Snicket, aka **Daniel Handler**. Handler was born in San Francisco and still calls the city home. Under his real name, he authored the black comedies *The Basic Eight* and *Watch Your Mouth: A Novel*. Erudite adults who have read his grown-up fiction say that he's one of the Bay Area's best novelists in a long time. Kids just like to say "Lemony Snicket."

Ambrose Bierce of *Devil's Dictionary* fame headed a number of San Francisco newspapers and wrote many short stories, "The Occurrence at Owl Creek Bridge" being the most famous one. He and Mark Twain (see photo) were friends, at one time working at the same newspaper in the Montgomery Block. Bierce earned the title "Wickedest Man in San Francisco" during his time here. He took pride in ruffling feathers, including those of other literati; when the flamboyant Oscar Wilde visited San Francisco in 1882 to give lectures on aesthetics and literature, Bierce wrote: "His lecture is mere verbal ditchwater – meaningless, trite and without coherence. It lacks even the nastiness that exalts and refines his verse." Bierce exited his life as he lived it; with flair. His disappearance at the age of 71, in the heart of Mexico, is dramatized in *The Old Gringo* by Carlos Fuentes, and then adapted into a film starring Gregory Peck as Bierce. It seems Bierce was getting restless in his old age and wanted to join the army of Pancho Villa as an observer. He dropped off the map soon afterwards, but not before sending a few letters to his daughter.

Tough guy to the end, one of these last letters reads: "Good-bye – if you hear of my being stood up against

The World According to the Wickedest Man in San Francisco

Some choice definitions from the old gringo himself, these definitions make it clear how Ambrose Bierce earned his "wickedest" title:

ACCOUNTABILITY, n.
The mother of caution.

CAT, n.
A soft, indestructible automaton provided by nature to be kicked when things go wrong in the domestic circle.

CONSULT, v.i.
To seek another's disapproval of a course already decided on.

CYNIC, n.
A blackguard whose faulty vision sees things as they are, not as they ought to be.

DEJEUNER, n.
The breakfast of an American who has been in Paris. Variously pronounced.

a Mexican stone wall and shot to rags please know that I think that a pretty good way to depart this life. It beats old age, disease, or falling down the cellar stairs. To be a Gringo in Mexico – ah, that is euthanasia!"

Although not trained as a historian, **Iris Chang** wrote *The Rape of Nanking* and brought to international consciousness the forgotten holocaust of World War II. More than 300,000 people were raped, tortured, and murdered in Nanking, China, by the invading Japanese army. The book made her a hero in China, especially to the people in Nanking, who for a long time had lived with the scars of an atrocity forgotten by the world at large. She received honorary degrees, woman of the year awards, and prestigious speaking invitations. In 2004, six years after the book's publication, the 36-year-old Chang was found in her car by the side of the road, dead by a self-inflicted gunshot wound. It seems that the woman who confronted evil face to face had suffered a mental breakdown when researching her book on the Baatan Death March and the memories of US soldiers who fought the Japanese. After she had been discharged from the hospital, she never fully resurfaced and the weight of history sucked her under. The people of Nanking were so grateful for her efforts, and saddened by her death, that they held a service for her at the Victim's Memorial Hall at the same time as her funeral in California.

The drug-addled genius **Phillip K. Dick**, PKD or even "Horselover Fat" to his legion of fans, wrote many of his paranoid and messianic masterpieces in the Bay Area. He was largely ignored outside of science fiction and counterculture circles during his own lifetime. *Blade Runner*, based on his novel, *Do Androids Dream of Electric Sheep?*, was the first in a series of movie adaptations that made millions – but he never lived to see it. *The Man in the High Castle* is Dick's most accessible novel set explicitly in San Francisco; it details an antique dealer's life in the city ruled by the Japanese-German powers after America loses half of its territory in World War II. *Humpty Dumpty in Oakland* was set in its East Bay namesake, and *The Broken Bubble* is set in San Francisco of the 1950s, when rock 'n' roll was starting to foment the cultural revolution to follow. Dick experienced visions throughout his life, and was convinced that the intervention of VALIS – Vast Active Living Intelligence System – saved the life of his young son. Dick was also convinced that our modern age was

FUTURE, n.

That period of time in which our affairs prosper, our friends are true and our happiness is assured.

IMMIGRANT, n.

An unenlightened person who thinks one country better than another.

LITIGATION, n.

A machine which you go into as a pig and come out of as a sausage.

MARRIAGE, n.

The state or condition of a community consisting of a master, a mistress and two slaves, making in all, two.

SELFISH, adj.

Devoid of consideration for the selfishness of others.

ZEAL, n.

A certain nervous disorder afflicting the young and inexperienced. A passion that goeth before a sprawl.

largely an illusion, and that we are still living in Roman-ruled Palestine shortly after the death of Christ.

Jack London (see photo) was born in San Francisco and grew up in Oakland. He lived a hard-scrabble existence until he catapulted to fame and became the highest-paid writer of his time. Although London is best known for his adventure novels *Call of the Wild* and *White Fang*, his range as a writer spilled over the constraints of stark realism. His portrait of his own lifelong love affair with alcohol in *John Barleycorn* greatly impressed fellow California resident Upton Sinclair: "Assuredly one of the most useful, as well as one of the most entertaining books ever penned by a man."

Mark Twain, born Samuel Clemens, is one of the most famous writers to call the area home. Twain wrote this description of San Francisco in his travelogue *Roughing It*: "San Francisco, a truly fascinating city to live in, is stately and handsome at a fair distance, but close at hand one notes that the architecture is mostly old-fashioned, many streets are made up of decaying, smoke-grimed, wooden houses, and the barren sand-hills toward the outskirts obtrude themselves too prominently. Even the kindly climate is sometimes pleasanter when read about than personally experienced, for a lovely, cloudless sky wears out its welcome by and by, and then when the longed for rain does come it stays."

Although Twain liked the rough and tumble nature of the city, and was ahead of his time in speaking out against anti-Chinese racism (he found early publishing success in a bilingual Chinese-English journal in San Francisco), he wasn't always fond of the weather. He most famously said that he'd never experienced a winter so cold as summer in San Francisco. He also wrote that he actually enjoyed the 1865 earthquake.

HOLD ON TO YOUR HAT
Selling out shows for more than 30 years, **Beach Blanket Babylon** at **Club Fugazi** *(678 Green St., 415-421-4222, beachblanketbabylon.com)* is a wacky musical revue where the one-liners and visual puns are tossed out in a never-ending staccato. Snow White is on a whirlwind, world-wide tour to find Mr. Right; a constantly changing cast of characters, reflecting the "it" celebrities of the moment, help or hinder her quest. Enormous hats are central to the show, and the one that appears in the finale is almost nine feet wide.

Photo: Stacey Lewis

BAND OF WRITERS

The Grotto *(sfgrotto.org)* is a writer and filmmaker collective started by a few friends who needed an office to work in, and so banded together to find affordable space. Now the Grotto is the working base for more than 30 writers. Some, like Po Bronson *(What Should I Do with My Life?)* are wildly successful, while others are still struggling. The Grotto also holds events on a quarterly basis and offers workshops and classes.

A 2004 survey put San Franciscans at the top of the list for spending on alcohol and books. The number of independent bookstores that are still alive and well here – while other cites have succumbed to chains – is testament to at least half of that finding. If it's true that smart people are usually melancholy people, then the bookstores explain the alcoholic half of the equation too. The Northern California Independent Booksellers Association *(nciba.com)* has a complete list of stores, from dog-only bookstores (books about dogs, not selling to them) to rare and antique tome shops. Below are some of the more interesting purveyors of books in the city:

Borderlands Books *(866 Valencia St., 415-824-8203, borderlands-books.com)*, is the mothership for used and new science fiction, fantasy, and horror books, video tapes, and DVDs. Neener-neener.

City Lights *(261 Columbus Ave., 415-362-8193, citylights.com)* has stayed true to its roots (see page 116) with a great selection of groundbreaking books.

A Different Light Bookstore *(489 Castro St., 415-431-0891, adlbooks.com)*, is the oldest and best-known book store in the city specializing in LGBT books.

European Book Company *(925 Larkin St., 415-474-0626, europeanbook.com)* is the best place in the Bay Area for books in French, German, Spanish, or Italian.

For the armchair traveler or soggy back roads trekker, **Get Lost Books** *(1825 Market St., 415-437-0529, getlostbooks.com)*, has maps, guidebooks, travel narratives, magazines, and live events – mixers for people on their way to Southeast Asia, slide shows from writers just back from Mongolia, and readings by visiting authors. The store's owner, Lee Azus, is a serious traveler himself and is happy to recommend books for a particular destination.

Ask a Bay Area bookworm what his or her favorite bookstore is, and you're most likely to hear **Green Apple Books** *(506 Clement St., 415-387-2272, greenapplebooks.com)*. The store sells new books, but its real draw is the used collection. Spend some time here, because the organization of the books, if there is one, is chaotic at best. There's a display with all the items found in used books: a marijuana leaf, postcards, pictures. Once, employees reportedly found a gun mixed in with a box of old books.

Isotope, the Comic Book Lounge *(326 Fell St., 415-621-6543, isotopecomics.com)*, is a lounge, event space, and bookstore for all things having to do with comic arts, from the latest edgy adult graphic novel to mimeographed zines.

A WEE BIT OF THE JUICE

It's hard to classify the **Edinburgh Castle Pub** *(950 Geary St., 415-885-4074, castlenews.com)*, but the Tenderloin neighborhood establishment is definitely a center of the homegrown arts and literary scene. It's where the world premiere of the stage play for Irvine Welsh's *Trainspotting* was held, serves as the headquarters for the Litquake festival, and regularly hosts readings and literary events. Edinburgh's resident writer/barman/owner/co-founder of the new publishing house Public House Press, Alan Black, is said to work and write like a man possessed; with so much going on, it's no wonder. "A pub is no better place to start [publishing books]. Ideas are born from sitting on the stools, the pillars of inspiration," he told us. Even on nights where no literary events are taking place, the bar is well worth a visit for the Scottish pennies, kilts, and the log used for Scottish log-throwing contests. Every January 25, the pub puts on a decidedly unpretentious (like the poet himself, organizers say) Burns Night, a tribute to Scottish poet laureate Robert Burns that's a woozy brew of Scottish-themed literature, performance, and lots of drinking. The drink of choice is scotch, of course. (A linguistic party trick and a good conversation starter at Edinburgh Castle Pub: in the Scottish Gaelic language, whiskey means "water of life.")

Lovers of Japanese culture need to check out **Kinokuniya Book Stores of America Company** *(1581 Webster St., 415-567-7625)*, in the heart of Japantown. Most of the books, CDs, and DVDs are in Japanese, but there is an English-language section with books about Japan, translated from Japanese, and learning the language.

Movie buffs and actors will enjoy **Limelight** *(1803 Market St., 415-864-2265, limelightbooks.com)*, with special actor editions of plays and scripts, screenplays, treatments, and storyboards.

Modern Times *(888 Valencia St., 415-282-9246, mtbs.com)* is a collectively owned and operated progressive bookstore in the Mission. They offer everything progressive and open-minded under the sun, including a well-stocked sexuality and gender section. Like City Lights, the store shares a name with a Charlie Chaplin movie.

Stacey's Bookstore *(581 Market St., 415-421-4687, staceys.com)*, is the oldest independent bookstore in San Francisco. Founded in 1923, the store now spans three floors and carries around 150,000 titles. It's the place to go for new books, with a friendly, helpful staff, and reading chairs on the second floor overlooking busy Market Street.

Bonnie & Clyde of the Barflies

Octavio Solis's play *The Ballad of Pancho and Lucy* is based on real incidents that took place when he moved to San Francisco in 1989. A couple was robbing bars in the Mission, gaining notoriety as a modern-day Bonnie and Clyde.

"Everyone had a different story about who they were, what they looked like, the way they got away," Solis told us. The head of Intersection for the Arts, where Solis has premiered many of his works, asked him at the time to do a play about the couple. Fifteen years later, when he and the theater managers decided a comedy or musical would be a nice change of pace, he returned to the crime spree that had fired the public imagination years before.

"So the actors and I, before I even had a script, we'd go do research in these bars, the **500 Club**, the **Elbo Room**, places like that," says Solis. "What was really funny was that all these classic dive bars, there were these local snaggle-toothed characters who know the bar scene very well. Some had been eyewitnesses to these robberies, and they were very helpful, telling me things like, 'They were just junkies,' then someone else would disagree and there'd be an argument, 'No, they needed money for their honeymoon.'"

He became more interested in the varied stories about Pancho and Lucy the regulars were telling him (and what those stories said about the tellers) than in what actually happened. Someone told him the pair waltzed into the bar like a gun-toting Astaire and Rogers; others informed him the pair were on a suicide pact and were having some last kicks.

In his new musical adaptation, "each time [a different version] gets told, Pancho and Lucy are played by two different actors," says Solis.

How did the two finally get caught? According to Solis, a cab driver watching the TV news saw a police sketch of Pancho, and heard the details of the bar he robbed. The driver had picked up the pair in front of that same bar seconds after the robbery, and dropped them off in a motel south of the city. The police soon arrested Pancho and Lucy, ending one of the city's more endearing crime sprees now immortalized by Solis. *500 Club, 500 Guerrero St., 415-861-2500; Elbo Room, 647 Valencia St. 415-552-7788. elbo.com*

The Pulitzer's the Thing

Here are some Pulitzer Prize winners who have called the Bay Area home:

Herb Caen, raconteur and journalist.

Czeslaw Milosz, Polish poet and essayist who called Berkeley home for much of his life. He also won the Nobel Prize in 1980.

William Saroyan, playwright of *Time of Our Lives*, which featured a location partly modeled on the famed Black Cat Café, one of the first openly gay bars in the city and a favorite Beat hangout.

The Play's the Thing

Many of the big live theaters in San Francisco are clustered between Union Square and Van Ness, north of Market; these offer good, tried-and-true, middle-of-the-road Broadway hits. One exception is **Exit Theatre** *(156 Eddy St. 415-931-1094, sffringe.org)*, one of the longest-running independent theaters in the city and home to the yearly San Francisco Fringe Festival.

A company dedicated to reviving the under-produced and under-appreciated musicals of yesteryear in a "staged concert" format, the **42nd Street Moon** *(Yerba Buena Center for the Arts Box Office, 701 Mission St., 415-978-2787, 42ndstmoon.org)* players take their name from a 1920s expression for the bright lights of Broadway. A staged concert is a fully choreographed production with minimal sets and costumes where the actors hold the script in their hands. Organizers explain this keeps costs down and allows the audience to focus on the story, dance, and music. Jazz hands, everybody!

Bindlestiff Studio *(505 Natoma St., 415-255-0440, bindlestiffstudio.org)*, the self-described "epicenter of Pilipino American Performing Arts," is the only performing arts space dedicated to Filipino artists in the United States.

Eureka Theatre Company *(215 Jackson St., 415-788-7469, eurekatheatre.org)* was thrust into the national spotlight after it commissioned and premiered the first installment of Tony Kushner's Pulitzer-winning *Angels in America*. The theater's main focus is on locally produced plays with a social conscience.

The world-famous **Magic Theatre** *(Fort Mason Center, Building D, 3rd Floor, 415-441-8822, magictheatre.org)* is the one of the most established of the independent theaters, and has launched the careers of many a famous playwright, including Sam Shepard and David Mamet. The company specializes in world premieres, and has seen the likes of Sean Penn and Nick Nolte on its stage.

Off Market Theaters and **C.A.F.E.** *(965 Mission St., 415-896-6477, cafearts.com)* offer inexpensive space for theater and improv productions, and classes like "introduction to stage managing." A sample production: *The Kung-fu Evangelist*, a one-man show about a disturbed deep-south evangelist who uses kung fu to make his point about our redeemer.

Gary Snyder, is a poet who has grown and matured beyond the Beats and still continues to write thoughtful essays and poems.

John Steinbeck, best known for *The Grapes of Wrath*, also won the Nobel Prize, in 1962. Although he had the reputation as a San Francisco-hater, in reality he hated the racism and political corruption that he found here, but loved the city itself.

Alice Walker, best known for *The Color Purple*.

Don't expect Marcel Marceau-style shenanigans from the **San Francisco Mime Troupe** *(855 Treat Ave., 415-285-1717, sfmt.org)*, but politically aware popular and experimental theater. The group's logo sports a red star as homage to its leftist leanings. The Mime Troupe is reportedly considering a name change – they're often booked for private events with the expectation that they're white-faced, striped-shirted performers pretending to be trapped inside a box.

"Queer Theatre for the Queer in Everyone" is how America's oldest and longest-running professional queer theater, **Theatre Rhinoceros** *(2926 16th St., 415-861-5079, therhino.org)* describes itself.

Victoria Theatre *(2961 16th St., 415-863-7576, victoriatheatre.org)* was built in 1908 as a vaudeville house and is the oldest theater in San Francisco still in use today. During its long life, it has housed a Spanish language cinema and a burlesque club; now, the venue hosts everything from independent film to comedy to performance art and plays. This Mission landmark has been used as a location in a few movies, and has seen two of the best comediennes of their generation perform on its stage; Mae West and Whoopi Goldberg.

THIS WAY UP

Rigo, born Ricardo Gouveia, has painted a number of large murals around the city that are an ironic commentary on urbanization. His most famous, "One Tree," is at the corner of Bryant and 10th Streets, and points to a lonely tree in the industrial area. Other murals include large faux traffic signs that point out birds, cars, or simply the ground beneath.

The city has more than 30 museums — one for every square mile-and-a-half of land. Some of the lesser-known and one-of-a-kind museums are listed below.

The **Cartoon Art Museum** *(655 Mission St., 415-227-8666, cartoonart.org)* is the only museum in the United States dedicated to the preservation and exhibition of cartoon art in all its twisted, sick and/or funny forms. It has an on-site research library and 6,000 pieces of cartoon art.

For conspiracy theorists and those with more than a passing interest in secret societies, the free **Henry Wilson Coil Masonic Library & Museum** (see photo) *(1111 California St., 415-776-7000, freemason.org)* contains more than 8,000 book titles and includes Masonic art and artifacts from California and around the world. Secret handshake not required.

SKETCHCRAWLING AROUND

Take a bunch of artists armed with paper and the drawing utensil of their choice, then let them loose on a city with the condition that they wander around and sketch everything they see. This was the idea of Enrico Casarosa, an Italian artist who lives and works in San Francisco. Casarosa got the idea after going on a bachelor party pub crawl, and now, international **Sketchcrawls** attract artists from Pittsburgh to Paris, Singapore to San Luis Obispo. *sketchcrawl.com*

On the second floor of the **Monadnock Building**
(685 Market St.) is a free gallery of modern art and
portraits of famous San Franciscans in the lobby fresco.

The **Museum of Craft & Folk Art** *(Fort Mason Center,
Building A, 415-775-0991, mocfa.org)* is a free
museum dedicated to contemporary craft, American folk
art, and traditional cultural art.

The **Museum of the African Diaspora** *(Third and
Mission Streets, 415-358-7200, moadsf.org)* is on the
ground level of the new St. Regis Museum Towers, and
hosts a variety of traditional and new media exhibits
showcasing African experiences locally and globally.

San Francisco Center for the Book *(300 De Haro
St., Suite 334, 415-565-0545, sfcb.org)* is a
bibliophile's paradise. Everything having to do with the
manufacture of books is on display here.

San Francisco **Museum of Craft & Design** *(550
Sutter St., 415-773-0303, sfmcd.org)* is a relatively new
museum that is making itself known for funky, eclectic
exhibits that move crafts beyond your mother's macramé
to the hip and interesting.

A PAINTED SCANDAL

North Beach gallery owner **Lori
Haigh** was forced to shut down her
Capobianco Gallery
(capogallerysf.com) in May 2004
due to a controversial painting
entitled "Abuse" by Berkeley artist
Guy Colwell. The painting, which
Haigh hung in the front window of
her gallery at the height of the Abu
Ghraib scandal, shows naked, hooded
prisoners connected to electrical wires
controlled by US soldiers.

There was some negative response:
Haigh was quoted as saying she was
punched in the face and spat upon,

Photo: Crawford Barton Papers. Courtesy of the GLBT Historical Society

The **GLBT Historical Society** *(657 Mission St. #300, 415-777-5455, glbthistory.org)* maintains one of the world's largest collections of source materials – letters, oral histories, newspapers, and all the other things that historians use as building blocks – on queer history. Focusing mainly on gay life in Northern California and open to the public, the archive includes: erotica from the 1930s to now; 2,300 periodical titles; a collection of buttons, T-shirts, and other memorabilia from bars, baths, and political campaigns; and the oral histories of more than 400 GLBT people, famous and not.

that her gallery was vandalized on a regular basis, and garbage was dumped on her sidewalk. Area artists, who took Haigh's story at face value, rallied to her aid.

People who know Haigh, however, describe her as a good-hearted but troubled person, and they have some reservations about her story. A quick Internet search on her name turns up stories about her receiving a $1.2 million payout from the Catholic Church for recovered memories of sex abuse, charges of embezzlement, and a history of harming herself.

In addition to the permanent collection in the archives, the GLBT Society museum has a number of changing exhibits. Recent shows include "Saint Harvey: The Life and Afterlife of a Modern Gay Martyr," which displayed rarely seen artifacts from the estate of Harvey Milk, including the clothes he wore at the time of his assassination; and "Sporting Life: GLBT Athletics and Cultural Change from the 1960s to Today," which detailed everything from the first gay vs. police softball games in San Francisco to the Mark Bingham games, named after the San Francisco gay man who fought against the hijackers of Flight 93 on 9/11.

The society is in the midst of securing funding (to the tune of $30 million) and a location for the proposed International Museum of Gay and Lesbian History, a state-of-the-art, immersive museum modeled on the Holocaust Museum in Washington, DC.

There are murals all over the city, but the highest concentration of them is in the Mission District, especially along 24th and Mission streets. Along the Mission Trail, there are more than 75 murals in six blocks in this area. A good way to get oriented is to visit the **Precita Eyes Mural Arts and Visitors Center** *(2981 24th St., 415-285-2287, precitaeyes.org).* The center offers classes, conducts workshops around the Bay for youth, and gives mural tours on the weekends. Prices vary, but are usually eight dollars for students, $12 for adults.

"We certainly encourage people to stop by or take a tour," says Joshua Stevenson, spokesman for the center. "Murals are a great way to improve the atmosphere in any neighborhood. What we encourage is for the community to come up with what they want to see in their community, as opposed to advertisements for corporations. We really think that communities should decide how their neighborhoods are going to look, not anyone else."

REVOLUTIONARY ART? NO PROBLEM

Unlike his mural at New York's Rockefeller Center that was removed because it included a portrait of Lenin, **Diego Rivera's** three murals in San Francisco — including one that was in the Stock Exchange for the West Coast and caused a stir — are still around today.

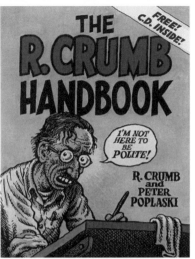

Robert Crumb sold his first comics on San Francisco street corners out of a baby stroller, legend has it, and came to hate the hippies who adored him.

"I found San Francisco to be a really sweet, elegant city after my experience of Cleveland, Philadelphia, New York, Chicago, [and] Detroit," he told us.

As it turns out, Crumb's brother, Max, once lived in the very same apartment as the authors of this book, and the landlord was surprised to hear that all those sketches he'd been given from his tenant's brother were from a famous artist.

Crumb was friends with **Phillip K. Dick**, and devoted issue #17 of *Weirdo* comic to Dick's odd religious experience/hallucination: *philipkdickfans.com/ weirdo.htm*.

In the documentary film *Crumb*, he talks about the proliferation of overhead wires in the city, and notes that he likes to include this high-voltage urban debris in his drawings whenever he can. It's hard to look at a Crumb drawing and not notice how many wires and electrical poles there are in the background.

"I used to like to 'hang out' at the **[Café] La Boheme**" *(3318 24th St., 415-643-0481)*, Crumb says. "I nicknamed the place 'The Lonely Guy Tea Room,' because there were always the same single men sitting by themselves, brooding over their cup of tea or coffee. Girls from the dance studio next door and upstairs would come in to get drinks to take out, and the single men, me included, would ogle longingly at the young dancer girls as they strode past, their noses in the air."

The Stock Exchange is now the members-only **City Club** *(155 Sansome St., 415-362-2480, cityclubsf.com)* (see photo of façade previous page), but is still home to Rivera's first US mural, "Allegory of California." For residents who want to see the mural, the City Club is often a special events venue. Anyone willing to pony up for some chi-chi cocktails will not only get to see Diego's large, stunning mural, but will be hobnobbing in one of the most well preserved Art Deco spaces in San Francisco.

Shit-faced on Photography

The city has a distinguished photographic pedigree; **Ansel Adams** was born and raised in San Francisco, and the **San Francisco Museum of Modern Art** *(151 3rd St., 415-357-4000, sfmoma.org)* was one of the first museums in the country to recognize photography as a fine art.

Now, some of the most innovative photography is coming out of the skate scene, with people like **Dylan Maddux, Ken Goto**, and others blending gritty social realism with technically accomplished prints to define a new style that's *Thrasher Magazine* meets Nan Goldin meets the immigrant experience.

To find out where photo and art exhibits are happening, check out the calendar on *fecalface.com*. Beware though; hipsters are drawn to Fecal Face-advertised events like flies are attracted to you-know-what. Even if you're not a hipster (and who says they are?), the booze is usually free and the art is usually pretty damn good, and the people, hipster or not, are usually nice. Drink it in, figuratively and literally.

Art, with a Twist

For people who enjoy art but don't enjoy the solemnity of hallowed halls, there are a number of galleries that are part drinking establishment, part art space. Although there are many bars in San Francisco with original paintings on the walls, these establishments make art central to their mission:

111 Minna

Come on a weekend night or during a musical event and the art will be hidden behind a mass of people, but on a weeknight or during the day, a good place to see what some of the best local artists are up to. *111 Minna St., 415-974-1719, 111minnagallery.com*

The Canvas Gallery

Across from Golden Gate Park, this expansive gallery always has an impressive line-up of changing exhibits, and on a typical night shows more art than some small museums. *1200 9th Ave., 415-504-0060, thecanvasgallery.com*

Creativity Explored *(3245 16th St., 415-863-2108, creativityexplored.org)* was founded in 1983 to give developmentally disabled adults interested in art a place to work on, exhibit, and sell their art. On any day, 60 or so artists will be at the main Mission studio and gallery. Visitors are warmly welcomed and often the artists are happy to talk about their work. Those who have preconceived notions about the abilities of developmentally disabled artists will be surprised – before we knew the story behind this place, we thought it was a gallery like any other. It is, but the openness of the staff and the artists definitely make it something special.

Their opening receptions are cool, too. At the "Aliens: The Green Ones" exhibit opening, visitors, of the terrestrial kind and otherwise, were encouraged to "dress for space." Considering the city's populace and love of dressing up, not much encouragement was needed.

The Gallery Lounge

A smaller space that's relatively new to the art-bar scene but gaining a strong reputation quickly. *510 Brannan St., 415-227-0449, thegallerylounge.com*

RxGallery

A cool artist-run Tenderloin wine and sake bar that opens for art and music events. *132 Eddy St., 415-474-7973, rxgallery.com*

Varnish Fine Art

A small bar tucked into the corner of a large, two-level art space. The gallery also hosts film and wine tasting events. *77 Natoma St., 415-222-6131, varnishfineart.com*

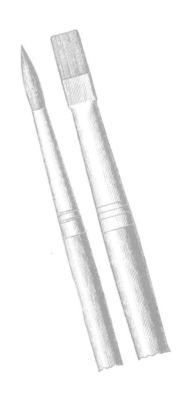

Don't tell San Franciscans that New York is the fashion capital of the US or they might take you on a tour of the eclectic boutiques and department stores to prove you wrong. Besides, as of 2004, San Francisco hosts its own Fashion Week – just like any other fashion-obsessed city.

A New You

A San Francisco company if there ever was one, **Guerilla Makeovers** makes reality TV dreams come true. For $90, the Guerilla Makeovers fashion gurus will figure out what it is you really want style-wise, and in three hours will transform you; kind of like the TV show *The Swan*, sans surgery. Stylists meet clients around 10 am any day of the week to first chat and strategize, and then hit the streets.

"Once we had a church group of kids from Florida, kids between 13 and 16 years old – so we took them to the Haight," says Jon Peahl, the owner. "We also had a dominatrix who wanted new whips and outfits so we took her to leather shops in SoMa [South of Market area]. Whatever it is you want, we can handle it."
866-293-7895, guerillamakeovers.com

The Dresser

Wilkes Bashford has been dressing San Francisco's elegantly conservative since 1966. He started as an employee of the White House department store, located at Grant and Sutter (now a Banana Republic). The White House was owned by French-born Raphael Weill, an arts and French cuisine connoisseur who arranged menus at the Bohemian Club for people like Sarah Bernhardt, Coquelin the Elder, and Jane Hading, whose performances in Moliere's plays made her famous. One of Bashford's most frequent customers is the well-groomed former San Francisco mayor Willie Brown.
375 Sutter St., 415-986-4380

the San Francisco look

Girls, get rid of those San Francisco fleece sweaters you bought at overpriced Fisherman's Wharf stores. "[San Francisco women] don't blindly follow whatever is in fashion," Ambiance store owner Donna O'Leary told us. "The San Francisco look is more vengeance-inspired. The girls don't want to look cookie-cutter here, they are very feminine too. Jackets, coats, sweaters, boots – that's very San Francisco. Think about it, it's cold here a lot!"

Here are some must-stop stores where you can perfect the San Francisco look.

Photo: courtesy of Ambiance

Ambiance

After working several years in retail, Donna O'Leary decided it was time she had her own store. The "famously romantic San Francisco stores," as O'Leary calls her three locations, all have a vintage feel, but the clothes are new. For prom dresses and black-and-white ball attire, O'Leary recommends her Haight store, where you'll find evening dresses that fit into most budgets, big or small. For a more contemporary look and more recognizable labels, head to the hip Union Street location; for young moms seeking a more casual look, the Noe Valley store is just what you're after. *1458 Haight St., 415-552-5095; 3985 & 3989 24th St., 415-647-7144 or 415-647-5800; 1864 & 1858 Union St., 415-923-9797 or 415-923-9796, ambiancesf.com*

Joe Pye
351 Divisadero St., 415-355-1051

Ooma
1422 Grant Ave, 415-627-6963, ooma.net

Red Dot Shops
508 4th St., 415-979-1597; 2176 Chestnut St., 415-346-0606, reddotshops.com

Best Bargains

Photo: courtesy of the Princess Project

Here's where you can find the best cheap clothes and second-hand threads in town:

Buffalo Exchange
1555 Haight St., 415-431-7733; 1210 Valencia St., 415-647-8332; 2585 Telegraph Ave., Berkeley, 510-644-9202, buffaloexchange.com

Crossroads Trading Co.
1519 Haight St., 415-355-0555; 1901 Fillmore St., 415-775-8885; 555 Irving St., 415-681-0100; 2123 Market St., 415-552-8740, crossroadstrading.com

Out of the Closet
A thrift store with a good cause – all donations fund medical care provided by AIDS Healthcare Foundation. Loads of clothes are added on a regular basis and with donors like Elizabeth Taylor, Bruce Willis, and Carol Burnett, you can find some real treasures. *100 N. Church St., 415-252-1101; 2415 Mission St., 415-920-9521; 1498 Polk St., 415-771-1503*

Thrift Town

2101 Mission St., at 17th St.,
415-861-1132

Worn Out West

This men's-only consignment store is a great place to find a worn-in pair of jeans, leather boots, or some leather collars and whips. Who ever said shopping can't be a learning experience? Check out the handkerchief poster in the back — you'll leave knowing what color handkerchief to wear in your back pocket depending on what your fancy is. Farmer John walking around with that red hanky in his pocket probably got quite an eyeful — or, fistful? *582 Castro St. (bet. Market and 18th Sts.), 415-431-6020*

Since 2002, Yvonne Chen and Jeremy Crown have been offering hip, one-of-a-kind clothes and accessories to those who don't abide by any animal products whatsoever. Both vegan themselves, they decided to open **Otsu** because there wasn't a place to shop for vegan lifestyle goods in the area. "The Bay Area had food fairly well covered, but not shoes and accessories. At the time, there were only three other vegan storefronts in the country," Chen says.

The word "Otsu" is Japanese and means stylish, quaint, tasty. "Apparently it's a pre-war term and not too common in today's Japanese vernacular so we thought it would work," Chen says. Turns out Otsu is also the capital of Shiga, Japan, and means "grass-like" in Turkish.

Otsu also carries a selection of cookbooks, comics, zines, music, paper products, and their own line of limited edition (and very cute) shirts.
3253 16th St., 415-255-7900 or 866-HEY-OTSU, HeyOtsu.com

Photo: courtesy of Jill Bliss

Blissful Art

Photo: courtesy of the Princess Project

A San Francisco native, Jill Bliss designs notebooks for publisher Chronicle Books, recently did a mural for **Doe** *(629-A Haight St., 415-558-8588, doe-sf.com)*, and sells her designs of shirts, wallets, and notebooks at **Otsu** and on *blissen.com*.

Notice Doe's logo – a cute orange deer on a silver board hung above the storefront – and the adjacent wall painting of a forest. The deer was feeling a little lonely, Bliss told us recently. "Learning about the different deer habitats in or near the Bay Area, I thought a redwood forest suited the deer and the shop the best, since they're both located on the shady, damp side of the street."

PROM QUEENS

Back in 2002, Kristi Smith Knutson and Laney Whitcanack met a high school student who told them that expensive prom dresses were often out of reach for graduating girls. The pair realized that they had numerous dresses and accessories they could donate and asked their friends to do the same; thus was born the **Princess Project**. They now get thousands of dresses each year and organize two events in the city where high school girls come looking for the perfect fit.

415-269-6667, princessproject.org

Photo: courtesy of Jill Bliss

Where to Play Dress Up

American Conservatory Theater (A.C.T.)

Callie Floor, Costume Manager at A.C.T., schedules one day a week for individuals to rent costumes used in past seasons. Prices range from $100 to $200 and rentals are for one week. "We do a full fitting, with alterations and everything, except for wigs," Floor told us.
Call for appt., 415-439-2379, act-sf.org

Photo: courtesy of Magaña Baptiste

Belly Dance Boutique

Magaña Baptiste is the founder of the first School of Middle Eastern Dance in San Francisco, which opened in the 1950s. She and her husband, Walt Baptiste, also opened the first Center of Yoga in the city in 1955. Although

Denim Kings

In 1853, a Bavarian immigrant by the name of **Loeb Strauss** became a US citizen and opened a dry-goods business in San Francisco. Nicknamed Levi, the man and his family ran a successful business.

In 1873, a Nevada tailor and customer of Levi, Jacob Davis, wrote him a letter to ask for help in paying for a patent. Davis wrote "the secratt of them Pants is the Rivits that I put in those Pockots and I found the demand so large that I cannot make them fast enough…. My nabors are getting yealouse of these success and unless I secure it by Patent Papers it will soon become to be a general thing everybody will make them up and thare will be no money in it. tharefor Gentlemen I wish to make you a Proposition that you should take out the Latters Patent in my name as I am the Inventor of it, the expense of it will be about $68, all complit and for these $68 I will give you half the right to sell all such Clothing Revited according to the Patent…."

Knowing a good idea when he saw one, Strauss accepted, and the two went on to make a fortune selling their riveted pants to miners. **Levi's Jeans** soon became the world's most famous jeans brand, a favorite of cowboys in Western movies, gay men in the Castro, and hipsters alike.

During World War II, the arcuate stitching design (the double row of stitching on the back pockets) was painted on the pockets due to government rationing of essential items such as thread.

Rivets were first used on 501 jeans in 1873 because miners complained that their pockets ripped under the weight of ore samples. The early jeans had rivets on the front and back pockets. Rear rivets were covered beginning in 1937 because of complaints that the rivets scratched school desk chairs and saddles. Since 1967, reinforced stitching has replaced the back pocket rivets.

Strauss's dry-goods business was located at 90 Sacramento Street. Now, the flagship store is at 300 Post Street (415-501-0100, levis.com), where customers can have their favorite jeans customized.

Clothes by Ben Davis, grandson of Jacob, can be purchased at: *Acme Surplus, 5159 Mission St.; Arik Surplus, 998 Market St.; Kaplan's, 1055 Market St., bendavis.com*

San Franciscans love their local designers, but we also know a good deal when we see one. **Loehmann's** *(222 Sutter St., 415-982-3215, loehmanns.com)*, which originated in Brooklyn, has been a favorite of bargain shoppers in San Francisco for many years. In the 1920s, Frieda Loehmann shopped Seventh Avenue designers' showrooms in New York, picking up their overstocks, samples, and cancellations, paying a fraction of the original wholesale price so she could resell them at greatly discounted prices. She would always pay in cash, which she carried in her stocking. The San Francisco store recently expanded and opened **Loehmann's Shoes** *(211 Sutter St., 415-399-9208)*. Today, frequent new arrivals and discount prices that get lower as the days pass make Loehmann's a great place to find a good bargain.

Prices at **Jeremys** *(Two South Park, 415-882-4929, jeremys.com)* are often higher than at Loehmann's, but it's worth signing up for their e-mail newsletter, where their best sales are announced.

the monthly fee was only $5, people were hesitant to take their classes, and those who did often asked teachers to not let their family and friends know they were learning what then sounded like an odd activity. The store sells and rents Middle Eastern costumes, including coin hip skirts for belly dancing. Yoga and meditation classes are offered here too.
730 Euclid Ave., 415-387-6833

Costumes on Haight
Great for last-minute Halloween shopping before heading down to the party in the Castro.
735 Haight St., 415-621-1356

Costume Party
The name says it all.
1050 Hyde St., 415-885-3377

Dez Demona
Online store that specializes in devil horn barrettes for that Beelzebub look.
dezdemona.com

Piedmont Boutique

At the corner of Haight and Ashbury streets, the once-hippie center of the world, Piedmont is a favorite of drag queens looking for glittery wear, colorful wigs, and satin gloves. You know you've found it if you spot the oversized legs sticking out of the window above the store (see photo). *1452 Haight St., 415-864-8075, piedmontsf.com*

Samba Do Coracao

Rent or buy carnival and masquerade costumes complete with feather headpieces. *By appointment only, 415-826-2588, sambadocoracao.com.*

Wasteland

Vintage warehouse. *1660 Haight St., 415-863-3150*

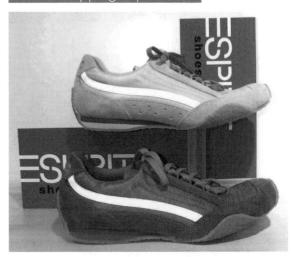

In 1964, Susie Russell, a twenty-year-old San Francisco resident on her way to Tahoe City to work as a keno runner for the summer, stopped her Beetle on the side of the road to give a young hitchhiker a ride.

The guy with the thumb out was Doug Tomkins, a twenty-year-old East Coaster who tried to impress Russell, to no avail. In Tahoe City, the pair went their own way but kept bumping into each other at social events. At the end of the summer, the two went on a trip to Mexico together and married later that year.

They decided to start a clothing business, Plain Jane, which they later renamed **Esprit**. Working out of a home office and using a van as showroom, they turned Esprit into a clothing empire. Stores opened worldwide, including a huge one in San Francisco, complete with a Caffe Esprit and Esprit Park across the street, and profits soared. But, as with all good things, the relationship came to an end, and the brand was sold to investors in 1996.

Susie Russell married Mark Buell later that year and is now very active in women's issues and politics. As for Doug Tomkins, he is the proprietor of 700,000 acres in Chile, which he turned into a preserve. Shoppers can still find Esprit clothes and accessories at Macy's – just one piece of advice: avoid going on Saturday afternoons if you don't like crowds.
Macy's, 170 O'Farrell St. (bet. Powell and Kearny Sts.), 415-397-3333

designs for divas

Hipsters crowd **American Apparel** (1615 Haight St., 415-431-4028; 2174 Union St., 415-440-3220, americanapparel.net), the Upper Haight's new store, every weekend to buy its cool yet 100% cotton merchandise. The Los Angeles-based company guarantees that all products are made in America and are sweatshop-free. American Apparel knows how to please customers while taking care of its employees – garment workers receive on-site massages, are paid twice the minimum wage, and can take free English classes if English is not their native language.

At **Forever 21** (7 Powell St., 415-984-0380, forever21.com), you'll find three jam-packed (by people and clothes) floors of cute styles of every color and cut, including jewelry, shoes, and purses at low prices. If you're brave enough to stand in the long check-out lines, you'll be rewarded with some cool merchandise and a bright yellow bag that reads, "John 3:16" at the bottom – something about accepting God in our hearts....

BLESSED CRAFTS

Confess your love of graphic tees at **ROCK n SHOP**, a semi-annual event where you can shop while enjoying drinks and live music. The event is organized by **She-Bible** and **Craft Nation** (craftnation.net). She-Bible shirts can be purchased year-round online at she-bible.com, or at **Ver Unica** (437-B Hayes St., 415-431-0688, verunica.com).

Here's a list of independent designers and clothing stores:

Babette
Known for her micro-fiber pleated coats.
361 Sutter St., 415-837-1442, babettesf.com

Dema
Twisted classics for independently minded women.
1038 Valencia St, 415.206.0500, godemago.com

Knitz and Leather
Knit-to-order sweaters, leather jackets, and bags.
1429 Grant Ave., 415-391-3480

Lotta Jansdotter
A great example of less-is-more design, this Scandinavian designer uses a lot of natural fabrics for her aprons, purses, and stylized fauna-inspired designs for housewares.
864 Post St., 415-409-1457, jansdotter.com

Manifesto
Vintage-inspired clothing for men, women, and children.
514 Octavia St., 415-431-4778, manifestoclothing.com

Minnie Wilde
Sassy vintage-inspired clothes made with love.
519 Laguna, 415-863-9453, minniewilde.com

Needles and Pens

Photo: Andrew Scott

Sewing machine queen Breezy Culbertson and independent zine buff Andrew Scott decided to open their small Mission store after traveling around the world. With so many independent designers and publications in the Bay Area, this was a much-needed space for the zine and DIY community. The friendly and laid-back couple hosts art shows, barbecues, and magazine launch parties.
483 14th St., 415-255-1534, needles-pens.com

PROPER ATTIRE

Fashion-conscious men shop the European collections, designer jeans, and shoes at **Rolo** *(2351 Market St., 415-431-4545)*. Fashion-conscious men on a budget prefer their outlet store, **Rolo Garage**. *1301 Howard St., 415-861-2097, rolo.com; Rolo Soma, 1235 Howard St., 415-355-1122*

Nisa

Hip urban wear that's comfortable.
3610 19th St., 415-865-0969, nisasf.com

Pink Stripes

A real Mission treat where girls can get both things they love: sweets and clothes.
1003 Guerrero, 415-642-4668, pinkstripessf.com

RAG (Resident Apparel Gallery)

A chic Hayes Valley boutique/co-op where local designers display and sell their designs.
541 Octavia St., 415-621-7718, ragsf.com

Sunhee Moon

Classic cuts that fit just right.
3167 16th St., 415-355-1800, sunheemoon.com

DIY Clothing and Accessories

Photo: Beth Snyder

After getting laid off from her job in medical research, Beth Snyder was looking for something that would keep her busy. She started crafting products at her kitchen table and soon realized they were good enough to sell. The only problem was finding the right store.

"The small batch market was just beginning to grow at that time, but it hadn't really gotten a toe-hold in any real way in the Bay Area," she told us. "So I decided to start my own boutique where I could make and sell whatever I felt like making that week, and where customers could come and watch me working in the studio and try some simple crafting projects for themselves, if they wanted to."

WRITINGS ON THE WALL

The most talked-about billboard in town was at 101 Powell Street in 2001, which announced "San Francisco's First Fcuk." City officials made **French Connection UK** take it down, but the clothing company quickly started posting the same ads (much smaller this time) on cabs around town.

San Francisco may be the birthplace of Levi's, Gap, Banana Republic, and Old Navy, but not everyone here wants chain-store fashion. In 2004, Hayes Valley became the first neighborhood to become a chain-store free zone. Two areas in and around the Haight followed — residents were able to stop Urban Outfitters from settling in and lobbied successfully for a say in what stores could move in. The city's latest victory over its possible Wal-Martization was in March 2005 when the North Beach commercial area around Columbus Avenue was also declared a chain-store free zone. Now if only San Franciscans were able to reclaim their independent coffee shops from ever-growing Starbucks....

As the **Wonderland Design Collective** *(2703 Seventh St. # 112, Berkeley, 510-843-3286, bethalyse.com)* got going, she started meeting other creative minds who were similarly producing goods at home and also having a hard time making money. She offered to bring them in as consignment artists and give them a place to sell their work.

The store sells locally-designed items such as towels, baby products, and stationery. It's also home to the Looking-Glass Studio, which hosts hands-on crafting workshops.

Start your DIY projects at **Britex Fabrics** *(146 Geary St., 415-392-2910, britexfabrics.com)*, a Union Square store that has been serving sewing machine experts and novices since 1952. Whether you know your stuff or have no idea how the hell someone can make a good-fitting dress out of a roll of cotton fabric, the friendly staff is here to assist you. Once you have what you need, head to **Stitch Lounge** *(182 Gough St., 415-431-3739, stichlounge.com)*, a women-owned business where Bay Area designers can come and mingle with other creative minds and make or buy clothing and accessories. Tools, supplies, resources, and advice are provided.

If you're heading to a DIY jewelry workshop, sift through the wide selection of beads at **Beadissimo** *(1051 Valencia St., 415-282-BEAD, beadissimo.com)*: you're bound to find some you like. Jewelry-making classes are offered in the back of the store.

mind the gap

Although rumor had it that **Gap** really meant "gay and proud" and that thousands of Republicans across the country were wearing gay-friendly clothes without knowing it, this urban myth is just that. Gap was actually named after the popular 1960s term "generation gap," and was founded by married couple Donald and Doris Fisher who lived in San Francisco.

Donald Fisher's six-foot-one stature and 34-inch waist made it difficult for him to shop, and he was tired of having to search the city for a good-fitting pair of jeans. He decided that others like him would appreciate a jeans-only store. At first, the couple sold jeans of all kinds, including Levi's, as well as record albums. Although the records didn't sell, the store was a success and Gap went on to become the all-American clothes empire we know today (an empire that includes Banana Republic and old Navy).

The late 1990s were a tough time for the brand, as sales slowed down. Thanks to either Monica Lewinski, who modeled the blue Gap dress in her after-hours play at the White House, or to the catchy songs and celebrities in their ads – or both – Gap made a comeback and is going strong once again.

Although most neighborhoods welcome Gap, Haight residents, well, hate it, and the big front window is often under repair because of the rocks and bricks that somehow seem attracted to it.

Gap
(includes BabyGap, GapBody and GapKids)
890 Market St., 415-788-5909;
100 Post St., 415-989-1266;
3521 20th Ave., 415-564-7137;
1485 Haight St., 415-431-6336;
3 Sacramento St., 415-391-8826;
2040 Chestnut St., 415-447-3986;

Photo: courtesy of Flight 001

READY FOR TAKE-OFF

Inspired by Pan Am's Flight 001, a flight from San Francisco that stopped in most of the world's major cities before finally landing in New York 48 hours later, **Flight 001** is the one-stop shop for all things travel. As the store's motto says, "Pre-flight, in-flight, or on arrival, the savvy traveler always moves in style." Not only do the white rounded walls make you feel like you've stepped into first class, the store is full of fun, fashionable, and practical travel gear that will make it look like you just joined the jet set. So get rid of your old suitcases and ugly passport covers and get set. Looking for a gift for the traveler who has everything? Pick up a Mile High Kit.
525 Hayes St., 415-487-1001, flight001.com

2159 Chestnut St., 415-929-1744;
3491 California St., 415-386-7517;
2169 Chestnut St., 415-771-9316;
1 Jefferson St., 415-392-8380;
4228 Geary Blvd., 415-751-0551;
83 Stonestown Galleria, 415-564-6523,
gap.com

Banana Republic
256 Grant Ave., 415-788-3087;
Embarcadero Center, 2 Sacramento St.,
415-986-5076;
3251 20th Ave., 415-753-3330,
bananarepublic.com

Old Navy
801 Market St., 415-344-0375;
2300 16th St., 415-255-1276,
55 Colma Blvd., 650-994-8183,
oldnavy.com

IT'S IN THE BAG

Although customers were concerned recently when the San Francisco company announced it was producing some accessories in China, rest assured the classic **Timbuk2** messenger bag is still as "city-born and street-tough" as it has been since the company started in 1989. The bag of choice for busy bike messengers (and those who like the bike messenger look), various colors and patterns are available in stores across town. *timbuk2.com*

Good Clean Deals

Fresh soaps displayed like edible cakes, colorful bath bombs, and stainless steel bowls of freshly made masks and scrubs are what made **LUSH** (2116 Union St., 415-921-5874; 240 Powell St. 415-693-9633, lush.com) so popular in the UK for ten years. The first US store opened in 2003 in Union Square. A smashing success throughout North America, LUSH recently opened a second location in San Francisco.

Pretty boys (and girls) can shop for bath salts, foaming milk bath, signature perfumes, "Butch" and "Fem," and logo shirts and caps which read "Tested On Boyfriends, Not Animals" at **Nancy Boy** (2319 Market St., 415-626-5021, nancyboy.com), the Castro's version of the Body Shop.

Pop Goes the Pop-up

Photo: courtesy of Method

Good things always come to an end – and so it goes with pop-up retail stores. To create a buzz, companies open a temporary store for customers to get a taste of what they offer, then abruptly close up shop to leave them begging for more.

Remember those colorful bottles of dish soap in Monica's kitchen on the TV sitcom *Friends*? That was the work of **Method** *(methodhome.com)*, a Bay Area company, and Karim Rashid, renowned product designer. For a few months, the company, whose slogan is "the people against dirty," tempted us with colorful and environment-friendly dish and hand soap in their pop-up store. Alas, the store is now closed, but you can still find their pretty products at Target and Linens N Things.

Weston Wear, an apparel brand for women designed by Julienne Weston, did the same with its Mission district pop-up store. The San Francisco native's clothes have appeared on TV shows like *Six Feet Under* and *Trading Spaces* and in the movie *Pretty Woman*, among others. Her clothes can be found at *westonwear.com*, and in stores around town (Anthropologie at 880 Market St., *415-434-2210*, Paparazzi at 230 West Portal Ave., *415-753-6576*; Haseena, 526 Hayes St., *415-252-1104*).

Although it's hard to keep track of all pop-up store comings and goings, websites like *stylemaven.com* and *eventme.com* let you in on shopping events.

Sole-ful San Francisco

In 1966, Margot Fraser discovered the comfort of **Birkenstocks** while on vacation in Germany. Her chronic foot pain vanished within months after she returned home to California, which convinced her that the shoes had health benefits Californians should know about. She began importing Birkenstock footwear, thus marking the beginning of Birkenstock Footprint Sandals, Inc., in the US. She then opened a small store in a San Rafael warehouse in 1971, and the rest is history.

Birkenstocks are still widely sold in the Bay Area, but here are some alternative shop options (apart from the Haight-Ashbury area where shoe stores are as plentiful as head shops):

Azalea
411 Hayes St., 415-861-9888, azaleasf.com

Jean and Jane Ford call themselves the right and left brain of **Benefit** *(2117 Fillmore St., 415-567-0242; 2219 Chestnut St., 415-567-1173; 1831 Fourth St., Berkeley, 510-981-9858, benefitcosmetics.com).* Starting in 1976 as the Face Place, the twins gave their customers what they wanted and it worked. Although Benefit prefers to keep quiet about its first product, we can't help but share the secret. One of their first customers, a local exotic dancer, was looking for a sweat-proof way to look naturally flushed all night – although the Benefit website says she used it for her cheeks, rumor has it that she used the Benetint liquid blush to keep her nipples rosy. They have since added to their selection, including products like Ooh La Lift, Boo Boo Zap, and Touch Me Then Try to Leave Me cream, and locals line up at the Brow Bar inside Macy's for a movie-star-perfect brow tweeze and wax.

If store-bought fragrances don't do it for you, why not ask local perfumer **Yosh Han** to make one just for you? Recently released signature scents include a sweet mix based on J.T. Leroy's book and movie, *The Heart is Deceitful Above All Things.* Han said that although she usually meets her customers in person in order to decide what mix will work, she has yet to meet the shy writer; all Q&As were done over e-mail. Signature scents cost around $500.

By appointment, 415-626-5385, eaudeyosh.com

Bulo Men

437-A Hayes St., 415-864-3244, buloshoes.com

Bulo Women

418 Hayes, 415-255-4939

Foot Worship

For (very) high heels and party queen platforms.
1214 Sutter St., 415-921-3668

Gimme Shoes

416 Hayes St., 415-864-0691, gimmeshoes.com

Bound for Leather

Photo: Fred Alert

Every year, 400,000 people attend the **Folsom Street Fair** (folsomstreetfair.com), a major leather event in September, where anything goes and five bucks gets you a public spanking. More than 12,000 people make it to the even more daring **Dore Alley Street Fair** in July, so you could say San Francisco's big on the leather scene.

Mr. S Leather & Fetters USA (310 7th St., 415-863-7764, mr-s-leather.com) shares a website with **Madame S Leather** (321 7th St. directly across from Mr. S, 415-863-9447) that includes message boards where visitors can plan scene ideas and read the latest product reviews.

Customers who want to make sure they get what they want can start a wedding and a dominatrix registry at **Stormy Leather** (1158 Howard St., 415-626-1672, stormyleather.com). And if it's boots you want, **Stompers Boots** (323 Tenth St., 415-255-6422, stompersboots.com), a boots-only store, sells everything you need.

For S&M books, videos, and classes, see blowfish.com and qualitysm.com.

HOME SWEET HOME

Walking into **Brown Eyed Girl**, situated in a Victorian house, is like coming back from a hard day's work to a warm, cozy domicile. You can sink in the comfy couch, catch up on reading by picking one of the books on the coffee table, try on some clothes hung in the closet, or chat with friends at the dinner table. And if this leaves you wishing your own home could look more like this one, you're in luck: everything you see here is for sale. Brown Eyed Girl sells clothes, accessories, and furniture. 2999 Washington St., 415-409-0214, shopbrowneyedgirl.com

California Dreamin'

Photo: Dylan Sanchez

Pipe Dreams *(1376 Haight St., 415-431-3553)* may not have the friendliest staff, but it's Haight-Ashbury's oldest smoke shop and is still owned by the same person.

Here are other head shops to check out:

Day Dreams
1589 Haight St., 415-554-0246

Distractions
1552 Haight St., 415-252-8751

Land of Sun
1715 Haight St., 415-831-8646

Psychedelic Sun
1746 Haight St., 415-668-5417

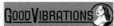

Good Vibrations, the woman-owned and -operated store that has made self-loving respectable also runs a vibrator museum and a NetFlix-like DVD-by-mail rental service that offers a number of sex-positive and couples-friendly selections. One of their latest designs is the world's first solar-powered vibrator. "What could be more sexually liberating and ecologically sound than a vibrator powered by solar energy?" author and staff sexologist Carol Queen said. The store has sold more than 120,000 vibrators since it opened, making the world is a much happier place.

Joani Blank, the founder of Good Vibrations, has moved on; she, along with a friend, recently started **Intimate Tattoos** (first called Titattoos), an online store that sells temporary tattoos designed to be worn on the breast. *intimatearttattoo.com*
603 Valencia St., 415-522-5460, 1620 Polk St., 415-345-0400, 2504 San Pablo Ave., Berkeley, 510-841-8987, goodvibes.com

Gem of a Fair

Christmas shopping can be stressful, but after a few drinks it's considerably less so. **Hayes Valley** merchants host a block party every year in December: the stores stay open late and offer cocktails, snacks, and live music. The best part is, you don't have to buy anything to get a drink ... although the merchants would appreciate it if you did. Check *sfstation.com* and local newspapers for dates.

Don't worry if you never get invited to the numerous secret sample sales around town: **Fashion Co-Op** *(fashioncoop.com)* is open to the less in-crowd too. For two dollars, you can take part in one of the biggest sample sales where up-and-coming designers show off their latest collections before they hit the stores. **Feria Urbana** is also a good place to check out. This urban fair is made up of approximately 25 artists and designers who sell jewelry, housewares, accessories, and more. To hear more about the twice-monthly upcoming events, sign up for the e-mail list at *feriaurbanasf.com*.

For other shopping events, *appelandfrank.com* and *chillinproductions.com* are worth checking out.

RAGS TO RICHES

Solomon Gump of **Gump's** has been importing one-of-a-kind furniture and accessories to San Francisco since 1861. His clientele may typically sip their tea with their pinkies raised, but Robert Livingston Gump, Gump's grandson, wasn't afraid of ruining Grandpa's reputation. In 1951, he eloped to Reno with Sally Stanford, San Francisco's last grand madam. Then again, Grandpa Gump himself was no stranger to bordellos — his store supplied many Barbary Coast establishments with eclectic items from around the world.
135 Post St., 800-766-7628, gumps.com

PARIS, CALIFORNIA

Starting as a makeshift store on his boat, Frenchman Felix Verdier realized that selling luxury items brought over from France was a lucrative business in the 1850s. He quickly expanded his business, building the **City of Paris** department store. The store lasted until 1970, and was replaced by the **Neiman Marcus** building *(150 Stockton St., 415-362-3900)* in 1981. Although most of the former building was torn down, Neiman Marcus agreed to retain a four-story rotunda which now houses the **Rotunda Restaurant** *(415-362-4777, rotundarestaurant.com)*. The rotunda's dome was temporarily taken down and sent to Massachusetts, where glass artisans cleaned and restored each of its 26,000 pieces.

A recent survey showed that 112 languages are spoken in the Bay Area, so it's not surprising that a cosmopolitan city like San Francisco would have many boutiques that specialize in goods from different parts of the world.

Champ de Mars *(347 Hayes St., 415-252-9434)* is a small Hayes Valley store, owned by French natives Pierre Moskovtchenko and Marceau Galliot, packed with miniature Eiffel Towers, old French street signs, and other trinkets *à la français* that the owners bring back from their regular trips to France. Patience and a good eye for small things hidden under piles of items is key to finding that one-of-a-kind piece.

With an entrance at basement level, you could easily walk by **Tazi Designs** *(599 Hayes St., 415-503-0013, tazidesigns.com)* without noticing it, but it's definitely worth the walk down the stairs. The softly lit room is full of neatly displayed Moroccan glasses, lanterns, and tagine bowls as well as furniture. The inviting music and friendly staff would make anyone want to stay for a cup of mint tea.

Walk one block north from the busy Haight and Ashbury streets and you'll find **Love of Ganesha** (photo above) *(1601-A Page St., 415-621-3071)*, a peaceful store full of embroidered pillows, tie-dyed shirts, incense, and jewelry. The best thing about it is the small back room filled with comfy pillows where you can sit and take a breather from shopping.

Full of sweet-smelling incense, one-of-a-kind boxes, bags, and jewelry the owner of **Life** *(604-A Haight St., 415-252-9312)* brings back from Bali and other parts of Southeast Asia, this store recently burned down and had to be closed for a while, but strong will and hard work helped the owner bring the store back to life.

Body Manipulations *(3234 16th St., 415-621-0408, bodym.com)* is the nation's oldest piercing studio, but piercing is just one of the many services they offer; branding, cutting, and tattooing are also available. The staff prides itself for having cut people open, "hung them from their skin, pierced them with hundreds of needles, and sewn a number of items into their skin." Paul, the owner, organizes a yearly Flying Tiger Circus event where you can see him hang from hooks.

Lyle Tuttle of **Lyle Tuttle Tattooing** *(841 Columbus Ave., 415-775-4991, lyletuttletattooing.com)* now a well-known speaker on the art of tattooing, got his start in San Francisco in 1960. He worked with the Department of Health to come up with standardized techniques to sterilize tattooing equipment. Some of his past customers include Janis Joplin, Cher, Peter Fonda, and Joan Baez. His store, now owned by Tanja Nixx, is still as popular as ever.

Think Before You Ink

Axl Rose, lead singer of Guns 'N Roses, warned you. If you're wishing you hadn't gotten that big heart with your ex-girlfriend's name tattooed across your chest, there are places in San Francisco that will make the bad memories disappear:

San Francisco Plastic Surgery & Laser Center
490 Post St., Suite 430, 415-392-5327, sfcosmeticsurgery.com

Second Chance, Central American Resource Center
Accepts San Francisco residents, 12-23 years old. Patients do community service in lieu of payment.
1245 Alabama St., 415-824-2330 x926, carecensf.com

Going, Going, Gone

The **Bonhams & Butterfields** *(220 San Bruno Ave., 415-861-7500, butterfields.com)* auction house made the news recently when it attempted to sell what appears to be Malcom X's bullet-riddled diary found in his coat pocket following his February 1965 assassination. The auction was cancelled due to the uproar, but you never know what will be up for auction next.

For the biggest rummage sale in the area, check out Oakland's annual day-long **White Elephant Sale.** "It's just like an estate sale but better because you don't have to deal with grieving relatives," reports Jason Ganz, a frequent shopper. *510-536-6800, museumca.org/events/elephant.html*

JAPANESE GEMS

In Japantown, check out the Japanese version of the dollar store at **Ichiban Kan** *(22 Peace Plaza)* where bowls, chopsticks, and bath minerals are all great deals, and for hip Japanese and local designer goods or live events, head to **Super7** *(1630 Post St., 415-409-4700, super7store.com).*

Colorful Designs, Dark Past

The Jackson Square interior design stores like **Design Within Reach** *(455 Jackson St., 415-837-3940, dwr.com)* and **Kartell** *(501 Pacific Ave., 415-839-4025, kartell.com)* will leave you dreaming of modern roomy houses, something you won't find in the city for less than a few million dollars. It's hard to imagine that this area was once known as Murderer's Corner in Barbary Coast days, a place where women lured men in bars with free drinks, only to poison them and steal all their belongings.

Cast A Spell

If you're looking for supplies for your next Santeria ceremony, head to **Botanica Yoruba** *(998 Valencia St., 415-826-4967)* where you can shop for magic potions, incense, and candles. While you're in there, listen carefully, and you may hear the live chickens that live in the basement. Most of the time, the music is too loud for people to hear them, but we know they're there – the owner recently showed them to a friend.

family jewels

From expensive rocks in Union Square to funky earrings in Upper Haight, jewelry stores can be found all around.

At **Jest Jewels** *(1869 Union St.,415-563-8839; 3 Embarcadero Center, 415-986-4494; 1791 4th St., Berkeley, 510-526-7766, jestjewels.com)*, you'll find feather phones and natural-feel silicone bra inserts to add a full cup size to your bust line, as well as earrings, necklaces, and pashminas.

Here are other stores to satisfy your jewelry needs:

683 Haight
683 Haight St., 415-861-1311

Bmod Jewelry
3994 Sacramento St., 415-867-0108, bmodjewelry.com

Global Exchange Fair Trade Center
2017 Mission St., #303, 415-255-7296, globalexchange.org

Avast, Ye Shoppers

826 Valencia, known as San Francisco's "only independent pirate store," was started by local author Dave Eggers. Inside you'll find designer glass eyes, pirate perfumes, a big tub of lard, and Karl the porcupine puffer fish, among other strange characters. Beware if you suffer from seasickness; a customer once had to leave the store because she felt nauseated when she entered. She blamed it on the fact that the floor is not level; we just think she needed some Dramamine. All proceeds from sales go to writing workshops for children, and more recently, adults. Check the website for the next thumb-wrestling contest and upcoming writing workshops and events.
415-642-5905, 826valencia.org

The ladies' restrooms on the sixth floor of **Macy's** Union Square store *(170 O'Farrell, 415-397-3333)* are probably as classy as restrooms get here, so if you gotta go, go there. These washrooms are the only rooms left from the upscale I. Magnin store that used to occupy this building. I. Magnin was mentioned in Hitchcock's movie *Vertigo* as the place where Kim Novak's character worked. When you're in the loo, contemplate the fact that Union Square is the third-largest shopping area in the United States, and this Macy's is the largest department store west of New York City.

A GALLERY OF FLOWERS

What looks like a disorganized art gallery featuring a display of bamboo and rocks on one side of the storefront and an amazing arrangement of branches and flowers on the other is actually **Ixia**, a flower shop where the owner sells Ikebana-style bouquets. *2331 Market St., 415-431-3134, ixia.com*

For unique landscaping tools, framed insects, animal bones, and stuffed animals – we don't mean the cute kind – there's **Paxton Gate** *(824 Valencia St., 415-824-1872, paxtongate.com)*. The two landscaping artists who opened the store originally had a landscaping store in mind, but they couldn't resist adding more and more "products." The store also offers a taxidermy class for those who want to learn how to stuff their own mouse.

In the East Bay, Ron Cauble's product selection is just as strange. He says he was just looking for an excuse to learn more about natural history when he opened the **Bone Room** *(1569 Solano, Berkeley, 510-526-5252, boneroom.com)* in 1987. The sale of animal bones and the like has apparently proven to be a profitable business as the store's selection has expanded to insect jewelry, fossils, shells, fossil and bone casts, and animal remnants. When choosing a skull, be sure to read the detailed descriptions. One we liked: "Male from China, seven teeth, damaged right orbital." Hundreds of moths from the store were used in Christina Aguilera's video "Fighter."

How's it Hangin'?

Part gallery, part consignment store, **Artist Xchange** *(3169 16th St., 415-864-1490, www.artist-xchange.com)* opened in 2003 to give local artists and residents a place to get together, hang out, and buy and sell some funky art.

Chuck Williams of **Williams-Sonoma** grew up in Southern California and started working at I. Magnin in Los Angeles shortly after his high school graduation in the 1940s. He then left for World War II and upon his return to America, went to Sonoma to help a friend build a house. He ended up staying and had plans of opening a hardware store there, but his plans changed yet again when he and his friends went to Paris on vacation.

Williams had always been a great cook and fell in love with French cuisine and its kitchenware. In 1956, French cookware was only available to chefs in the US, so Williams decided to open a store in Sonoma with all the French utensils he had discovered in Paris. It wasn't long before he moved the store to San Francisco, and with the help of Julia Child and her televised French cuisine lessons, his business went from one store to 250 today. Williams expanded and also opened Pottery Barn, Hold Everything, and West Elm.

340 Post St., 415-362-9450; Two Embarcadero Center, 415-421-2033; 2000 Chestnut St. 415-929-2520; 3251 20th Ave., 415-242-1473, williamssonoma.com

Located on classy Maiden Lane with big brand neighbors like Chanel and Hermès, **Sur La Table** is another foodie favorite where you can sometimes spot Alice Waters of Chez Panisse fame, the East Bay chef who helped to create California Cuisine.
77 Maiden Lane, 415-732-7900

JOY FOR TOYS
Remember the wooden toys you loved so much as a kid? Well, thank Pamela Byars and her daughter Temple at the **Ark Toy Company** *(3845 24th St., 415-821-1257; 1812 Fourth St. Berkeley, 510-849-1930)*: they sell all your old favorites in their San Francisco and Berkeley stores.

Hammers in Harmony

Before opening the family-run **Cole Hardware** store on Polk Street, owner Dave Karp was kind enough to call **Brownie's Hardware**, another family-owned hardware store that has now been in business for more than 30 years; Karp wanted to make sure it was fine to open a store within seven blocks of theirs. To date, both stores remain friendly competitors.

Brownie's Hardware
1563 Polk St., 415-673-8900

Cole Hardware
2254 Polk St., 415-674-8913,
colehardware.com

Chinatown has tons of great stores where you'll find inexpensive housewares, clothes, and tacky San Francisco souvenirs. If you have a foodie in the family, be sure to check out the **Wok Shop**. It's full of all the kitchen gadgets you'll ever need, including cleavers, bamboo steamers, wok tools, dim sum supplies, dishes, garnishing tools, cookbooks, baskets, and bamboo utensils (as well as lottery tickets).

"The store opened right after President Nixon's trip to China in 1971, the first trip to China by a United States official since 1949," store owner Tane Chan says. "There was so much interest and curiosity about Communist China after that."

"We originally had a gift shop in Chinatown called Yum Yum. I decided to start selling woks because the only place you could find them was a Chinese grocery store whose staff couldn't speak English, so non-Chinese people were intimidated."
718 Grant Ave., 415-989-3797, wokshop.com

According to a 2002 market research study, nearly a quarter of San Franciscans make an online purchase each month. Of the 25 largest US markets, the San Francisco Bay Area leads the nation in online shopping.

San Francisco was the Dot Com center of the late nineties and although many online stores have gone belly up, there are survivors:

King of online auctions, **eBay.com** is a Bay Area favorite that led the way for many other online shopping sites. They also created a niche market for those wanting to unload unwanted possessions but were too lazy to do it themselves. Websites like **foundvalue.com** can come scope out your home for hidden treasures: representatives handle all postings on eBay and shipping to customers for a small fee.

High-end customers can go brand crazy on **eluxury.com** and **sephora.com** – both have corporate offices and customer service centers in San Francisco, but are owned by the French group LVMH.

Although Macy's department store had its start in New York, **macys.com** started in San Francisco.

The San-Francisco-based **redenvelope.com** has been a favorite of trendy shoppers ever since Oprah recommended the website for its customizable gifts.

Catwalking for Cats (and Dogs)

You may laugh at Paris Hilton's chihuahua Tinkerbell and her absurd designer outfits, but shopping for your pet is no laughing matter at these two shops, where you can gear up your soon-to-be-hip urban pet.

Puppycat
289 Divisadero St., 415-621-5911

Vavadog
735 Fillmore St., 415-409-3900, vavadog.com

music to my ears

Amoeba Music
(1855 Haight St.,
415-831-1200,
amoebamusic.com)
opened its first store
in Berkeley in 1990
when most
independent music
stores were being eaten up by big chain stores. It is the
largest independent record store in the US and
according to music buffs, could very well be the best
music store in the world. The store donates a portion of
its profits to the Rainforest Action Network; to date they
have helped save over one million acres of rainforest.

Jack's Record Cellar (254 Scott St., 415-431-3047)
is a small, quiet store and the oldest record shop in the
city. Here, you'll find 78 RPMs as well as LPs, and Roy
Loney, former lead singer of the 1960s band the Flamin'
Groovies, behind the counter.

There are almost as many DJ record stores as there
are hair salons here, and it seems that everyone and
their mother spins.

BPM

573 Hayes St., 415-487-8680, bpmsf.net

In House Records

988 Mission St., 415-543-4003, throwdown.com

Tweekin Records

593 Haight St., 415-626-6995, tweekin.com

If Sparky needs a home, a pet
palace may be a solution. Pets
Are Wonderful Support (**PAWS**,
pawssf.org) is a local organization
that helps people living with AIDS
by providing financial support so
that they can keep their pets.
Each year, the organization hosts
Petchitecture, a live auction
where people can bid on pet habitats
(such as the Bachelor Pad 2000,
the Pavilion Empress Wu, and the
Murderin' Murdoch) designed by
some of the Bay Area's top
designers and architects.
(pawssf.org/ptech2002/
download_images.html)

Photo: Tom Bross, San Francisco Convention and Visitors Bureau

From hippie bands living in communes to independent magazines that are all about the L word, San Francisco is a city where anything goes and everyone is accepted – except conservatives. Its entertainment is like its residents: anything but mainstream. Back in the 1970s when David Bowie was on tour and his concert failed to sell out here, he reportedly told the press, "They don't need me. They have [disco icon] Sylvester."

Tough Guy
in the City of Love

They call him Dirty Harry because he always gets stuck with the job no one wants to do. Well, it turns out that's kind of how **Clint Eastwood** got the part. The title role was originally intended for Frank Sinatra, who had to decline because of a hand injury. It was then offered to John Wayne and Steve McQueen, among others, but Eastwood was the only one willing to do it.

Same goes for the role of the Scorpio Killer, although the original actor's fate was a lot more tragic than Sinatra's injured hand. Audie Murphy was approached to play the role, but died in a plane crash before he could accept the offer. Although his character was inspired by the Zodiac Killer, a serial murderer who tortured and killed couples in the Bay Area in the late 1960s, **Andrew Robinson**, the actor who eventually got the role, was far from the violent type. Legend has it that he was so terrified of guns that every time he had to pull the trigger for a scene, he would close his eyes. Director Don Siegel stopped production for a week so that Robinson could learn, with the help of a gun expert, to work a firearm without flinching. When the film was released, Robinson received death threats because of his role, and was forced to get an unlisted number.

Danny Glover, Annette Bening, Denzel Washington, Benjamin Bratt, and Winona Ryder were all students of the **American Conservatory Theater** *(30 Grant Ave., Sixth Floor, actactortraining.org)*. This three-year MFA program includes classes in speech, voice, movement, and acting; part of the curriculum includes performing for the public with the A.C.T. theater troupe *(act-sf.org)*. Ryder returns to the city on a regular basis as her parents still live in the Bay Area — her father Michael Horowitz owns **Flashback Books** *(flashbackbooks.com)*, which specializes in rare books and periodicals from the 1960s.

PORN-SHOPPING NANNY

While filming *Mrs. Doubtfire*, **Robin Williams**, a San Francisco resident since the age of 16, liked to keep his makeup and nanny outfit on between scenes and walk around town incognito. Williams has said he liked to walk into porn stores and ask for videos behind the counter in his kindly, old-lady voice.

The Nightmare Before Christmas, the animated film produced by Tim Burton, was made entirely at the now-closed San Francisco Studios at 375 Seventh Street. Other features produced there include *James and the Giant Peach* (filmed on Treasure Island), *Twisted* with Ashley Judd, and *Sweet November* with Keanu Reeves. The TV series *The Streets of San Francisco* starring Karl Malden and Michael Douglas and *Nash Bridges* with Don Johnson and Cheech Marin also were filmed in San Francisco.

When Birds Attack

For the movie *The Birds*, director **Alfred Hitchcock** was inspired by a 1961 incident in which seabirds attacked residents of Monterey Bay. Recent research has shown that the birds were suffering the effects of ingesting contaminated plankton, but at that time, the then-inexplicable "revolt of the birds" helped Hitchcock devise the simple but horrifying "what if" premise.

High Crimes

In *Dirty Harry*, the Scorpio Killer's first victim is a girl swimming in a **Holiday Inn** rooftop pool *(750 Kearny St., 415-433-6600)*. The scene was shot from the **Bank of America Building** *(555 California St.)*.

DA ACTOR

Actors often become politicians, but former San Francisco mayor **Willie Brown** went the opposite direction, albeit briefly — he played a politician in *The Godfather Part III* and a judge in *Just One Night*.

Follow That Car

Don't try following in **Steve McQueen**'s footsteps. The infamous car chase route in the classic 1968 film *Bullitt* is entirely fictitious. The scene took three weeks to film and segments were cut and pieced together during editing. Part of the route should have taken the drivers onto the Golden Gate Bridge, but the director was denied a filming permit.

Two Mustangs and two Dodge Chargers were used for the chase scene. All the cars were trashed except for one Mustang; a Warner Bros. employee is said to have purchased it after production. A few years later, he supposedly refused to sell it to McQueen, even though the car was sitting in a garage not being used.

Stan Woo Loves Hollywood

Thanks to Ron Howard's 1999 movie *EDtv*, featuring Matthew McConaughey and Woody Harrelson, Stan Woo's small **North Beach Video** store got its fifteen minutes of fame – well, more like a few seconds, but it was worth it. The store owner says that in the weeks following the film's release, sales increased and people came from all over the country to see his store. Woo also got a new counter courtesy of Universal, as well as free movies because the studio thought he didn't have enough in stock. It was probably Ron Howard's doing: although he was friendly, Howard told Woo that he should think about stocking more of his movies.
1398 Grant Ave., 415-398-7773

Hollywood Sparks

The city became Hollywood North for a few weeks in 1973 when Paul Newman, Steve McQueen, Faye Dunaway, Fred Astaire, and OJ Simpson were in town to film *The Towering Inferno*. It was in this movie that Astaire, then 75 years old, danced on screen for the last time (it was also the only film for which he was nominated for an oscar). Co-star Susan Blakely was a former model and was not yet known as an actress when she appeared in the movie. "Fans didn't know who I was, so I would say I was Faye Dunaway to make them happy," Blakely recently told the *San Francisco Chronicle* with a laugh. "A lot of people in San Francisco who think they have her autograph really have mine."

**SHAKING IT UP
AT THE OPERA**

The opera scene in *Pretty Woman* was supposed to be filmed at a San Francisco opera house but the October 17, 1989 earthquake prevented them from doing so. A set was created in Southern California instead.

Moviegoers may have loved Sharon Stone and Michael Douglas's sexy 1992 thriller *Basic Instinct*, but local gay rights activists were not amused. While the movie was being filmed, 50 San Francisco riot police had to be present at every location to deal with picketing gay and lesbian activists, who were protesting the way the film's gay characters were portrayed. In response, director Paul Verhoeven printed fake call sheets to trick the protesters into going to unused locations.

When the movie was released, protesters handed out flyers at local theaters saying "Catherine did it" to ruin the plot for moviegoers. This didn't seem to have much of an impact on its success, as the film went on to become one of the highest grossers of the year.

A JAZZY AD LIB

Al Jolson's famous line in 1927's *The Jazz Singer* – "You ain't heard nothing yet" – was an ad lib that the director wisely left in. *The Jazz Singer*, the very first talking feature, was filmed in San Francisco – one of the scenes shows **Coffee Dan's** at the corner of O'Farrell & Powell Streets.

HIGH CONCEPT, LOW BUDGET CINEMA
PRESCRIPTIONS FILLED
-AT THE
san francisco usa and beyond...
HI/LO FILM FESTIVAL
APRIL 14-17 2005

APRIL 14-16
Red Vic
Movie House
1727 Haight Street
San Francisco, CA

APRIL 17
Parkway
Theater
1834 Park Blvd
Oakland, CA

HIGH CONCEPT, LOW BUDGET
HI/LO FILM FEST

NO REFILLS - DR. AUTHORIZATION

MAY CAUSE EUPHORIA, DIZZINESS...

Red Vic Movie House in San Francisco

14 Thursday
7:15 pm - shorts 1
9:15 pm - shorts 2

15 Friday
7:15 pm - shorts 3
9:15 pm - shorts 1

16 Saturday
5pm - "Skateboarding is not..." w/shorts
7:15 pm - SF Graffiti Documentary, Piece By Piece w/shorts
9:15 pm - Shorts 2

Tix: $8 / $5 for Saturday 5pm show
Buy at www.hilofilmfestival.com
Info at 415.558.7721

Parkway Theater in Oakland

17 Sunday
6pm - Shorts 3

FESTIVAL
SPONSORS
bitch

Photo: Keith Telek

If there's a particular community that makes films, chances are it has a festival here. One of them is the **hi/lo Film Festival**, put together by Killing My Lobster *(killingmylobster.com)* (see also 185). High-concept and low-budget shorts and documentaries are shown every year at the **Red Vic Movie House** *(1727 Haight St., 415-668-3994, redvicmoviehouse.com)*, and the **Parkway Theater** *(1834 Park Blvd., 510-848-1994, picturepubpizza.com)* in Oakland.

The festival started in 1997 mainly as an excuse for Killing My Lobster to showcase their short film *Space Chocolate*, about a piece of chocolate flying through space. Marc Vogl, executive director of Killing My Lobster and organizer of the festival, told us, "It ain't Hollywood. The films are not slick, but it proves that a silly idea can become a fun movie." *hilofilmfestival.com*

Wall of Shame

Yes, these movies were made in San Francisco, but please don't remind the locals.

The Bachelor (1999) with Chris O'Donnell, Renée Zellweger, Ed Asner, Brooke Shields, Mariah Carey, Hal Holbrook, Peter Ustinov, and James Cromwell.

Bedazzled (2000) with Brendan Fraser and Elizabeth Hurley.

40 Days and 40 Nights (2002) where Josh Hartnett and Shannyn Sossamon can be seen at **Crepes on Cole** *(100 Carl St.)* and **Caffe Trieste** *(609 Vallejo St.)*.

Hulk (2003) transforms at Vallejo and Sansome Streets.

Sister Act 2: Back in the Habit (1993), where Whoopi Goldberg taught her music class in North Beach. One of the students was then unknown Lauryn Hill, who later became the lead singer of the Fugees and a big star in her own right.

other film festivals

American Indian Film Festival

Showcasing Native American and First Nation films, this annual festival, which takes place in November, brings together Native music and comedy, at the **Palace of Fine Arts Theatre** (*3301 Lyon St., 415-567-6642, palaceoffinearts.org*) and the **United Artists Galaxy Theatre** (*1285 Sutter St., 415-474-2835*). *aifisf.com*

Berlin & Beyond

German-language film festival in December that provides highlights of recent European cinema. Movies are shown at the **Castro Theatre** (*429 Castro St., 415-621-6120, castrotheatresf.com*). *goethe.de/sanfrancisco*

Black Film Festival

Showcases African American films. Also organized by the San Francisco Black Film Festival (*sfbff.org*) is the annual **Urban Kidz Film Festival** (*African American Art & Culture Complex, 762 Fulton St., Suite #300*), a one-day event that exposes kids to movies that stimulate the imagination. Both festivals take place in June. *ukff.org*

Cinemayaat – Arab Film Festival

Features movies that counter "violent, racist images of the Arab world." The festival takes place in September. *aff.org*

Festival Cine Latino! – Cine Acción

This festival focuses on Latino movies and takes place in September. *cineaccion.com*

The Sweetest Thing (2002), Cameron Diaz, Christina Applegate, and Selma Blair live at 1151 Kearny Street.

Twisted (2004) starring Ashley Judd, Samuel L. Jackson, and Andy Garcia.

The Wedding Planner (2001) featuring Jennifer Lopez and Matthew McConaughey.

When a Man Loves a Woman (1994), in which Meg Ryan and Andy Garcia booze it up at the Buena Vista Café in Fisherman's Wharf. It was here that America's first Irish Coffee was created in 1952. The movie is based on notes written by Orson Welles. Unlike others on this list, this film is not bad.

Festival of Independent Cinema

A selection of independent features shown in November.
filmarts.org

Frameline: San Francisco International Lesbian and Gay Film Festival

The world's oldest and largest LGBT film festival happens every June.
frameline.org

Human Rights Watch Bay Area Film Series

Every first Tuesday of the month at the **Yerba Buena Center For the Arts** *(701 Mission St.)*, this series focuses on documentaries with a human rights theme.
ybca.org

International Black Women's Film Festival

Presents films directed, produced by, or prominently featuring black women in non-stereotypical roles. The festival takes place in June.
ibwff.com

Jewish Film Festival

Showcases movies made by Jewish filmmakers; takes place in July.
sfjff.org

Latino Film Festival

This November festival promotes Latino films.
latinofilmfestival.org

HOLLYWOOD IN THE PARK

Drive-in movies may be long gone here, but thanks to the **San Francisco Neighborhood Theater Foundation**, we're getting free movies in the park. Showings happen at Washington Square and Dolores Park. Check *sfneighborhoodtheater.org* for dates and times.

Mad Cat Women's Film Festival

International festival that exhibits independent films and videos directed by women around the world; the festival takes place in September.
madcatfilmfestival.org

National Asian American Telecommunications Association San Francisco International Asian American Film Festival

A long name to describe the biggest event in North America dedicated to the exhibition of Asian American and Asian cinema. This March festival features more than 130 films and videos from around the world.
naatanet.org

Nob Hill Adult Theatre Gay Adult Film Festival

A festival in February that celebrates gay porn.
nobhilltheater.com

Noir City: San Francisco Film Noir Festival

Presents film noir movies in January.
filmnoirfoundation.org

Resfest Digital Film Festival

A traveling festival that focuses on the relationship between film, art, music, and design. The festival starts in New York in September and travels to San Francisco and to other major North American cities before heading to Europe, Asia, and the South Pacific.
resfest.com

PACK IT UP

Ever wonder what happens to movie sets when filming is done? Sometimes they go to good causes. For *The Matrix Reloaded,* filmed in Oakland and Alameda, the crew had built an entire freeway at the Alameda airfield. When the film wrapped, "They dismantled the highway and shipped all the wood and metal to a non-profit organization that builds houses for low-income families in Mexico," according to Scott Trimble, location manager.

San Francisco Black Lesbian/Gay/ Bisexual/Transgender Film Festival

Held at the **San Francisco Gay and Lesbian Community Center** *(1800 Market St., in the Rainbow Room)* in December.
sfcenter.org

San Francisco Independent Film Festival

This festival, which takes place in February, organizes several indie fests throughout the year in addition to the Independent Film Festival itself. Past festivals have included the **SF Horror Fest** *(sfhorror.com)* and the **Documentary Film Fest**.
sfindie.com

San Francisco International Film Festival

Features films from more than 50 countries that with an emphasis on those haven't secured US distribution.
sfiff.org

San Francisco Ocean Film Festival

Films that celebrate the sea, marine life, and the people who live, work, and play in or near the ocean, shown in January. A children's festival is also included. Held at the **San Francisco Maritime National Historical Park** *(Building E, Fort Mason Center, 415-447-5000, nps.gov/safr)*.
oceanfilmfest.org

Favorite Theaters

George Lucas showed the first *Star Wars* film at the **Coronet Theatre** *(3575 Geary Blvd.)* in 1977 and since then has had most of his premieres there. Unfortunately, the theater closed in March 2005, a few months before the release of *Episode III: Revenge of the Sith*.

A list of other theaters around town:

Balboa Theatre
3630 Balboa Ave., 415-221-8184

Bridge Theatre
3010 Geary Blvd., 415-751-3212

Castro Theatre
429 Castro St., 415-621-6120

Clay Theatre
2261 Fillmore St., 415-267-4893

Embarcadero Center Cinema
1 Embarcadero, 415-352-0810

Empire Cinema
85 West Portal Ave., 415-661-2539

San Francisco Silent Film Festival

Silent films accompanied by live music; takes place in July.
silentfilm.org

Sex Worker Film and Arts Festival

Films by and about sex workers, as well as live performances by sex worker artists. The festival takes place in May.
bayswan.org/swfest2005/

Zeitgeist International Film Festival

A June festival held in the backyard of Zeitgeist – a favorite local bar in San Francisco's Mission District *(199 Valencia St.)* – it features a secret projection technique (Beer-O-Scope) involving projectors, white painted walls, and plenty of beer. The organizers say Beer-O-Scope has the effect of making every film or video an award-winning masterpiece.
overcookedcinema.com

Four Star Theatre
2200 Clement St., 415-666-3488

Lumiere Theatre
1572 California St., 415-267-4893

New Mission Theater
2550 Mission St.

Opera Plaza Cinemas
601 Van Ness Ave., 415-352-0810

Presidio Theatre
2340 Chestnut St., 415-776-2388

Roxie Cinema
3117 16th St., 415-863-1087

In 1980, a group of political activist friends decided to start a collectively run business. They figured a movie theater was a good idea, since one of them had worked at one while in high school and most of the others were film buffs.

From 1980 to 1990, the **Red Vic Movie House** was located on the first floor of a red Victorian building that also housed the building owner's **Red Victorian Bed, Breakfast & Art** *(1665 Haight St., 415-864-1978, redvic.com)*. Films were shown in 16 mm and customers were seated on donated couches. "Our landlady was not very prompt about fixing the often leaky roof," Martha Bowen, one of the owners/workers told us. "I remember once when playing *Das Boot*, a film that takes place in a damaged submarine, it rained that night and water was dripping on our patrons."

In 1990, the theater moved down the street to where the **Full Moon Saloon** used to be. Since the theater was no longer in a Victorian building, they shortened the name to the Red Vic. In the storage room behind what used to be the stage of the nightclub, workers can still see graffiti drawn by musicians who hung out there before their gigs.

Although the Red Vic's funky couches are gone, it's probably the only theater in town where popcorn is organic, can be ordered with yeast or without, and is served in wooden bowls; large soda cups are normal, not the gallon-size ones you find in multiplexes. It's also the best movie theater in town to celebrate 4-20 in. Show up with some pot at the 4:20 pm showing of *The Big Lebowski*, shown at this time only on April 20. Lights out, light up, and chill out with "The Dude."
*1727 Haight St., 415-668-3994,
redvicmoviehouse.com*

TUBE TESTED
In 1927, **Philo T. Farnsworth** invented **television** in a laboratory at 202 Green Street. Although the city installed a plaque commemorating the invention a long time ago, you'll notice that it still looks pretty new. That's because the first plaque was stolen and had to be replaced.

Zoetrope Dreams

Headed by **Francis Ford Coppola** and **George Lucas, American Zoetrope** (916 Kearny St., 415-788-7500, zoetrope.com) started out as a collective of young filmmakers, based in an old warehouse at 827 Folsom Street. Although they scored a seven-film deal with Warner Bros., *THX-1138* (1971) was the only movie they released because Warner Bros. didn't approve of the rest; two of the seven scripts Coppola had offered to Warner Bros. were *Apocalypse Now* and *The Conversation*.

In the 1980s, Coppola released *One From the Heart*, which flopped; Zoetrope was on the verge of closing. Shortly after that film's release, Coppola received a letter from a group of teenagers who asked him to make a movie based on the S.E. Hinton novel *The Outsiders*. Coppola gave it a chance knowing that if the film didn't bring in money, he would close his studio. The film was a success and Zoetrope was saved.

Now, Coppola is known for masterpieces like *The Godfather* but the local filmmaker got his start by directing soft porn movies such as *The Playgirls and the Bellboy* and *Tonight for Sure* while studying at UCLA. These days, he's busy making wine in Napa Valley, while keeping cinema the main family business (the director's daughter Sofia won an Oscar for her *Lost in Translation* script, and nephew Nicolas Cage is an Oscar-winning actor). He can also be seen working in his Zoetrope studio, in the offices of his literary magazine, **Zoetrope All-Story** (all-story.com, 415-788-7500), and doing his duties as the San Francisco Honorary Ambassador of the Central American nation of Belize.

Just outside of the city, George Lucas founded the force at his own production studio, **Skywalker Ranch** (lucasfilm.com). Although the ranch will stay open for business, Lucas is now back in town at the **Letterman Digital Arts Center** in the Presidio. Fans not lining up for his latest *Star Wars* epic can hope to catch him at the complex's restaurant.

PRIME TIME

San Francisco's various television stations broadcast in numerous languages other than English, representative of the Bay Area's ethnically diverse population.

In Name Only

Numerous TV shows past and present are said to take place in San Francisco, but in reality most are filmed in L.A. studios. Here some of them:

Photo: Scott Davis courtesy of the SF Film Commission

Dharma & Greg with Jenna Elfman and Thomas Gibson.

Full House with Bob Saget, Candace Cameron, John Stamos, and the Olsen twins. The opening credits show the family having a picnic at Alamo Square (see photo).

Party of Five starring Neve Campbell, Matthew Fox, Scott Wolf, and Jennifer Love Hewitt.

Phyllis, a *Mary Tyler Moore Show* spin-off which starred Cloris Leachman, Lisa Gerritsen, and Liz Torres.

Please Support Public Television

KQED, the call letters for San Francisco's public television and radio station, is an acronym for the Latin *quod erat demonstrandum*, which means, "which was to be demonstrated." In 1954, with funds received from local foundations, KQED started broadcasting two shows a week using a transmitter placed on the roof of the Mark Hopkins Hotel *(999 California St., 415-392-3434)*. However, money ran out quickly. Hoping that viewers would help, the KQED staff organized an auction; among the items they sold were two Himalayan rabbits, an oil painting of Death Valley, a church seat, 25 hours of Arthur Murray dance lessons, three cases of Hills Bros. coffee, and a lifetime certificate for lube jobs at Eddy Howard Motors. As a result, the station was back in business.

Seeing the effectiveness of auctions, donations, and pledges, public stations across the country started organizing their own fundraising drives. Next time your favorite programming is interrupted by a pledge drive, you can thank San Francisco.

YOU'RE ON TV!

A new addition to San Francisco's TV landscape is **Current** (also known as INd TV), a satellite channel for the young and hip who want more than CNN's predictable headlines. Al Gore and the Google guys are behind this venture. *current.tv*

Graffiti Police

When the local NBC station decided to stop broadcasting through KRON4's transmitters in favor of KNTV in San Jose in 2002, they lost a lot of San Francisco viewers – the reception was so bad after the move that even the last episode of *Friends* wasn't worth wrestling with an antenna for. NBC finally figured out that the move was not a good one and they have been working on transmitting closer to the city to please their viewers ever since.

Just as locals were about to tune back in, NBC suffered another public relations nightmare when it spray-painted sidewalks around town to promote its upcoming show *The 4400*, which was to be shown on the USA Network, owned by NBC. The city spent $4,000 scrubbing off the stenciled messages, which read, "The 4400 are coming," according to the *San Francisco Chronicle*. The city attorney's office spent an additional $3,000 investigating the incident, which NBC agreed to cover as well as pay $96,000 to the San Francisco Clean City Coalition. When asked what they thought about *The 4400*, most San Francisco residents said they had never watched it.

KTSF Channel 26 has been featuring Asian-themed programs since 1976. It's the only station in the United States broadcasting nightly live news in both Cantonese and Mandarin. It also features programs in Japanese, Korean, and Hindi.

Here's My Stick, Now Beat Me

In the Barbary Coast days of the late 19th century, entertainers had to earn their way to the top the hard way. **Oofty Goofty** knew this fact when he willingly covered himself in tar and horse hair and stood in a cage on Market Street to entertain passersby. For a week, he was the talk of the town, but he had to stop the show when, unable to sweat under the tar, he was rushed to the hospital.

Goofty later found a job as a dancer and singer in a local bar where, after performing one act, he was literally thrown out. Landing on the sidewalk, the comedian realized that he felt no pain. And so he found his next act: for the next 15 years, Goofty walked around town carrying a baseball bat and charged people 25 cents to hit him with it. Goofty may have carried on longer if boxing champion John L. Sullivan hadn't hit him as hard as he could on the back with a pool cue. Oofty Goofty never fully recovered, thus ending his career.

San Francisco celebrities in the 1960s, **the Cockettes** were a wild and wacky hippie performance troupe who shared living quarters (the Cockettes' house is believed to have been at 946 Haight St.), meals, and almost everything else. Comprising both gay and straight members, they confused and amazed audiences with their counterculture, pansexual stage shows. Film director **John Waters**, an early fan, described them as "hippie acid freak drag queens." "We would buy crab meat and have huge dinner parties. Housewives in the supermarket would almost beat us up when they would see us buy crab meat with emergency food vouchers – not even food stamps," Waters has said.

At one time, **Allen Ginsberg** was lovers with **Hibiscus**, the Cockettes' charismatic founder. "It was difficult to sleep on the sheets because there was this sort of glitter stuff there," Ginsberg has said. "And it was always on our lips and in our butt holes. You knew it was always around. You couldn't quite get it out."

It's said that the Cockettes paved the way for the glam rock of David Bowie and audience participation à la *The Rocky Horror Picture Show*. In 1972, the Cockettes went their separate ways in part because some members disagreed on whether they should be paid for performing. For a fascinating glimpse into their world, rent the 2002 documentary *The Cockettes*.

THE UN-SOCIETY

In the 1960s, a theater group called **the Diggers** (an outgrowth of the San Francisco Mime Troupe) distributed free food in Panhandle Park (starting at Stanyan St. and ending at Baker St., between Oak and Fell St.) every day to local residents. While Lyndon Johnson proclaimed the nation as "The Great Society," the Diggers declared the Haight as "The Great Un-society" and also ran the Free Store at 1090 Cole Street, where shoppers could get jeans, jackets, books, and magazines at no charge.

MIGHTY SYLVESTER

Sylvester started performing with the Cockettes and went on to become a huge disco star in the 1970s, releasing the hits "You Make Me Feel (Mighty Real)," "Do You Wanna Funk," and "Dance (Disco Heat)." The disco queen has since earned legendary status in San Francisco; his life paralleled the rise of the gay community in the Castro and its battle with the AIDS pandemic. In 1988, the theme of the annual Castro Street Fair was "A Tribute to Sylvester." Although too weak to participate, Sylvester could hear the crowd chanting his name in the streets. He died of complications from AIDS later that year.

Photo: Marc Vogl

The performance troupe **Killing My Lobster** is a local favorite for its wacky plays and cabarets. It began in the mid-1990s; according to Marc Vogl, its executive director, San Francisco was a great environment to get started in because "you get an audience that's excited to see weird shows." The troupe has put on shows like *The Wonderful World of Science*, *Killing My Lobster Kisses a Toad*, and *Killing My Lobster Owes You Money*. (See page 174 for info on their festival.)

KLM got its name at a party when one of the founders couldn't remember the name of the Roberta Flack song "Killing Me Softly" that was made popular again by the Fugees. The tipsy founder forgot the words, and instead sang "killing my lobster, with his words…" thus inspiring the troupe's new name.

Their first show took place on Valentine's Day 1997 at the Grasshopper Palace; Vogl told us, "with 24 chairs, it wasn't much of a palace." But the crowd was impressed, and the troupe started doing shows at bigger venues like **Venue 9** *(252 9th St., 415-646-0868)*, **Exit Theatre** *(156 Eddy St.,415-673-3847)*, and **Victoria Theatre** *(2961 16th St., 415-863-7576)*. *killingmylobster.com*

We don't want to claim that everything started in San Francisco, but it just so happens that while experiments on radio prototypes were being done on the East Coast, San Francisco had its own radio genius. **Francis J. McCarty** started testing his "wireless telephone" in 1903 and was able to show his invention to the press in 1905. He set up the apparatus at the Cliff House while reporters stood a mile down the beach and listened to McCarty singing into his wireless telephone. The experiment got him the attention he wanted and he was soon giving lectures and demonstrations all over the city.

Unfortunately, McCarty's life was cut short in 1906 on his way home from work. When the streetcar he was riding in had to stop suddenly to avoid a pedestrian, McCarty was thrown out and is said to have crashed, ironically, into a telephone pole.

4-20 LOUIS, DUDE

According to Steven Hager, editor of the stoner magazine *High Times*, the term "4-20" was coined in 1971 by a group of about a dozen pot-smoking friends at San Rafael High School who called themselves the Waldos. The term was shorthand for the time of day the group would meet — by the campus statue of Louis Pasteur — to smoke pot. "Waldo Steve," a member of the group, says the Waldos would salute each other in the hallway and say, "4-20 Louis!" The term stuck and spread beyond San Rafael with the help of the Grateful Dead and their dedicated pot-smoking fans. *waldo420.com*

THE GRASS IS GREENER

The Bay Area is home to a lot of musicians, including the bands **Metallica**, **Rancid**, and **Green Day**. Billie Joe, the singer of Green Day, picked up the phrase "green day" from friends while hanging out and smoking pot in the basement of a Berkeley University building. He wrote the song "Green Day" about his first pot experience, and the group changed their name from Sweet Children to Green Day in 1990. To hang out with Mike Dirnt, Green Day's bassist, head over to **Rudys Can't Fail Café** in Emeryville *(4081 Hollis St., 510-594-1221, rudyscantfailcafe.com).* He owns the place.

Photo: Mark Altamine

Stan Shaff has been composing and performing at the **Audium** since 1975 and has attracted lots of curious visitors. He likes to remind people that the Audium is not a business venture; we think of it as a sound museum where one can get away from city noise and experience changing sound exhibits. Every Friday and Saturday, attendees can sit in one of the 49 chairs in the dome-shaped room and enjoy the composer's eclectic mix of sounds bouncing off walls and traveling from speaker to speaker. Hope you're not afraid of the dark, though, since the show takes place in total darkness; Shaff and his equipment designer, Doug McEachern, believe that visuals get in the way of the experience.
8:30 pm; Fridays and Saturdays, 1616 Bush, 415-771-1616, audium.org

Legendary musicians Janis Joplin, the Grateful Dead, Jefferson Airplane, and Crosby, Stills, Nash & Young lived within a mile or so of each other in the Haight Ashbury days of the 1960s when hippies lived in communal harmony and buses full of tourists came to see what the counterculture looked like close up. Thousands of people emigrated to what is now the Upper Haight area in order to find peace and love; many left broke and more confused than before, but some found stardom.

Country Joe McDonald and the Fish lived at 638-640 Ashbury – And it's one, two, three, what are we fighting for?

Janis Joplin and Country Joe McDonald lived at 112 Lyon Street in apartment #3 when Joplin recorded the

Sounds of the Bay

The Bay Area may be known for 1960s hippie bands, but new musicians and bands are discovered all the time. From the legendary Summer of Love days to Oakland's hip-hop scene, here's a list of artists and bands from the Bay Area (decades indicate when these acts became popular):

1960s:
Beau Brummels
Big Brother and the Holding Company
Blue Cheer
The Charlatans
Country Joe and the Fish
Creedence Clearwater Revival
Flamin' Groovies
Grateful Dead
It's a Beautiful Day
Jefferson Airplane

Kingston Trio
Moby Grape
Mother Earth
Quicksilver Messenger Service
Santana
Sly and the Family Stone
Steve Miller Band

1970s:
Elvin Bishop
Pablo Cruise
Dead Kennedys
Doobie Brothers
Graham Central Station
Norman Greenbaum
Sammy Hagar

Dan Hicks and the Hot Licks
Jefferson Starship
Journey
Eddie Money
Montrose
Pointer Sisters
Boz Scaggs
Sylvester
Tower of Power
The Tubes

"Cheap Thrills" album in 1967. She was evicted for having a pet, a collie mix named George. Joplin also lived at 635 Ashbury at one point (see photo, previous page). The hard-living rock star died of a heroin overdose in Los Angeles at the age of 27; her ashes were scattered along the Marin County coastline.

The Jefferson Airplane bought a four-story mansion for $70,000 in 1968 at 2400 Fulton Street and turned it into their studio, office, home, and party pad for more than 10 years. **Dan Ackroyd** and **John Belushi** of the **Blues Brothers** stayed here following the New Year's Eve 1979 show at the Winterland Ballroom.

Jimi Hendrix once lived at 1524A Haight Street.

Any day of the week, you can walk past the **Grateful Dead's** old house at 710 Ashbury Street (see photo) and see fans still lighting up a joint in homage to the late Jerry Garcia.

Head of the Dead

On August 1, 1942 at Children's Hospital in San Francisco, rock legend **Jerry Garcia** was born; he was named Jerome John Garcia after Jerome Kern, the composer of classic Broadway musicals like "Show Boat" and "Roberta." Garcia grew up at 121 Amazon Avenue in the Excelsior, a working-class neighborhood; his father was a professional musician and his mother ran the **Four Hundred Club**, a bar always full of sailors named for its location at 400 First St. (now the Bank of America tower). In 1947, Garcia went fishing with his dad and tragically witnessed him drown. As a result, he, his brother, and his mother moved in with his grandparents at 87 Harrington Street.

Although he's mostly remembered as the leader of the Grateful Dead, Jerry Garcia said he wasn't comfortable with the role. He spent the last five years of his life playing with Old and In the Way, a bluegrass band he started with David Grisman.

Jerry Garcia passed away in August 1995. Some of his ashes were thrown into the Ganges River in India and the rest were scattered in the San Francisco Bay on the morning of April 15, 1996.

1980s:

Digital Underground

Faith No More

Flipper

Huey Lewis and the News

Chris Isaak

Jellyfish

Greg Kihn

Metallica

Night Ranger

Primus

Jonathan Richman

Joe Satriani

Tommy Tutone

Tony! Toni! Tone!

Romeo Void

Tom Waits

Vote for Kennedy

With a long history of celebrity politicians in California including "The Terminator" as governor, it may not be surprising to some that raucous punk singer **Jello Biafra** of the Dead Kennedys would run, albeit not seriously, for mayor in San Francisco. Some, though, didn't think the joke was funny; in 1994, long after he lost the election, a slam dancer crashed on to Biafra at 924 Gilman Street Project, a Berkeley collectively-run punk dance club that launched the careers of Rancid and Green Day. Biafra asked for the guy's I.D. but he was laughed at; then a group of the guy's friends, recognizing Biafra, started kicking him, calling him a "rock star sell-out." Biafra suffered a broken leg, damage to the ligaments of one knee, and a head wound. *510-525-9926, 924gilman.org*

1990s:

4 Non Blondes
Counting Crows
En Vogue
Green Day
MC Hammer
Mr. Big
Rancid
Smash Mouth
Stroke 9
Third Eye Blind
Too $hort
Train
Tupac

2000+:

AFI
Creeper Lagoon
The Donnas

DJ Shadow

flower power cheat sheet

January 14, 1967

A **Human Be-In** took place at the Polo Grounds, Golden Gate Park. Speakers included Jerry Rubin, Allen Ginsberg, Lawrence Ferlinghetti, and Timothy Leary. Participants were encouraged to bring food to share, flowers, beads, costumes, feathers, bells, cymbals, and flags. The Jefferson Airplane entertained.

December 6, 1969

The Rolling Stones gave a free concert at the **Altamont Raceway & Arena** *(17001 Midway Rd., Tracy, 925-373-7223)* near Livermore after they were denied use of Golden Gate Park. People attended from all over the country. The Stones asked members of the Hell's Angels to help out with security, not knowing that many of those present that day were neophytes. We're not sure if it was the free beer, or the drugs the audience was on, but while the Stones played the Hell's Angels started pushing people back from the stage; a member of the Black Panthers took out a gun and was then stabbed and killed by a Hell's Angel. For many, Altamont marked the end of the San Francisco era of peace and love.

The Stones were performing "Sympathy for the Devil" at the time; during the concert, Mick Jagger told the audience that every time they played that song, something weird happened. They only found out what that "weird" thing was the following day. As a result, they refused to play the song again in concert for six years.

The home of the Hell's Angels was at 715 Ashbury Street.

the beat goes on

The dot-com real estate boom of the 1990s forced many live music venues out of the city, but those that remained have managed to keep on truckin'. From the Make-Out Room to Bottom of the Hill to the famous Warfield, the beat goes on.

12 Galaxies

This bar is named after local street celebrity Frank Chu and his cryptic sandwich board.
2565 Mission St. (at 22nd St.), 415-970-9777, 12galaxies.com

Avalon Ballroom

From its first concert in 1966 – which marked the start of the career of a Texan woman with a whole lot of soul, Janis Joplin – until 1968, the Avalon showcased the best of the "San Francisco Sound." Chet Helms, also from Texas, was the owner of the Avalon and manager of the band Big Brother and the Holding Company. When he found out that the band was looking for a female lead singer, he gave his Texan friend a call and told Joplin to come to San Francisco.

Helms also convinced the then-unknown Grateful Dead and others to perform at the ballroom. His musical taste was great, but his business skills were lacking, unlike his former business partner Bill Graham. In 1968, the city seized his sound permits and the place closed shortly after.

The Avalon Ballroom remained closed for a long time until Morning Spring Rain, a concert promotion company led by a hippie entrepreneur/ex-commune member named Steve Shirley, reopened it in 2003. The first band to play in the renovated space was Big Brother and the Holding Company. Since then, however, the Ballroom has closed once again and is now a mattress designing facilities.
1300 Van Ness Ave., 415-730-4061, morningspringrain.com

Records-R-Us

Bay Area-based record labels:

3 Acre Floor Records
(alternative, pop) *3acrefloor.com*

625
(punk, thrash) *625thrash.com*

ABB Records
(hip-hop) *abbrecords.com*

Alternative Tentacles
(rock, punk) *alternativetentacles.com*

Arhoolie
(country, tejano) *arhoolie.com*

Badman Recording Co.
(rock, moody)
badmanrecordingco.com

Cheetah's Records
(rock, punk) *painlessdistro.com*

Devil in the Woods
(indie) *devilinthewoods.com*

Dreams by Degrees
(electronic, pop)
dreamsbydegrees.com

Drunkenfish Records
(rock) *drunkenfishrecords.com*

Bimbo's 365 Club

In the TV series, *The Chris Isaak Show*, the character of Mona, who appears undressed on a rotating table, is based on a real woman known in San Francisco as "Dolphina." In a nightclub in the 1930s, a magician placed a series of mirrors that would project an image of a nude mermaid who was lying on a rotating table in the basement up into the fish tank located behind the bar. For 25 years, the character of "Dolphina" was played by Donna Powers who worked at the club. It was also here that customers could watch a woman, known then as Rita Cansino, dance on stage. She later changed her name to Rita Hayworth.
1025 Columbus Ave. (at Chestnut St.), 415-474-0365, bimbos365club.com

The Boom Boom Room

Although rumor around town has it that bluesman John Lee Hooker owned this place, he only licensed his name to the club for five years. The bar was named after his hit "Boom Boom," and people still come here for the cocktails, live blues, and soul music.
1601 Fillmore St., 415-673-8000, boomboomblues.com

Bottom of the Hill

All-you-can-eat barbecues on Sundays, local and up-and-coming bands, and the outdoor patio make this place a local favorite.
1233 17th St. (at Missouri), 415-621-4455, bottomofthehill.com

Eighth Note Records
(pop, piano composers)
eighthnoterecords.com

Fat Wreck Chords
(hardcore, punk) *fatwreck.com*

The First Time Records
(pop, rock) *tftrecords.com*

Full Frame Records
(rock, hip-hop) *fullframerecords.com*

Function 8
(trip-hop, progressive) *function8.com*

HighTone Records
(country, rock) *hightone.com*

Kamikaze Records
(R&B, funk) *kamikazerecords.com*

Lookout Records
(rock, hardcore, punk)
lookoutrecords.com

Magnetic Motorworks
(quirky, intelligent)
magneticmotorworks.com

Paris Caramel Records
(indie, pop)

Café du Nord

A dark and cozy bar with good food and great shows.
2170 Market St., 415-861-5016

Great American Music Hall

San Francisco's oldest and grandest nightclub, opened in 1907. The club has quite a rocky past; it served as a restaurant/bordello named the Music Box from the early 1900s to the dark days of the Great Depression. During the 1950s, the club was taken over by members of the Moose Lodge, a fraternal social organization. Eventually, the building fell into ill-repair and was set for demolition. A last-minute reprieve saved it from being destroyed, and it reopened in 1972. Over the decades many famous acts have graced the hall with their presence, including Duke Ellington, Van Morrison, Sarah Vaughn, and the Grateful Dead. The hall still hosts a wide variety of acts each week.
859 O'Farrell Street, 415-885-0750, musichallsf.com

The Fillmore

During his engagement at The Fillmore, **Otis Redding** stayed on a houseboat in Sausalito. While there, he wrote his last song and greatest hit: "(Sittin' On) The Dock of the Bay."

Music entrepreneur Bill Graham could very well be called the father of San Francisco entertainment. With the **Fillmore Auditorium**, the **Warfield** *(982 Market St., 415-567-2060)*, the **Punchline Comedy Club** in San Francisco *(444 Battery St., 415-397-4337)* and

Radio Khartoum

(electronic, pop) *radiokhartoum.com*

Revenge Records

(eclectic, world) *revengerecords.com*

Six Degrees Records

(world) *sixdegreesrecords.com*

Six Weeks Records

(punk, grind) *sixweeksrecords.com*

Slumberland Records

(pop, moody) *dropbeat.com/slrland*

Subterranean Records

(hardcore, industrial)

subterranean.org

Tigerbeat6 Records

(noise, hip-hop) *tigerbeat6.com*

Toyo Records

(noise, rock) *toyorecords.com*

Weapon-Shaped

(hip-hop) *weapon-shaped.com*

Sacramento (2100 Arden Way, Suite 225, 916-925-5500), and **Winterland** (at the corner of Post and Steiner Streets, now home to a Burger King), he had every type of live music venue covered. Graham died in a helicopter crash on October 25, 1991.
1805 Geary Blvd., 415-346-6000, thefillmore.com

Grant and Green

In the 1960s, this place often showcased talented musicians of the period; it was known as the Coffee Gallery at that time.
1371 Grant Ave., 415-693-9565

The Lost and Found Saloon

Creedence Clearwater Revival launched its career here and the place still delivers great live rock music.
1353 Grant Ave., 415-981-9557

Make-Out Room

Tracy Chapman has been known to sneak in and give shows here.
3225 22nd St., 415-647-2888, makeoutroom.com

The Matrix

When it opened on August 13, 1965, the Matrix was San Francisco's first folk music night club. Its owner, Marty Balin, was part of a new band that performed that first night; the band was the **Jefferson Airplane**. Other artists who played there include Janis Joplin, the Grateful Dead, The Doors, and Bruce Springsteen. The bar closed in 1972 but was recently renovated and reopened under the same name.
3138 Fillmore, 415-563-4180

SINGING OUT
The San Francisco Gay Men's Chorus made its official debut on December 20, 1978, though it first appeared informally singing a memorial hymn on the steps of the San Francisco City Hall the previous month, the evening Mayor George Moscone and Harvey Milk were assassinated. The group, one of the oldest gay men's chorus's in the world, performs throughout the year at theaters, churches, and opera houses in the area. Although new performances are added from year to year, annual favorites include *Home for the Holidays*, *Cabaret*, and *The Annual Pride Concert*.
sfgmc.orgi

phoenix stories

Photo: Joie de Vivre

Chip Conley, owner of Joie de Vivre Hospitality, has turned many buildings around town into unique boutique hotels. One of his first successes in the hotel industry was to transform a building in the heart of the gritty Tenderloin district into the **Phoenix Hotel** *(601 Eddy St., 415-776-1380)*, now considered a high-end oasis for stars when they're in town. Hotel staffers have plenty of celebrity stories to tell; here are some that Pam Wright, the hotel's general manager, shared with us.

Booted Out

Over the years, it has become a tradition of sorts for bands that have stayed here to plaster the yellow maids' carts, and one of the hotel's storage room doors, with their band stickers. Two of the older (and thus well-stickered) carts have become part of the hotel's sculpture garden. But when a disruptive band member recently threw one of the carts into the pool in the early hours of the morning, the band, which management declined to name, was ordered to fish the cart out and was then booted from the hotel.

Photo: Joie de Vivre

Play That Funky Music

A list of Bay Area music festivals and street musicians:

Bay City Luv

This acapella street group has been singing their gospel songs in front of the American Conservatory Theater's Geary Theater *(corner of Geary and Mason Sts.)* for six years, Tuesdays through Saturdays.

Jazz Festival

Takes place in October.
sfjazz.org

Music for People and Thingamajigs

Annual spring festival where sounds are produced from made and/or found objects and alternate tuning systems. The participating musicians use exotic and traditional instruments made from materials like bamboo, glass, metal, phonographs, wood, and electronics.
thingamajigs.org

A Good Host

John Kennedy Jr. was the best man at a wedding that took place in the courtyard the weekend after the Loma Prieta earthquake in 1989. He forgot his cufflinks but Conley was able to run home and get his own to loan to John John.

Give the Man a Guitar

Several years ago, while musician Ben Harper was staying here, he surprised the hotel night auditor – a musician himself – with a guitar to replace the one that had just been stolen from his car.

Mysterious Art

When actor Vincent Gallo stayed here in 2004, he awoke one morning to find a large and very elaborate piece of artwork, made as a kind of tribute to him, outside his room. The identity of the artist and how the piece got into the hotel courtyard is still a mystery. But the piece has found a permanent home at the hotel, hanging just outside of what was Gallo's room.

San Francisco Blues Festival
The oldest blues festival in the world, at Fort Mason every year in September.
415-979-5588, sfblues.com

San Francisco Electronic Music Festival
Takes place every summer at the SomArts Cultural Center.
934 Brannan St., sfemf.org

Tape Music Festival
Takes place in January.
sfsound.org/tape

The Vowel Movement
This monthly event features performers who use only their voices as instruments.
thevowelmovement.com

World Music Festival
Takes place in September.
sfworldmusicfestival.org

where are they now?
(bay area version)

Tom Ammiano

Nicknamed "The Mother of Gay Comedy," Tom Ammiano was one of the first openly gay comedians when he started doing stand-up comedy in 1980 at the Valencia Rose Cabaret. A well-known entertainer and an openly gay teacher, a rarity in the 1980s, Ammiano was featured in the documentary *The Life and Times of Harvey Milk* and interviewed in national publications. Ammiano is still a gay activist but now works in politics; he had a major role in creating the San Francisco Domestic Partners Ordinance which provides equal benefits for employees of companies that contract with the City and County of San Francisco, and he's now a city supervisor.

Lynn Duff

Lynn Duff, a 16-year-old lesbian, made national news when she escaped from the Rivendell psychiatric institute in Utah where she was being forced to go through aversion therapy. The lesbian-made film *But I'm a Cheerleader*, which was released in 1999, was inspired by Duff's story. Duff went to live with foster parents in San Francisco and started *24-7*, a zine for kids who have been locked up. She now works as a counselor at a homeless youth shelter in Oakland.

William Hung

Getting the boot from the TV show *American Idol* was the best thing that could have happened to Hung. He charmed the audience with his off-key singing – well, everyone except the judges, and went from being a UC Berkeley nerd to a local celebrity with a CD. *williamhung.net*

BILLIE HOLIDAY BUSTED
Guests at the **Executive Hotel Mark Twain** *(345 Taylor St.)* can easily figure out that the famous jazz singer **Billie Holiday** stayed in Room 203 – a plaque commemorating her visit is on the wall. The hotel chose its words carefully; the plaque reads: "Billie Holiday occupied this suite." The part about her getting busted for possession of opium and a pipe when the police raided her room is politely left out.

Walks of Fame

San Francisco may not compare to Tinseltown when it comes to sidewalk "stars," but at least we've got three (small) walks of fame to call our own:

Seventh Street sidewalk
7th St. bet. Folsom and Harrisson

Hotel Diva sidewalk
440 Geary St.

Bill Graham Civic Auditorium
99 Grove St.

Puck and the *Real World* Gang

MTV's *The Real World San Francisco* captured the nation's imagination at a time when "reality TV" was still a novelty. For six months, Cory Murphy, Judd Winick, Mohammed Bilal, Pam Ling, Pedro Zamora, David Rainey (aka Puck), and Rachel Campos lived at 953 Lombard Street and exposed their lives and personalities to America. For anyone who was happy when smart-ass bike messenger Puck got kicked out, or cried when Pedro, one of the first AIDS sufferers to be seen regularly on television, passed away, this house is worth the walk. The house is barely recognizable, though – that's because Martin Eng, the owner, had to renovate the place after a fire in 2000. He says that he agreed to have the show filmed on the second floor of his house (he lived on the ground floor) because he didn't know the MTV show would become so popular. "Puck came back a few times, but he told me to take his picture off my website," he tells us. "I remember I took pictures of him getting in a fight with a guy outside."

These days, Cory Murphy is married, and lives in Anaheim where she teaches middle school. Pam Ling and Judd Winick married in 2001 and still live in San Francisco; Ling is Assistant Professor in Residence in the UCSF Department of General Internal Medicine. As for Winick, he has published graphic novels and syndicated a comic strip; his animated series *The Life & Times of Juniper Lee* premiered in June 2005. Mohammed Bilal, along with a friend, created The Color Orange, a hip-hop theater group focusing on healing disparate black/white, Jewish/Muslim relationships; he is also a writer, poet, musician, and actor. Puck got married during an epsiode of MTV *Real World/Road Rules Battle of the Sexes*. He now has a child and has been seen in small roles in TV shows such as *Law and Order*. Rachel Campos-Duffy, who was with Puck until he was kicked out of the house, now lives in the Midwest with her husband Sean Duffy (also a former *Real World* cast member) and her two children. As for Pedro Zamora, he was publicly praised by Bill Clinton for his efforts in educating high school students about the AIDS epidemic. He passed away in November 1994.

Linda Perry

Linda Perry, lead singer of 4 Non Blondes, released a solo album after the band split up, but it didn't sell well. In 2001, emerging singer Pink asked her for help on her album; Perry co-wrote and produced much of *M!ssundaztood*. She has since helped Christina Aguilera win a Grammy for her hit "Beautiful," and she's worked with other artists such as Jewel, Courtney Love, Gwen Stefani, Robbie Williams, Melissa Etheridge, Solange, Gina Gershon, Gavin Rossdale, Lisa Marie Presley, Fischerspooner, Unwritten Law, L.P., Kelly Osbourne, and Enrique Iglesias.

Wavy Gravy

The famous hippie clown who got his nickname from B.B. King now lives in Berkeley and is the founder of CampWinnarainbow, a circus and performing arts camp.
campwinnarainbow.org

Spot the Celebrities

"Hot" places change all the time, but here are some reliable celebrity favorites:

Ana Mandara
We're not sure if it counts as a star-sighting if the stars are investors, but then again, we're not sure that Don Johnson and Cheech Marin are still considered stars.
891 Beach St., 415-771-6800

Photo: Joie de Vivre

Bambuddha Lounge
This isn't your typical hotel bar. On any given night, you may spot Tracy Chapman, Sean Penn, or Green Day lounging in the outdoor patio. Then get a room at the adjacent Phoenix Hotel; that's probably where they're sleeping too.
601 Eddy St., 415-885-5088, bambuddhalounge.com

Don't Mess with Beth

In 1999, **Beth Lisick**, now a *San Francisco Chronicle* columnist, author, and organizer of Porchlight story-telling evenings *(porchlightsf.com)*, was interviewed by the *Chronicle* and asked about The Beth Lisick Ordeal gig at Lilith Fair, Sarah McLachlan's all-women music tour. She said the band had a good time, but it would have been nice if they had received the $250 they were promised. She added: "And you know, Sarah, I think we gave at least $250 worth of love to the Lilith Fair audience. Maybe even $275. Now please pay us or we're gonna kick your ass." The morning the article was published, Lisick received 16 phone calls from Sarah McLachlan's manager and the Lilith Fair people. The check was FedExed and they got it the next day. Ah, the power of the press.

Not Your Mother's Newsstand

Fog City News is the place to go for international magazines, newspapers, and hard-to-find chocolates from around the globe *(455 Market St., 415-543-7400, fogcitynews.com)*. For French magazines and newspapers, a few good titles can be found at **Café de la Presse** *(352 Grant Ave., 415-398-2680)*. Local independent titles and zines can be found at **Naked Eye News & Video** *(607 Haight St., 415-864-2985)*. Naughty readers can also stock up on old – we don't want to say used – porn magazines that date as far back as the 1940s at **Magazine** *(853 Larkin, 415-443-2212)*.

Harry Denton's Starlight Room

Hillary Clinton, R.E.M.'s Michael Stipe, and Mikhail Gorbachev, among others, have made appearances in this hotel bar.
450 Powell St. (in the St. Francis Drake Hotel), 415-395-8595

Hemlock Tavern

Courtney Love has been known to head to Hemlock after a show. A hot SF band, The Donnas, play here from time to time too.
1131 Polk St. (at Post St.), 415-923-0923, www.hemlocktavern.com

The Prescott Hotel

The Prescott has made the beds of a long list of celebrities including Madonna, the Red Hot Chili Peppers, and Elizabeth Taylor.
545 Post St., 415-563-0303, prescotthotel.com

In Hearst Place

In his early twenties, **William Randolph Hearst** took over his father's newspaper, the *San Francisco Examiner*, and made it a financial success by sensationalizing the paper's front pages and introducing banner headlines and lavish illustrations. Hearst's technique was inspired by Joseph Pulitzer and became known as "yellow journalism."

Hearst is also believed by many to have initiated the Spanish-American War of 1898 in order to boost newspaper sales. When illustrator Frederic Remington asked him if he could return from Havana since not much was happening there, Hearst told him, "Please remain. You furnish the pictures and I'll furnish the war."

William Hearst's Editorial Guidelines

To make sure that every staff member was on the same page, Hearst distributed these guidelines:

1. Make a paper for the nicest kind of people from the great middle class. Don't print a lot of dull stuff that people are supposed to like and don't.

2. Omit things that will offend nice people. Avoid coarseness and a low tone. The most sensational news can be told if told properly.

3. Make your headlines clear and concise statements of interesting acts. They should answer the question: What is the news? Don't allow copyreaders to write headlines that are too smart or clever to be intelligible.

4. The front page is your forum. Put important items and personal news about well-known people there. Sometimes condense a big story to go on the first page rather than run it longer inside the paper.

Tosca Café

A favorite of Marin resident Sean Penn and regular tourists Johnny Depp and Nicolas Cage.

242 Columbus Ave. (between Broadway & Pacific), 415-986-9651

The Grind

A neighborhood breakfast place and a favorite of singer PJ Harvey when she's in town.

783 Haight St., 415-864-0955

5. Nothing is more wearisome than mere words. Have our people tell stories briefly and pointedly. Let people get the facts easily. Don't make them work at it.

6. Please instruct copyreaders to rewrite long sentences into several short ones. And please try to educate the reporters to write short sentences in the first place.

7. Photographs of interesting events with explanatory diagrams are valuable. Make every picture worth its space.

8. If you cannot show conclusively your own paper's superiority, you may be sure the public will never discover it.

The Butler & The Chef

French bistro favorite of local band Third Eye Blind.

155 A South Park St., 415-896-2075

The Clift

Celebrity sightings include Salman Rushdie, Danielle Steele, Woody Allen, and George Lucas.

495 Geary St., 415-775-4700, clifthotel.com

Bay Area magazines

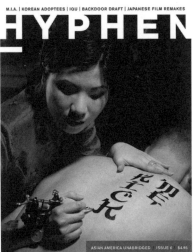

When the dot-com boom in the Bay Area went bust, so did a lot of magazines. But the ones that survived or were born in the post dot-com landscape are feistier than ever. "While the Bay Area may be no New York in terms of publishing, we are a hotbed for independent media," Melissa Hung, *Hyphen*'s editor in chief, recently told us. "Because of our culture of activism, people here aren't afraid to just dive into something, even something as crazy as starting a magazine."

"There was an infusion of money and talent during the dot-com boom in the Bay Area," said Richard Landry, executive director of the **Independent Press Association**. "When the bubble burst, there were a lot of talented people with a lot of time on their hands. They put their creativity to work and San Francisco became a very interesting city in publishing as a result of that."

The Independent Press Association, a local non-profit that helps independent media get heard, got its start when a group of publishers got together in 1996 in San Francisco and realized that although it was impossible to change big media corporations, an organization could give independent media more power by encouraging independent magazines and giving them financial help.

Many of the titles listed here are members of the IPA. For more titles, check their directory at *indypress.org*.

The Believer
Literary magazine started by *McSweeney's* founder Dave Eggers.
www.believermag.com

Bitch
The magazine that describes itself as "A Feminist Response to Pop Culture."
bitchmagazine.com

Curve
Magazine that covers lesbian-related celebrity interviews, news, politics, style, travel, and social issues.
curvemag.com

Dwell
Focus on innovative architecture.
dwellmag.com

Girlfriends
The word on lesbian lifestyle.
girlfriendsmag.com

Hyphen
A non-profit news and culture magazine covering Asian America.
hyphenmagazine.com

San Francisco Documented

There are tons of documentaries on San Francisco; here's a list to get you started if you want to learn more about the Bay Area and its denizens:

24 Hours on Craigslist
A random day with some of San Francisco's *craigslist.org* visitors.

Berkeley in the '60s
A two-hour report on what was probably the most radical city in the nation at the time.

Casey Kasem's Rock 'n' Roll Goldmine: The San Francisco Sound
A brief showcase of some of the popular Bay Area bands in the '60s.

The Cockettes
Shows the rise to stardom of a fabulous group of hippie theater acid freaks.

Golden Gate Bridge
The controversial history of the landmark bridge.

Grateful Dawg

A look at a quiet side of Jerry Garcia's life and his music sessions with David Grisman.

Pursuit of Equality

A film on the 2004 Winter of Love when same-sex marriages became "legal."

Raider Nation

A look at the Oakland Raider "family."

The Rolling Stones: Gimme Shelter

The infamous Altamont concert at which Hell's Angels were hired by the Stones as security, resulting in the death of an audience member. Rumor has it that George Lucas was one of the cameramen for the documentary, but unfortunately his camera broke after shooting about 100 feet of film. The footage was unusable.

Streets: San Francisco

Profiling well-known skateboarders and skate spots around town.

Mother Jones

A legendary liberal non-profit that publishes investigative news articles. *motherjones.com*

ReadyMade Magazine

A bimonthly print magazine for people who like to make stuff, *ReadyMade* is a great read for the Stitch and Bitch crowd and the MacGyver in all of us. The magazine features step-by-step DIY projects with used materials. *readymademag.com*

Salon

A smart online publication that remains a leader in publishing savvy Internet articles. *salon.com*

San Francisco Bay Guardian

Technically not a magazine but a family-owned weekly with feature-length articles and event listings. *sfbg.com*

Skinny

A quarterly guide to the Bay Area for "residents and visitors with discriminating tastes, a discriminating budget, and an interest in local talent, art, personalities, and flavor of all kinds." *skinnymag.com*

Wired

A magazine that was smart enough to report on the progress of technology and the Internet in its early days, it remains one step ahead of everyone else when it comes to hi-tech news. *wired.com*

Nightlife

Photo: Greg Wellborn

Even though the fun in San Francisco seems a bit forced at times – one too many pirate parties can leave you feeling seasick – there's plenty of true-blue oddities and swingin' (in all senses) good times to be had. Bars come and go with alarming regularity, and even "institutions" change ownership in a heartbeat. That's why you can't go wrong showing up in the happening neighborhoods and staying open to whatever comes your way.

Herbal Alternatives

There's more to nightlife in San Francisco than alcohol – there's ecstasy, marijuana, cocaine, crystal meth, and recently, a lot of interest in prescription painkillers. Of course, most of these drugs don't lead to much good in the long run, but in one of the ironies of life, the liquid that makes people crazy and obnoxious (if you're not one of them) is legal, and the little plant that makes people mellow, forgetful, and giggly, is not. The good news is, in San Francisco, pot is effectively legal – for those who pony up the $150 to visit one of the doctors who advertise for referrals and then go to the department of health downtown to fill out some forms and pay the $25 for their medicinal cannabis card.

For those who don't have such a card, possession of less than an ounce of the chronic (away from school grounds) is only a misdemeanor. Selling any amount however is a felony.

There are 43 pot clubs in the city (they outnumber McDonald's), and as of this writing, city officials are in a bind about them. On the one hand, they want to regulate the clubs, but on the other, since California state law is much softer on pot than federal law, city officials don't want to aid what they see as draconian federal laws by creating a paper trail. City officials had adopted an unofficial don't-ask, don't-tell policy with regard to pot clubs until someone tried to start one on the ground floor of a long-term-stay hotel that housed people in a city-run substance abuse program.

Industrial by day, DJ and dance central by night, this area packs a lot of diamonds into rough streets. Say "Folsom Street" to a local, and they'll think you're going to the daddy of all leather fests, Folsom Street Fair (see Living), but the **Folsom Street/South of Market** (SoMa) area is lively for gay and straight people all year round. When the lights go down, the auto repair shops close and the bars and clubs open.

The Eagle *(398 12th St., 415-626-0880, sfeagle.com)* is not a chain, but there's one in nearly every major city and it's always the headquarters for the leather-set. It's the place to go for Folsom Street Fair-like atmosphere anytime of year. The sixty-plus-year-old establishment has a monthly male mud wrestling event and regular events staged by the Gay Softball League *(sfgsl.org)* and the Sisters of Perpetual Indulgence *(thesisters.org)* – best described as AIDS activists who party like sailors and dress like nuns – and the like. The leather-curious would do well to start at The Eagle, or visit: *sfleathercalendar.org*

For dance and DJ fans, **1015 Folsom** *(1015 Folsom St., 415-431-1200, 1015.com)* may not be the very best club in the city – electronic music fans say that the claim to that title changes each night of the week, depending on who's throwing the party – but it's a definite mainstay in a city where clubs can come and go at breakneck speed. 1015 Folsom has a main dance floor with a mind-blowing sound and light system, and three other rooms that each have their own vibe – it's kind of like a dance department store for house, break beats, and trance music. It's crowded and has a definite Marina crowd element with high-class hoochie mamas, as we affectionately call them. A "Marina crowd" is local short-hand for the BMW set who deign

Local Potables

Cable Car
Invented at **Harry Denton's Starlight Room** *(450 Powell St., 415-395-8595, harrydenton.com)* on top of the **Sir Francis Drake Hotel** (photo above), a cable car is served in a cocktail glass with cinnamon sugar, and usually consists of spiced rum, curaçao, lemon juice, and, at the Starlight Room, simple syrup, though many recipes call for a sweet & sour substitution. The Starlight Room is one of many well-touristed hotel bars and probably has the best view of them all.

to impose their Gucci loafers and open shirts on SoMa night spots. Rightly or wrongly this crowd is much maligned, but in fairness it doesn't take much to seem like you're putting on airs here. As a visitor from out of town once remarked about local fashion: "San Francisco fashion is kind of what homeless people look like where I come from."

Other notable bars in the area include the **Cat Club** (1190 Folsom St., 415-431-3332), next door to 1015. It's smaller and feels a little funkier (in a good way) than 1015, and specializes in the glam '80s. **Luna Lounge** (1192 Folsom St., 415-626-6043) is hit or miss; the crowd can be a little on the trendy side, but that's part of the SoMa experience. The saving grace is the smoking room: with white plastic walls and the hum of an air purification system, it feels like you're in a futuristic submarine.

If it's not a good night at Luna Lounge, head over to **ANU** (43 6th St., 415-543-3505, anu-bar.com), which seems more low-key and chill, but is just as fun and attracts some of the best local DJs around.

DNA Lounge (375 11th St., 415-626-1409, dnalounge.com) is a space built for the serious clubber. Hard-core music lovers heart the DNA Lounge. The owner is Jamie Zawinski, open source hero and a key developer of the Netscape web browser. In the spirit of the open source movement, Zawinski's DNA Lounge site has all the code for the computer programs that run his light and sound systems, links to all the permits needed to open a night club in San Francisco, and honest ramblings about recent shows DNA has put on. Zawinski had to fight to start DNA – with the gentrification of the area came complaints from the newly-arrived gentry – and he doesn't pull punches about his patrons or acts. As he wrote in an October 2003 blog entry after describing a band's act as "karaoke" because nothing was live: "I spent a fortune building this venue from the ground up, and we operate it as, essentially, a charity. I receive no salary, and I haven't had a single dime of my investment repaid. This club is a gift from me to the world. That means that I don't have to blow sunshine up your ass."

Cosmopolitan

There's some dispute whether this drink was actually invented here or by members of the gay community in Provincetown, Massachusetts. A published interview with Toby Cecchini, the New York mixologist often falsely credited with "inventing the cosmo," relates a more complicated story: a friend of his had tried a drink called "a cosmopolitan" in the Life Café in San Francisco. Cecchini and his friend smoothed out the rough edges of the drink and made it the tasty version most people know today from *Sex and the City* – cointreau, cranberry juice, lemon juice, lime, and vodka.

Butter *(354 11th St., 415-863-5964, smoothasbutter.com)* is one of the best bars in the city, and definitely merits a visit. It's anti-fancy, with white trash cuisine (Twinkies, Tater Tots, White Castle burgers), and takes the "trailer trash" concept to new heights by using a vintage trailer as the kitchen – the waitress picks up your drinks through the trailer's window. Whereas sometimes the fun at themed bars can seem a little forced, this place is as self-conscious as a hooting NASCAR fan – i.e., not at all. Even better, an amiable, diverse crowd and good DJs make this place feel like a neighborhood bar, with benefits.

Somehow the aptly named **EndUp** *(401 6th St., 415-646-0999, theendup.com)* is where partiers in the Mission or on Folsom seem to end up – probably because the bar usually stays open (though alcohol-free after 2 a.m.) until 8 a.m., and then lets people back in two hours later, if they are so chemically inclined. It's probably the most well-respected club in the city, a SoMa institution since 1973 that almost always meets and exceeds expectations. The "Other Whirled" new DJ

Blue Blazer

This one isn't served much these day; silver mugs are hard to find and lighting drinks on fire isn't so popular here after the 1906 earthquake and blaze. Made with scotch, lemon, sugar, and boiling water, servers ignite it then quickly pour the flaming brew from one silver mug to the other. This drink, all the rage in the gold mining days, was invented at the now-defunct **El Dorado Bar**.

Irish Coffee

The owner of the **Buena Vista Café** *(2765 Hyde St., 415-474-5044 thebuenavista.com)* wanted to recreate a drink he'd enjoyed at Shannon Airport in Ireland. He and international travel writer Stanton Delaplane tried a number of different recipes, consulted with the city's mayor, and finally came up with a pitch-perfect drink. Today, Buena Vista Café serves 2,000 Irish Coffees every day. Delaplane, by the way, won a Pulitzer Prize in 1942 for his reporting on a few California and Oregon counties that wanted to secede and form a new state.

talent showcase starts at 6 a.m. on Saturdays and is for serious house music freaks who want to dance until noon. **Fag Fridays** *(fagfridays.com)* start at 10 p.m. Friday nights and go until six the next morning. The event, organizers say, "is an exercise in redefining the world – Fabulous!"

Cherry Bar & Lounge *(917 Folsom St., 415-974-1585, thecherrybar.com)* is a newer Folsom bar that's mainly for women and the women who love them. Recent Sunday nights have had **Miss Kitty's Scratching Post**, a "gentlewomen's club" that features the best butch, femme, andro, and trans strippers in town, Miss Kitty claims. *misskittysscratchingpost.com*

The Mission

When an out-of-towner asks where to go out at night in San Francisco, "the Mission" is usually the first response from any well-irrigated local. **The Mission** is the place where locals go for serious bar-hopping; a cover charge is a rarity and Friday and Saturday nights turn whole streets into impromptu block parties. There's a definite energy here that brings professional drinkers from all around the Bay Area at night. There is also many a cheap burrito place in the area, along with more expensive, sometimes trendy restaurants, to keep the party going.

The heavily Hispanic Mission has something for everyone – a strong lesbian community, one of the most sexually and racially mixed bars in the city, live music venues, and the best venues for new art and culture. Don't be put off by the neighborhood's gritty character; stepping out of the 16th and Mission BART Station can be a little overwhelming the first time because of all the people seemingly just hanging around and the confusion of cheap stores, pedestrians, and traffic.

CAMA *(3192 16th St., 415-864-5255, camasf.com)*, a "bed bar lounge," is one of the newest bars in the Mission and sits on one of the best corners to launch an evening from. Across from the main bar, **CAMA** has a few beds in alcoves in the wall where patrons lie and chat, sip their drinks, and get to know each other better. There's also a smoking patio in the back and a smaller room for more private conversations.

JonBenet Ramsey

Available at the Outer Mission/ Bernal Hill **Argus Lounge** *(3187 Mission St., 415-824-1447)*, a JonBenet Ramsey is one part ginger ale, one part vanilla Stoli vodka, and one crushed cherry.

Mai Tai

Invented by Victor J. "Trader Vic" Bergeron at the original Trader Vic's in Oakland (since closed) in 1944. Though it has been modified a few times since, the original formula was: two ounces of 17-year-old J. Wray & Nephew Jamaican rum; half an ounce of French Garnier Orgeat; half an ounce of Holland DeKuyper Orange Curacao; one-quarter ounce of Rock Candy Syrup; juice from one fresh lime. The mix was then shaken and garnished with half of the lime shell inside the drink and a sprig of fresh mint.

Doc's Clock (2575 Mission St., 415-824-3627) is a slightly infamous – for many, this bar fits into the "favorite place to go where anything can happen." It's the only place we've seen customers cheer after someone who vomited all over the women's bathroom got carried out while flashing the "rock on" sign. The night before this particular incident, there was a barroom brawl – that's the kind of place **Doc's Clock** is on the weekends, but during the week, it's definitely more of a neighborhood bar. Maybe the big neon sign out front has something to do with the weekend craziness – like moths to a flame, if there's one bar a drunk person can find, it's Doc's Clock. Doc's is also one of the few bars in the city that has shuffleboard.

For lesbians, the **Lexington Club** (3464 19th St., 415-863-2052, lexingtonclub.com) is the tried and true place to see and be seen. Some sisters of Sappho say that the "tried and true" is the good and the bad part of this institution – a young crowd and excessive drama are the two complaints we hear the most. Regardless, the self-described "friendly neighborhood dyke" bar has *The L Word* viewings, and a few nights a week feature $10 all-you-can-drink happy hours.

For some reason, people either seem to love or hate **Zeitgeist** (199 Valencia St., 415-255-7505, sonic.net/~wwpints/zeitgeist/). It's usually called a biker bar, but most of the bikes here are of the pedal power variety. Zeitgeist sports a black sticker-laden interior, a wait staff that sometimes seems overworked, and one of the biggest and best outdoor patios in San Francisco. Despite its gruff exterior, people here mind their own business and have a good time. Looking at it, most people would think this is the last place in the world to score a date, but randy heterosexuals do well

Martini

Said to be invented at the now-closed **Occidental Hotel**, the story goes that a customer who was about to take the ferry to the East Bay city of Martinez wanted something stiff enough to keep him comfortable during the long journey. The bartender named the potent gin-based drink after the man's final destination. Today, the martini is available, and well-done, almost everywhere in San Francisco, but the upscale **Bob's Steak & Chop House** (500 California St., 415-273-3085, bobssteakandchop.com) is the best place to watch the vestiges of the old-boy network/two-martini lunch crowd drink themselves toward cirrhosis of the liver.

Martuni's (Four Valencia St., 415-241-0205, martunis.citysearch.com) on the edge of the Castro is a much more laid-back place to enjoy martinis. It has a strong gay clientele, but everyone will feel comfortable here, especially as the piano keys start a-tinklin' and patrons join in a big sing-along.

here, and the lesbian regulars say that it's the perfect place to meet a new friend-of-a-friend. Zeitgeist's well-priced pitchers, good burgers, and large outdoor space encourages getting a big group of friends together, so it's a natural to make new connections here. The bar also operates a Guest Haus (their spelling, not ours) in case you're too drunk to get home or make a new friend. On sunny weekend days, the patio is very crowded.

12 Galaxies (2565 Mission St., 415-970-9777, 12galaxies.com) is the only bar we know of named after a living local celebrity. Most people think that Frank Chu, who mans a Financial District corner every morning with his sign proclaiming inter-galactic conspiracies, is advertising this bar on the sign he's holding up. The confusion probably arises because some businesses do advertise on his sign – a local record store and an international shoe retailer. Chu is a regular at the bar, and gets free beer there. In interviews, he says he's honored that they named a bar after him, and that he likes the "progressive rock" they play there. Besides his insistence that Bill Clinton ruined his acting career and owes him royalties, Chu is a pretty cool guy to hang around with. He's the latest in a long line of local characters that residents take a special shine to – he gets a new sign every week from a local copy shop and can always be seen downtown chatting with bike messengers. He's said he goes skiing once a year near Lake Tahoe, but does not ski with his sign.

El Rio (3158 Mission St. 415-282-3325, elriosf.com) is a neighborhood bar that has a number of good things going for it, but best of all is probably the free oysters on the half-shell every Friday while they last. The owners describe El Rio as a "neighborhood bar with a Bay Area-wide clientele who enjoy being in a culturally, racially, and sexually mixed environment."

Here are few more Mission favorites: **500 Club** (500 Guerrero St., 415-861-2500), **Elbo Room** (647 Valencia St., 415-552-7788, elbo.com), **Make-Out Room** (3225

Mimosa

Half orange juice and half champagne, some stories have Alfred Hitchcock inventing the Mimosa at the legendary Jack's Restaurant (a yesteryear hangout for high rollers, with private rooms for quick encounters on the second floor) after a hard night of drinking. Other sources, though, say that the Mimosa was invented at the Ritz Hotel in Paris.

22nd St. 415-647-2888, makeoutroom.com), and **Hush Hush Lounge** *(496 14th St., 415-241-9944)*. It's a neighborhood made for bar-hopping, so don't be afraid to hop on in to any other bars you spot along the way.

If you close down any of these bars, expect to see **"The Tamale Lady,"** as she's known, selling fresh tamales to calm stomachs filled with more combustionable juice than the Space Shuttle Columbia. The Tamale Lady (Virginia Ramos is her real name) is an institution, and Zeitgeist throws her a big birthday party every June 28.

Lower Haight

In the trinity of San Francisco neighborhoods that fill up most nights of the week with revelers, Lower Haight is the most compact, but it also offers the biggest variety of scenes in the tightest space. Lower Haight (as opposed to the much more touristy Upper Haight) runs a few blocks on either side of Haight Street from Webster to Divisadero. Two caveats – it's the most hetero of the three main party neighborhoods, and many of the bars are wine and beer only (coincidence?).

Like the Mission, there are plenty of good places to refuel on food, and many of the restaurants specialize in take-out or quick meals – perfect when visiting local bars. People don't seem to bar-hop as much here as in the Mission, but it happens. Most visitors don't even know this neighborhood exists, but it has the highest concentration of DJ-only record shops, medical marijuana clubs, and good bars within a few square blocks than probably anywhere else in the city.

Although the Lower Haight is safe enough on the main streets while everyone else is around, it's not wise in this neighborhood – or any other that attracts a lot drunk visitors (which in turn attracts muggers looking for easy marks) – to wander on dark and lonely streets. This is especially true east of Fillmore, where gang-related

WE'RE HERE, WE'RE QUEER, GIMME A DRINK

The first rule of **Guerrilla Queer Bar** *(guerrillaqueerbar.typepad.com)* is to have fun outside of the "gay ghettos" of Castro and SoMa and introduce a friendly form of queer culture to straight bars every few months or so. The Guerrilla Queer Bar crew pick an area of the city and show up, 200-or-so strong, to take over a predominantly straight bar with "we're here, we're queer, gimme a drink" revelry; confused patrons are either happy to see the place liven up or they head for the door. Started in 2000 in San Francisco, there are now Guerrilla

shootings happen once in a while, and a few people walking quieter streets late at night have been relieved of their wallets.

Let's go on a walking tour of the places that are safe during typical bar hours (at 2:30 a.m., the streets start getting pretty empty). At the corner of Waller and Fillmore is where **Movida** used to stand; a skateboarder and neighborhood hangout for years and one of the best bars in the city, the place closed in April 2005.

Pay your respects with a beer at the new, friendly **Café du Soleil** (200 Fillmore St., 415-934-8637) in Movida's old spot, and move on up to Haight Street. Cross the street and make a right; walk past wild party and dance spot **Nickie's** (we'll be returning there shortly) to **Underground SF** (424 Haight St., 415-864-7384, undergroundsf.com), which was formerly the **Top**. Underground SF has goth and glam nights, metal nights, and "Crip Nights, for thugz and the men who love them."

Most Deadheads know this, and almost everyone else doesn't – **Nickie's** (460 Haight St., 415-621-6508, nickies.com) is the only place in the city with a regular Grateful Dead night, a surprise because the area is fairly anti-hippie most other nights of the week. Whereas Zeitgeist advertises itself as a "patchouli-free zone," on Monday nights Nickie's is a patchouli-friendly zone. This is one of the better dance spots – it's a veritable rainbow coalition on hip-hop nights, and one of the most attitude-free places to dance in the city.

Cross Fillmore Street, walk past a few storefronts, and head into **Mad Dog in the Fog** (530 Haight St., 415-626-7279), a favorite place for international sports fans. But American sports fans should beware; if it comes down to soccer or American football, soccer will always win. They have Boddington's and Old Peculiar beer on tap. We're well acquainted with the first, but don't know the latter – it seems to make British people very happy, though.

Queer Bars across North America, as well as one in London. Some past events include: "Love Me Tender Tendkerknob," "Take Back the Marina," and "Papal Smear," to celebrate (ironically) the selection of the new pope. The suggested drink menu for the Papal event: 1) Piss Christ: A Robert Mapplethorpe inspired drink made with of a pint of beer with a shot of Midori; 2) Nun with a Ruler: Equal parts tequila and Jagermeister; 3) Altar Boy Reacharound: Frangelica, half & half, and a maraschino cherry with the stem pulled out.

Cross the street to **Toronado** (547 Haight St., 415-863-2276, toronado.com). No exaggeration, beer lovers from around the country come to the Lower Haight just to visit this place. At last count, Toronado had a whopping 45 beers on tap, and at least that many bottled beers. Most of them are either from Northern California, Germany, or Belgium. Don't ask for a beer that's not on the board (and horror of horrors, do not ask for a watery budget beer like Budweiser), or you'll get a sharp response from the bartender.

Next, an optional stop at **Molotov's** (582 Haight St., 415-558-8019). A definite punk/speed metal vibe, Molotov's is fun in a nihilistic death metal sort of way. Then visit **Noc Noc** (557 Haight St., 415-861-5811), a very funky bar in an already funky neighborhood and probably the oldest bar in the Lower Haight. Noc Noc's windows are decorated with what seems like trash. Inside, this cave-like establishment has a lot of low-slung tables and places to chill and talk. It's definitely a conversation/hangout type of venue. Noc Noc looks

like it serves hard liquor, but it doesn't; the Chimay beer, which has a pretty stiff alcohol content, will do the trick quickly enough, though. Many nights Noc Noc has DJs, but even when they're spinning you might not know they're there — people who have visited say they like the eclectic mix of music, but didn't know that the bar has a well-hidden DJ booth.

BUDGET FOR THE DEPARTMENT OF PARTYGOING

Submitted by the Partygoers to the City of San Francisco:

• One (1) 1974 Ford Econoline van with mushroom shaped bubble window ($8,237)

• Interior floor to ceiling shag carpeting (burnt orange) for said van. ($218.14)

• Office space in the Western Addition — location TBD ($1,250/month)

Party Crashing as an Art

Anti-authoritarianism is in the air – there's no other way to explain why people here get such a kick out of crashing parties they weren't invited to. During the dot-com days, lavish parties were thrown for every half-baked business idea on the Internet – this was supposedly a "new economy," not prone to the booms and busts that had plagued the old one.

SF Girl *(sfgirl.com)* was a group of girls, superheroes of sorts, and although they have disbanded, their legend lives on. They managed to insinuate themselves into a number of dot-com parties, and the party pictures on their website were a roll-call of companies that burned brightly in San Francisco and were then snuffed out.

The Partygoers *(thepartygoers.com)* were in many ways the male counterparts to the SF Girl crew (though the Partygoers did have one female member eventually). They who were big on "spreading goodwill through the spontaneous visitation of social gatherings and celebrations." One of the best things about the Partygoers was that they took pictures of the parties they went to and recorded their impressions and critiques afterwards. As the Partygoers explained, their goal was to turn good parties into great ones. (Apparently, they were good conversationalists and had a talent for making margaritas.)

The Partygoers once had a bench dedicated to them at Alamo Square Park – even though they made and posted the plaque itself, and it's since been removed, or "vandalized," as the Partygoers said. They also petitioned then-mayor Willie Brown to consider a Department of Partygoing (see their proposed budget in the sidebar).

Their last communiqué to the world was a press release entitled, "Urgent! The Party Spirit of San Francisco Is Dangerously Low." They've since either gone deeper underground, or the party spirit was so low there were no more parties to "visitate" – like animals who lose their natural habitat, the Partygoers became extinct.

• Second-hand furniture for office – includes sleeper sofa, love seat, egg-shaped stereophonic listening chamber, bar stool. ($1,462)

• Two (2) copies of the "White Album" ($17.99/each)

• One (1) antique bottle dispenser stocked with Pabst Blue Ribbon beer and assorted 40s ($1,743.11 + weekly beer refills estimated @ $100/week)

• Two (2) Technics SL-1200Mk2 turntables ($599.99/each)

• One (1) portable 8" electric disco ball ($38.99)

Whatever the orientation, San Francisco has something for everyone. Straight people have the least number of choices, but thanks to a fairly recent addition at the **Power Exchange** *(74 Otis St., 415-487-9944, powerexchange.com)*, kinky straight couples and single women have a new home in the city.

The Power Exchange is one of the biggest sex clubs in the world, and **Level 3** is a 10,000-square-foot floor dedicated to couples only almost every Friday and Saturday night. The third Saturday of the month is Fetish Ball Night, where the floor turns into an anything-goes zone — within the safety guidelines and rules.

The Power Exchange Gay Sex Club, on the top floor, is for men only and is open Thursday through Sunday. For the women, the only "just show up" sex club (not counting public bathrooms at a number of Mission bars) is the **Lezbi Inn**, and other women-only nights at the Power Exchange.

Although everyone thinks bathhouses when they think gay sex clubs in San Francisco, in fact they were shut

FOR STUDS AND DADDY'S

Daddy's *(440 Castro St. 415-621-8732, daddysbar.com)*, a two-level gay leather and Levi's bar with theme nights, begs the question: Who's your daddy? If you want one or want to play one for an evening, this place is for you. Daddy's is not just a bar, but a destination for gay visitors from around the world.

down in 1984 because they were allegedly key in spreading HIV. At the time, the gay community was divided over the city's decision. On the one hand, bathhouses had a culture of unsafe sex that was hard to change; on the other, unsafe sex in general spreads diseases, not unsafe sex in specific kinds of places, and some members of the gay community felt that shutting down the bathhouses was a form of homophobia hiding behind public health measures.

Regardless, there are still bathhouses in the greater Bay Area, with **Steamworks** *(2107 4th St., Berkeley, 510-845-8992, steamworksonline.com)* the biggest and most well-known – there's a workout room for men who want to pump up before pumping up, and private rooms of different sizes with slings available for a low fee.

In the city, **Eros** (see photo, previous page) *(2051 Market St., 415-864-3767, erossf.com)* is the only pure sex club in the Castro. Set on Market Street across from the "Gay Safeway," this place is easy to miss from the outside, but the inside boasts play rooms, professional massages, and a lounge to chat and hang out.

Blow Buddies *(933 Harrison St., 415-777-3767, blowbuddies.com)* is serious about no cell phones or fragrances, and they welcome out-of-towners who are there to play, not gawk. As might be obvious from the name, Blow Buddies, which has other locations in North America, bills itself as a no bullshit place to get nasty – they have events for bondage buddies, underwear buddies, and golden shower buddies throughout the month. Film director John Waters once said that if he ran for public office, his campaign would call for as many Blow Buddies as Starbucks. Note that sex clubs in the city do not have any completely private spaces – that was made illegal after the 1984 bathhouse closings.

Stud *(399 9th St., 415-252-STUD, studsf.com)* reputedly has a bit of a rough crowd, but if that's your thing.... This SoMa institution turns into **Tranny Shack** *(heklina.com)*, one of San Francisco's longest running clubs, one night a week, and has a number of other theme nights throughout the week.

Featuring plus-size go-go dancers and other delectable oddities, **Stinky's Peep Show** is one of those unique events that could only happen in San Francisco. Originally the weekly event was at the divey **Covered Wagon** (R.I.P.), then bounced around for awhile until finally landing at **Café du Nord** *(2170 Market St., 415-861-5016, cafedunord.com)*

"Stinky's is a fairly underground thing – it's always a party and it's definitely a rock 'n' roll crowd," says Audra, who founded the show in 1997. She says that the events usually feature punk or rock music, live or via DJ, accompanied by the jumbo gyrations of the big and beautiful dancers. Audra says if they're tipped well, the dancers are nice; if not, they're likely to kick over your drink when you're not looking.

The back room features a peep show. "It's not a typical backroom peep show," Audra told us. "We have some sort of current event theme from the Pope to Bin Laden. We once had a woman who pretended to be Pablo Picasso and used her breasts to paint pictures. We also had naughty nurses and witches, and a woman with an electric chair; when she sat on it, she got a mild shock. Then an article of clothing fell off. It's not meant to be sexual, it's meant to make you laugh and possibly even disgust you."

Audra is the beautiful mind behind another event that started in San Francisco but has since gone big with European tours and a movie: **Incredibly Strange Wrestling** *(incrediblystrangewrestling.com)*. The first "ISW Snackdown" video features a bout between El Homo Loco vs. El Pollo Diablo, in a "cock fight," among many other tongue-in-cheek pleasures. Incredibly Strange Wrestling live shows happen every six months or so, often at **DNA Lounge**.

Drinking in Historic Proportions

The Saloon *(1232 Grant Ave., 415-989-7666)* in North Beach is the oldest surviving bar in the city, built in the early 1860s. Although now famous as one of the best jazz bars in San Francisco, this institution has doubled as a house of prostitution and a speakeasy at various times. The bar survived the fire of 1906 because the men of the area did their best to make sure the place didn't burn to the ground.

The only employee-owned strip club in the nation, the **Lusty Lady Theatre** *(1033 Kearny St., 415-391-3991)* almost shut down after the dot-com bust but is now alive and shimmying up a storm. When management said they just couldn't make a profit at the unionized club and would have to zip it up, the workers banded together and negotiated a buyout price. Now, for $300, any employee can buy into the company and potentially get a big stack of quarters that customers keep pumping (ahem) into the slots to keep the show going. The 2000 documentary *Live Nude Girls Unite!* follows the unionization efforts of the dancers in sometimes drawn-out, unedited detail. But the documentary confirms something one hears often in San Francisco – the Lusty Lady boasts some of the most well-educated exotic dancers in the city.

It's just one of many strip clubs near the Broadway/Columbus intersection in North Beach – testaments to the area's pre-gentrification days when it was an inexpensive immigrant neighborhood.

Out of the slew of strip clubs in this area, **The Hungry I** *(546 Broadway St., 415-362-7763)*, deserves a mention. The original Hungry i (with a lowercase "i") was a comedy club a few blocks away that helped solidify the careers of Jonathan Winters and Mort Sahl, among many others. Lenny Bruce did his routine there as well, and it was actually in San Francisco in 1961 that he was first arrested for obscenity.

Hungry i, started by Enrico Banducci (who also started the recently revived **Purple Onion** comedy club, which has seen surprise appearances from Robin Williams), stood for "hungry intellectual," and helped make San Francisco the breeding ground for an edgier humor than most Americans had ever heard before.

On one occasion Winters, who has since spoken publicly about his bouts with mental illness, stepped out of character during a Hungry i performance and started raving about Alcoholics Anonymous, among other things. The story goes that when his cigarette lighter

---

Other historic bars in the city include:

• The **Beach Chalet** (*1000 Great Hwy., 415-386-8439, beachchalet.com*), between Golden Gate Park and the Pacific Ocean, is packed on the weekends, but almost every table in the second-floor restaurant offers great ocean views. The microbrews here are especially tasty, and they'll sell them by the bottle for those who want to enjoy them on the beach (technically illegal but discretion is the better part of valor) or back at home. The first floor, built in 1925 by famed architect Willis Polk, is a visitors center for the Golden Gate Park that has a scale model of the park and WPA-era fresco murals, including a rendering of William Randolph Hearst taking a photograph.

didn't work, the comedian burst into tears and ran out of the club all the way to Fisherman's Wharf. There, he climbed up into the rigging of a historic ship and proclaimed to police that he was the man in the moon. He spent the night in a psychiatric ward.

Tender Loins in the Tenderloin

Most of the nightlife in the Tenderloin is centered around trading sex for money or drugs. There are a few bars, most notably **Lush Lounge** (*1092 Post St., 415-771-2022, thelushlounge.com*) and **Edinburgh Castle Pub** (950 Geary St. 415-885-4074, castlenews.com).

Lush Lounge is well known for its transvestite clientele. Many of the working girls stop in between tricks to have a drink in the upstairs room that overlooks the main floor. Edinburgh Castle is best known as a center of Scottish culture in one of the most unlikely neighborhoods. There's a large selection of scotch whiskies, live bands, and very often there are literary events here.

How the Tenderloin got its name is not entirely clear. It is definitely one of the least touristed regions of the city, and for good reason – the down-and-out congregate here, thanks in part to the large number of rundown single residence occupancy (SRO) hotels that charge by the night or by the week.

One story about the naming of this area claims that because it was always a rough section of town, the beat cops who walked these mean streets received extra pay and could afford to buy the more expensive cuts of tenderloin beef. Others say that the term started in New York City, and that old-time cops there were paid so much to ignore the drug and prostitution houses that they could buy the best meat with their bribe money.

No matter what the story, it's best not to walk alone late at night, and no matter what the time, walk confidently and don't flash a guidebook, camera, or map.

• **Li Po** (*916 Grant Ave., 415-982-0072*) is one of the best and oldest bars in Chinatown. When it opened in the late 1920s, there was an opium den in the basement where the bathrooms are now. Bartenders there say that the ghosts of opium addicts still come to the bar looking for a fix. Whether or not this is true, there are strong spirits here, at least in the bottled variety. Ng ka py (pronounced "ingapay"), a type of Chinese whiskey made with herbs, is called "opium in a bottle" by some, and Li Po is one of the very few bars in the city to serve the stuff. The buzz feels like more fun than the law allows, but apparently there are only legal herbs in this wonderful potion. The Beat writers came here often to toast Li Po himself, a famous Chinese poet of the Tang Dynasty.

San Francisco's not just a wine city, damnit. There are plenty of places that either brew their own or offer a big selection of beers on tap. **Anchor Brewery** *(1705 Mariposa St., 415-863-8350, anchorbrewing.com)*, which has been making beer in San Francisco since 1869, is one of the biggest in Northern California, and many would say the best.

The brewery is most famous for **Anchor Steam** beer, one of seven brews it makes in San Francisco. It offers free tours every weekday afternoon, but it's necessary to call ahead. These tours usually last around 45 minutes, and are extremely popular with locals and visitors, thanks in part to all the beer you get to taste at tour's end.

Although very popular during its first 80 or so years of production, steam beer – as Anchor and many other West Coast brews were known because of the way they were made – started losing market share in the 1950s because of mass-produced competitors like Miller and Budweiser.

• **The Little Shamrock** *(807 Lincoln Way, 415-661-0060)*, right next to Golden Gate Park, is generally acknowledged as the second-oldest bar in the city and is infamous for its "ghoul pool" (guessing what famous person will die next). A cozy place with mismatched furniture, it's the go-to bar for St. Patrick's Day and a historic stop while wandering Golden Gate Park.

As luck would have it, the **Old Spaghetti Factory**, where many of the original beatniks ate because of the huge portions and dirt cheap prices, served only one beer on tap – Anchor Steam. In 1965, an heir to the Maytag fortune was enjoying his Anchor Steam at the bar and the restaurant's owner, Fred Kuh, told the man that if he liked the beer so much he better go visit the historic brewery sooner rather than later because it was on the verge of shutting down. Fritz Maytag was smitten, and bought a majority share in the company for a few thousand dollars just in the nick of time – there was only $128 in the brewery's bank account. On another note, thethe Old Spaghetti Factory's original location now houses **Bocce Café** *(478 Green St. 415-981-2044)*.

Beat Bars

Spec's Twelve, also known as the **Adler Museum Cafe** *(12 Adler St., 415-421-4112)*, is a funky hole-in-the-wall featuring a collection of Navy-related oddities and WWII posters. The bar is tucked into an alley across the street from **City Lights** bookstore and has seen its share of Beats, drunks, and business people from the nearby Financial District. One of the bartenders tells us she limits customers to one Irish car bomb (Guinness, Bailey's Irish Cream, and Jamieson whiskey) per night, or things get a little too rowdy for this eclectic place. Although now it has a little bit of the tourist trap vibe, **Vesuvio** *(255 Columbus Ave., 415-362-3370, vesuvio.com)* was another watering hole favored by the Beats and their hangers-on. The only thing that separates Vesuvio from City Lights is **Jack Kerouac Alley**. The bar has a drink named after Kerouac, its most famous regular. This is ironic, but Kerouac would be happy – he died at the age of 47 from health problems caused by a life of heavy boozing.

• San Francisco Brewing Co.
(155 Columbus St., 415-434-3344, sfbrewing.com) is another North Beach favorite and used to be the main hub of Barbary Coast nightlife. In 1913, Jack Dempsey, who eventually became a world famous boxing champ, worked at the bar, then called the Andromeda Saloon. In 1939, the FBI captured notorious gangster Baby Face Nelson here. In 1985, the bar became one of the first microbrew pubs in San Francisco and only the fourth in the US. Today, San Francisco Brewing Company serves beer made on the premises and offers live music almost every night of the week.

Ima Kara, OK!

San Francisco seems to draw the kind of people who like to travel, and people who love Asia are especially abundant here because the city is a hub of affordable flights in that direction. Liking Asia by necessity means that you at least don't hate karaoke, and if you do, well, that year in Japan is going to be a very long one.

San Francisco has a list of **karaoke bars** where you can caterwaul in public, and karaoke boxes where you do your warbling in a private room with friends. Alcohol is officially off-limits, but at two Japantown favorites don't ask, don't tell is the unwritten rule (and don't bring any glass bottles; employees who have to clean up afterwards hate them).

Those who have been to Japan will especially love **Do Re Mi Music Studio** *(1604 Post St,. 415-771-8884)* with songs in Japanese, Korean, and plenty in English. Seemingly nonsensical videos that accompany the songs are all just another authentic part of the Japanese karaoke experience.

SMELL THE GLOVE

Bondage a Go-Go *(bondage-a-go-go.com)* is a recurring event that's still going strong as San Francisco's "longest running fetish dance party." Started in 1993 by a group of BDSM aficionados, Bondage a Go-Go *strongly* discourages gawkers and has a dress code that encourages fetish and/or goth attire. It's not a sex club per se, but is definitely a sexually charged environment for those who find a thrill in the smell of latex or leather. A typical event features any combination of music, stage show, and rope/play demonstrations by BDSM professionals.

Harlem of the West Coast

In its previous incarnation as **Club Morocco**, the stage at **Club Waiziema** *(543 Divisadero St., 415-346-6641)* has seen the likes of Tina Turner, James Brown, Marvin Gaye, and Billie Holliday perform. Back then it was a favorite hangout of former mayor Willie Brown and other city big shots. Today, it features local artists, live music, special events, great Ethiopian food, and super cold beer on tap.

At a City Hall meeting we attended to support the bar's petition to stay open later, one of the officials on hand marveled at the number of residents who came out on a Thursday afternoon to support Waiziema. Lower Haight/Upper Panhandle regulars know that all it takes is a beer at the bar and a few questions and Ebbe, one of the owners, will happily tell you everything he knows about the place before he bought it.

Club Morocco was one of the main stops in this area back when it was the "Harlem of the West Coast," bounded by Fillmore and Divisadero streets. Look for the African-American bookstores, African art stores, and Caribbean restaurants that still survive as remains of the area's past.

Brew Crew

Lagunitas Brewing Co. *(1280 N. McDowell Blvd., Petaluma, 707-769-4495, lagunitas.com)* brews their especially tasty beers in Petaluma, 40 miles north of San Francisco, and they invite beer lovers to give them a call if they want a tour. The brewers used to have parties every Thursday afternoon that were open to the public, but as of this writing they'd been discontinued.

Takara Sake Factory *(708 Addison St., Berkeley, 510-540-8250, takarasake.com)*, in Berkeley, doesn't make beer but is worth visiting. There's a museum that details the history and process of sake-making, and a tasting room that's the most authentic one can find this side of Tokyo.

Magnolia Pub & Brewery
(1398 Haight St., 415-864-7468,
magnoliapub.com), the only
brewpub in the heart of hippie-
holdout Haight Ashbury, and Financial
District/SoMa spot **21st**
Amendment *(563 2nd St., 415-*
369-0900, 21st-amendment.com)
both deserve a mention for good
atmospheres and quality beers that
will help any beer lover forget he's in
the heart of wine country.

With wine country just outside city limits, it's no surprise that San Francisco is serious about wine. You can get wine recommendations from corner store owners and a wine selection at your most humble convenience store that rivals upscale restaurants in other states.

There are a number of wine bars throughout the city, but two in particular have a special place in the heart of local oenophiles. The **London Wine Bar** *(415 Sansome St., 415-788-4811)*, started in 1974 as the first wine bar in the US and is probably the most casual one in San Francisco. Friendly servers in this Financial District space have a knack for setting those who don't know much about wine, besides the fact that they enjoy it, at ease.

VinoVenue (photo above) *(686 Mission St., 415-341-1930, vinovenue.net)*, in the SoMa area near the **San Francisco Museum of Modern Art**, democratizes wine in a different way. A newcomer to the wine scene, VinoVenue puts the concept "try before you buy" into practice with self-serve wine-tasting machines. The wines are sorted by type, with an "adventure" kiosk that's always a lot of fun. Seating is limited, though, so it's good for brief tasting sessions.

Notoriety

Photo: Liz Abbott photographed by Audra Morse

From the Beat poets to the brightest lights of the flower power generation, dreamers of all stripes have lived, loved, and lost in San Francisco. From a modern Cain and Abel story set in the city's most famous strip club to the 1976 dinner where longtime local politico Willie Brown praised cult leader Jim Jones – of Kool-Aid mass suicide fame – not everyone's dreams turned out exactly as planned in the City by the Bay.

Homeless, Not Hopeless

San Franciscans are fairly generous to those in need and the city has a number of programs to help – some say perpetuate – homelessness. It's a difficult issue, made more so by local hotels and restaurants who claim the huge homeless population is discouraging tourism.

Almost as if to illustrate the point, an unbalanced homeless man attacked a woman near Union Square who was in town for a convention in May 2003. Ironically, the woman was part of a group of psychiatrists attending the national meeting of the American Psychiatric Association. The woman was hospitalized after the man, who had a history of mental illness, hit her from behind for no apparent reason.

Many out-of-towners are surprised by the sheer number of homeless people here, and even locals, though sympathetic, can find the constant barrage of panhandling annoying. At last official count in January 2005, there were 6,248 homeless people in the city, down more than 25 percent from the last official count in 2002. Many credit Mayor **Gavin Newsom**'s controversial **Care Not Cash** program, which offers the homeless a place to stay while cutting welfare checks from a high of $410 to $59 a month.

Most of the bad people who have been caught in California are serving time in **San Quentin**, California's oldest and best known prison still in operation. Only 18 miles north of San Francisco, this prison that sits beside San Francisco Bay covers 432 acres.

It was established in July 1852 at Point Quentin in Marin County as "an answer to the rampant lawlessness in California at the time," prison officials say. During its construction, inmates slept on the prison ship, the Waban, at night and labored to build the new prison during the day. San Quentin housed both male and female inmates until 1933 when the women's prison at Tehachapi was built.

San Quentin also contains the state's only death row gas chamber for male inmates. The prison is one of the toughest and most violent in California, in part because it holds almost twice the number of inmates it was designed to.

The Monolithic Prison System

Photo: Daniel Halvorson

The California Department of Corrections and Rehabilitations (CDCR) is the largest prison system in the United States, and the largest state employer in California. Below are statistics from the CDCR, which operates all state prisons, oversees community correctional facilities, and supervises parolees.

Budget:
$5.7 billion (2004-2005)

Average yearly cost:
per inmate, $30,929; per parolee, $3,364

Staff:
49,073 employees

Total offenders under CDCR jurisdiction:
301,181 (parolees and prisoners)

A serial murderer whose identity is hotly disputed, the **Zodiac Killer** terrorized the Bay Area in the late 1960s and into the early 1970s, making himself the most notorious criminal the city has ever experienced. He was never caught or positively identified – he could be alive and reading this today. One suspect, Arthur Leigh Allen, has strong circumstantial evidence against him; the police questioned him in 1992, but DNA and fingerprint tests were inconclusive.

The Zodiac Killer usually killed young couples in secluded areas; on at least a few occasions he wore a black outfit that covered entire body, including his head, and was decorated with his odd brand of ancient symbols. Taunting police through letters to the media, the killer included bizarre charts (see image) that he said were clues. After the first few letters, the killer took to starting his communications with, "This is the Zodiac speaking."

In addition to his regular letters, the killer sent four others that were completely encoded using his symbols. Only one of these four messages was ever decrypted, and it wasn't done by professionals, but by amateur sleuths. One-time Bay Area resident Ted Kaczynski, the **Unabomber**, was originally a suspect, but was cleared by the FBI and local police. Experts say that Kaczynski probably got the idea of sending egotistical missives to the media from the Zodiac Killer.

Whoever he is, the last confirmed Zodiac sighting was in March of 1970. A man offered to help a young mother and child who were stranded on the side of the road in their car, but instead apparently disabled it. Supposedly taking the pair to the nearest service station, the man drove, apparently aimlessly, for two hours. The would-be killer was asked by the woman if he always helped stranded motorists. "By the time I'm done with them, they won't need help," he responded. The woman jumped from the car with her child and later identified the man as fitting the police composite sketch of the Zodiac Killer.

FACILITIES

32 state prisons ranging from minimum to maximum custody; **40 camps**, minimum custody facilities located in wilderness areas where inmates are trained as wildland firefighters; **12 community correctional facilities**; and **5 prisoner mother facilities**.

PRISON POPULATION

All institutions: 163,939

Prisons: 154,161

Camps: 4,146

Community facilities: 5,473

Outside CDCR: 1,702

Escaped: 254

Additionally, the US Citizenship and Immigration Services holds 17,226 people in California who are in the US illegally.

Richard Ramirez, aka the **Night Stalker**, was a serial killer who committed a string of murders, rapes, and other crimes that started tentatively in 1984, then turned into a full-on orgy of depravity in 1985. The Zodiac Killer looks like a nice guy next to Ramirez, whose actions took place mainly in Los Angeles but included San Francisco; when he attacked a couple, he would usually shoot the man in the head and rape and torture the woman in front of the dying man's eyes. He also left satanic symbols written in his victims' blood on their bodies and the walls of their homes. Los Angeles residents were terrified; police sketches of the killer's gaunt face, based on the recollections of the few who survived their encounters, were everywhere. As a result, Ramirez relocated for a time to the Bay Area, where he had lived before LA.

On August 18, 1985, an elderly Bay Area Chinese couple was found in their bloodied bed. Both had been shot in the head, but the woman survived. She had been sexually assaulted and was paralyzed for life. An inverted pentagram and lyrics from a heavy metal song were scrawled in lipstick on the wall of their home; police matched the bullet the intruder used to the Night Stalker killings in Los Angeles.

San Francisco police searched their unsolved homicide cases and found two probable matches from earlier that year. On February 20, 1985, two sisters, 50 and 70, had been stabbed to death in their apartment on Telegraph Hill. Additionally, on June 2, 1985, a day after the Night Stalker killed a pair of elderly sisters in Los Angeles, a man was shot in the head as he lay sleeping in his apartment in the Cow Hollow neighborhood. His girlfriend was then violently raped, but survived.

The Bay Area found itself in the same vice-grip of fear that Los Angelenos were living in, and Mayor **Dianne Feinstein**, in an effort to calm citizens,

PRISONER CHARACTERISTICS:

Males: 93 percent

Females: 7 percent

Parole violators: 12 percent

Race:
37 percent Hispanic;
29 percent white;
29 percent black;
6 percent other

Offense:
51 percent crimes against persons;
21 percent property crimes;
21 percent drugs;
7 percent other

Lifers: 27,251

infamously mentioned some of the details of the case, including the fact that the police knew what kind of shoes the Night Stalker wore (he'd left bloody footprints at crime scenes). Detectives weren't amused, and noted that the Night Stalker most likely immediately dumped his shoes – the Avia's he wore before the announcement were never found.

A manager at the **Bristol Hotel**, a residence hotel in the Tenderloin, called police and told them that someone who matched the Night Stalker's description had stayed there a few times over the previous year and a half. The man had checked out on the day the elderly couple was attacked, and police found satanic symbols drawn in the room.

While San Francisco police were scrambling to find the Night Stalker, Ramirez struck again in Los Angeles, killing a man and repeatedly raping his fiancée while making her swear allegiance to Satan. The woman survived and was able to tell police what kind of car the attacker drove. An observant teenager had written down the license plate. When police located the car, they found a fingerprint that they were able to link to Ramirez from a previous arrest for theft. That same print was found at the home of the elderly Bay Area couple.

Soon, the inaccurate police sketches of the Night Stalker were replaced with photographs of Richard Ramirez, who was eventually found as he was trying to steal a car in a Hispanic area of Los Angeles. In the ensuing chaos, he was nearly beaten to death by a mob of angry residents.

During the topsy-turvy trial (one juror was shot to death by her boyfriend, and other jurors were reportedly terrified that indeed Lucifer was on the side of the defendant), Ramirez attracted a host of female admirers despite (or perhaps because of?) his crimes. Found guilty, he received 19 death sentences for 13 murders and 30 other serious charges. Now living on death row in San Quentin, he continues to receive mail and explicit pictures from his female fans. In 1996, he married a freelance magazine editor, **Doreen Lioy**.

Lifers without possibility of parole:
3,168

Condemned to death: 637

Average reading level:
seventh grade

Average Age: 36

Employed: 53.6 percent

Average sentence: 52.9 months

Average time served:
26.1 months

Commitment rate:
446 per 100,000 California population

Although the Zodiac Killer and the Night Stalker are the two most notorious killers to strike in San Francisco, there have been other bad apples who have called the Bay Area home.

Theodore Kaczynski, the **Unabomber**, was a mathematics instructor at the University of California, Berkeley in the late 1960s. He was interviewed by police during the Zodiac Killer investigations and is best known for his rambling anti-technology manifesto and his decades-long quest to topple the industrial system by sending letter bombs to universities and businesses. He sent two of his bombs to his old university in Berkeley and one to a San Francisco researcher.

Charles Manson and his group of followers, known as **The Family**, lived in the Haight area for a short while. Reportedly, the competition here among charismatic leaders looking for lost souls was too much for Manson and he moved

The Family down to Southern California. In August of 1969, Manson directed his followers to spark what he felt were imminent race wars by killing high-profile white people – one of the victims was actress **Sharon Tate**, wife of **Roman Polanski** and nine months pregnant at the time – and trying to make it look as if the Oakland-based **Black Panthers** were responsible. Manson, the mastermind of the killings, and most of the members of The Family who committed the crimes, remain in prison.

One of Manson's followers, **Lynette "Squeaky" Fromme**, attempted to assassinate President Gerald Ford in Sacramento in September of 1975. She claims she did it because she assumed Manson would have testified at her trial, and she wanted to give her idol a platform to preach his message to the world again.

Just a few weeks later, a woman named **Sara Jane Moore** tried to kill President Ford in front of San Francisco's **St. Francis Hotel**, supposedly to get back

The Zodiac Killer: A Timeline

Dec. 20, 1968

Two young people are shot to death as they sit in a parked car on a lover's lane near the Vallejo, about 30 miles north of San Francisco.

July 5, 1969

Again near Vallejo, a 22-year-old woman is killed and her friend, a 19-year-old man, survives after a man with a flashlight approaches their car and opens fire. An hour later the man who would gain infamy as the Zodiac Killer calls the Vallejo police department and reports what he thinks is his latest double murder. He takes responsibility for the killing of the other young couple killed in December.

into the good graces of her radical terrorist friends; the FBI had been using her to try to get information on the kidnappers of publishing heiress **Patty Hearst**, but her radical pals were suspicious of her. (Obviously, 1975 was not Gerald Ford's year, nor is Northern California likely one of his favorite places to visit.) **Oliver Sipple**, a former Marine who moved to San Francisco and was active in Harvey Milk's political campaigns, was just another spectator in the crowd that day, but when he saw Moore's gun he tried to wrestle it away from her – Moore got off one shot, but Sipple had saved the president's life. Sipple, a gay man who had not come out of the closet to his mother, was deeply disturbed by the attention given to his sexual orientation. When *San Francisco Chronicle* columnist **Herb Caen** mentioned his sexuality in print, Sipple sued him, but was unsuccessful. At the time, Sipple said, "My sexual orientation has nothing at all to do with saving the president's life, just as the color of my eyes or my race has nothing to do with what happened in front of the St. Francis Hotel."

Leonard Lake was born in San Francisco and was caught by an on-the-ball South San Francisco police officer. Lake, who had given a fake name to the cop, was hauled into the police station for having an illegal silencer on his .22 caliber pistol. Under questioning, he told police his real name and then quickly swallowed cyanide pills that he'd taped to the inside of his coat; he lapsed into a coma and eventually died. Police from the SFPD's Missing Persons' division took over the case when it was discovered that the car Lake was driving belonged to a missing San Francisco man. Police followed the clues to a compound in Wilseyville, 140 miles northeast of San Francisco, which contained secret rooms used for sexually torturing and killing his victims, as well as a mass grave. Twelve bodies were dug up, including two entire families, but police believe there were probably around 25 victims in total.

Charles Ng, Lake's accomplice in the horrific crimes (some of which were videotaped), was still on the loose, but had a weakness for shoplifting – he was caught in Calgary, Canada by store security guards. The Canadian and United States governments sparred over his extradition, since a death sentence for Ng was almost a certainty. Eventually returned to the US, Ng used his knowledge of the law to make his trial one of the costliest the country has ever seen – but he was eventually sentenced to death for killing six men, three

July 31, 1969

Three Bay Area newspapers receive a copy of a letter signed with what was to become the Zodiac's symbol, a simple design of a cross in a circle. The writer claims he's responsible for the July 5 shootings. An encrypted part of the message is decoded: "When I die I will be reborn in paradise and the [people] I have killed will become my slaves."

Sept. 27, 1969

A pair of young co-eds are picnicking at Lake Berryessa in Napa County (in a place locals now call "Zodiac Island") when they are approached by a tall man wearing a hooded costume. He ties them up with rope and stabs them with a long knife. The woman dies but the man survives. The killer uses a magic marker to draw his trademark design on the door of the man's Volkswagen.

women, and two infants. Ng is awaiting execution at San Quentin.

Scott Peterson, a two-timing Bay Area fertilizer salesman who went fishing the day his pregnant wife disappeared in December 2002, sparked one of the most closely watched trials since O.J. Simpson's (a former San Francisco resident). First, it came to light that he was having an affair with a massage therapist before and after his wife disappeared. The woman, Amber Frey, approached police and started recording conversations with her suitor after a friend saw Peterson on the news. The body of his unborn son and the badly decomposed body of his wife washed up four months after she disappeared, not far from where Peterson went fishing. He was apprehended near the Mexican border with his hair bleached blond and a huge wad of cash. In 2004, he was convicted for the murders of his wife and son and is now one more resident on California's crowded death row at San Quentin.

The Hungriest Cop in San Francisco

In November 2002, three off-duty policemen, apparently intoxicated, had just shut down a bar after a police get-together celebrating the promotion of a new assistant chief. The three cops noticed two men walking down the street with a takeout box full of savory Mexican food – one of the men was a bartender whose bar had just hosted "Taco Tuesday," and he had the leftovers.

Mexican food is great to eat when you're a little bit tipsy, and the cops told the guys to drop their takeout and slowly step away from the tortillas. A scuffle ensued and one of the men with the food received a beating. A

Oct. 11, 1969

A San Francisco cab driver is shot and killed by a customer at 3898 Washington Street (at Cherry Street) in Presidio Heights. A dispatcher mistakenly broadcasts a lookout for a black suspect. Two cops stop a white man who may have been the killer on a nearby street before letting him go.

Oct. 13, 1969

The *San Francisco Chronicle* gets a letter containing a bloody patch of the cab driver's shirt and a threat to shoot children on a school bus. Bay Area police start escorting buses to schools.

Nov. 10, 1969

The *San Francisco Chronicle* receives another letter from the Zodiac containing detailed plans for a "death machine" to blow up a school bus.

swarm of police arrived on the scene, but many of the usual protocols weren't followed – the off-duty cops weren't given a blood-alcohol test for hours, were allowed to talk with each other (and potentially get their stories straight), and weren't lined up for a positive I.D. by the victims. Scandal ensued; one of the hungry cops, **Alex Fagan Jr.**, was the son of the newly promoted assistant chief, Alex Fagan Sr.

Fajita Gate, as it was to be called, saw seven of the top SFPD officials indicted by a grand jury. No one in the entire case was ever convicted, though Fagan Jr. did lose his job. More than the food itself, the case became a study in high-caliber political feuds and questionable decisions on the part of the district attorney Terrence Hallinan. Many say he bungled the case by handing the grand jury a blank check to indict whoever they saw fit, and he admits that he was surprised by their sweeping indictments.

There was a big shakeup at the department – Heather Fong was appointed as the city's first female police chief, and many of the indicted left their jobs. Inside and outside the police department, African-Americans were not pleased that Chief Earl Sanders, a civil rights hero to many, was publicly humiliated with an indictment at the end of a long and respectable career. They also wonder why it took a brawl with two white guys for Fagan Jr., who had racked up numerous complaints from citizens when he was starting his (short-lived) career in a black neighborhood, to get the boot.

In March of 2004, both Alex Fagan and his dad were arrested at a Scottsdale, Arizona hotel when the younger Fagan started smashing up the place after an apparent argument with dad – maybe Fagan was hungry again for Mexican food in the culinary capital of the desert Southwest?

In any event, Fagan Jr. had been drinking, and when dad tried to step in and take control of the situation after the Scottsdale police arrived, he too was cuffed, but not stuffed; they let him go but did haul Alex down to the station. Fagan Sr., by the way, was reportedly a big fan of the *Dirty Harry* movies and ran with the **Cowboy Cops**, a group of hard-nosed S.F. narcotics detectives in the 1970s.

March 22, 1970

A young mother, 22, escapes with her newborn daughter from a man the mother identifies as the Zodiac Killer.

July 26, 1970

The *San Francisco Chronicle* receives another letter from the Zodiac. He claims to have killed 13 more people, but none of those deaths are confirmed.

July 8, 1974

In his last verified letter to the media, the Zodiac complains to the *San Francisco Chronicle* about the superiority complex of one of their columnists.

Like most successful entrepreneurs, **Jim Mitchell** started small – while in college in San Francisco he paid girls $5 to go topless so he could photograph them. He sold these photos to adult stores and the profits accumulated quickly. Once he had mastered the business of still photos, he moved up the adult entertainment ladder by making short porn movies. Jim and his brother Artie became two of the more infamous in a long line of San Franciscan entrepreneurs – known for hiring the best girls in town and offering live shows in which these girls wore nothing more than a hat.

Ever the patriots, the brothers opened the **O'Farrell Theatre** on July 4, 1969. Despite (or thanks to) the frequent police raids, complaints, and trials, the establishment set the standard, or lack thereof, for strip clubs across the country. Although the theater can't claim to have invented the lap dance, it certainly helped bring it back to center stage. Nicknamed "the Carnegie Hall of public sex in America" by journalist and one-time head of security Hunter S. Thompson, the theater was just the beginning of the brothers' career. Fortune and fame came quickly after the release of their first feature-length porn movie, *Behind the Green Door*, in 1972.

Now considered a classic in the porn movie industry, *Behind the Green Door* was a huge hit in America and even made it to the Cannes Film Festival. Although graphic enough to shock more than one seasoned

QUICK ON THE DRAW

San Francisco homicide detective **Dave Toschi** became well-known because of his work on the Zodiac case. Toschi favored a type of custom-made quick draw holster that Steve McQueen copies in the movie *Bullitt*, whose title character is modeled on Toschi. Toschi was taken off the Zodiac case in 1978 when it was discovered that he was sending anonymous letters to *Tales of the City* writer and *San Francisco Chronicle* journalist Armistead Maupin praising his own work on the case. Toschi's superiors brought in a handwriting expert to compare Toschi's writing with the Zodiac's, but a connection was ruled out.

devotee, the film didn't make waves simply because of its edginess. The lead actress, **Marilyn Chambers**, had worked as a model before gaining entry into the adult movie business. Around the time the movie was released, clueless marketing executives for Ivory Snow declared Chambers the company's new poster girl and put a picture of her on every container of their laundry detergent. The Mitchell brothers jumped on the publicity opportunity and wrote press releases that described the model-turned-porn-star just as the soap ads did: "99 and 44/100's percent pure." (Chambers has since been able to keep her spot on the small screen – she ran for vice president on the Personal Choice Party ticket in the 2004 US presidential election.)

The 1980s was a sad decade for AIDS-affected San Francisco, and although some might have seen this as a deterrent, the Mitchell brothers saw it as an opportunity. In 1986, the brothers released the first safe-sex porno: *Behind the Green Door: the Sequel.* But money, drugs, and alcohol flowed freely, and as with all good things, the brothers' success came to end – Artie was found shot dead in his Corte Madera home in February of 1991. Not only was his death devastating, the fact that Jim Mitchell was the murderer made it all the more shocking.

Although Jim's lawyers claimed that the shooting was an accident and that he had come to his brother's house to talk to him about quitting drugs and alcohol, the prosecutors noted that Jim had kicked the front door down and shot Artie three times, including one bullet to the brain.

Jim served approximately half of his six-year sentence in San Quentin, and was released in 1997. The O'Farrell Theatre continues to be a very popular adult venue in San Francisco and Jim Mitchell still is involved in the business. The Mitchells' story was the subject of a TV cable movie, *Rated X*, starring brothers Charlie Sheen and Emilio Estevez.

A SCANDALOUS RECIPE

The recipe that started the whole Fajita Gate scandal, in the words of the cook who made them, as he testified to the grand jury: "I put meat, and, after two or three minutes, put bell peppers, green peppers, and onions, and then I just took tortillas, flour tortillas, and I put in the white container and that's it."

Jim Jones was one of the charismatic dreamers who came to the City by the Bay with big plans, many of which actually panned out, but then his methods became madness, culminating when he forced his followers to commit the biggest mass suicide in recent history. Jones made San Francisco the headquarters of the **People's Temple Christian Church** in the early '70s and was much praised by city leaders for his work with drug addicts and homeless people; long-time San Francisco politician **Willie Brown** lauded Jones at a 1976 city shindig for the racial tolerance Jones' followers practiced and preached. But as the church grew, so did Jones' demands on his followers, whose family members started to complain. Although he managed to keep an arrest for solicitation at a cruisy park a secret, Jones was getting freer in his interpretations of what "love thy neighbor" really meant, especially towards the wives of his followers. Amid a custody battle, mounting negative publicity about "miracle healings," and financial exploitation, he decided it was high time for him and about 1,000 of his followers to relocate to the 300-acre farm known as **Jonestown** in the South American nation of Guyana.

In November of 1978, Congressman **Leo Ryan** of San Francisco left for Guyana with concerned relatives and reporters to investigate bizarre stories leaking out about Jonestown. In public, church members put on a happy face for Ryan, but in private, they begged to leave with him. Tensions mounted, and after a knife attack by a loyal People's Temple follower, Ryan and some of the cult members rushed to a nearby airstrip where two planes were waiting. As they were getting ready to board, a truck pulled up and men with machine guns started shooting. Ryan, three journalists, and a defecting People's Temple member were killed. Some survivors managed to crawl off into the jungle.

Surely knowing that the end was near, Jones

Mitchell Brothers Filmography

Although it might seem that the **Mitchell Brothers** were avid fans of German geography with all of their "Grafenberg" movies, in fact, Ernst Grafenberg is the German doctor and scientist that the G-spot was named after. No pervert, Grafenberg contributed greatly to our modern understanding of how cancer spreads and invented an early IUD birth control device. Here's a list of movies from the Mitchell Brothers:

Rabin's Revenge, 1971

Rampaging Nurses, 1971

Woman of the Night, 1971

immediately gave the order for the much-practiced suicide drill – this time it was for real. When the Guyanese army showed up the next day, more than 900 people were dead, the majority from drinking a cyanide-laced Flavor-Aid concoction, the rest from strangulation, or, like Jones himself, from a gunshot wound to the head. (Jones had conducted suicide drills called "white nights," a term that was to take on a much different connotation in the gay community the next year; see page 243.)

The world, but in particular San Francisco, was shocked; today, there are still memorial services every year for the city's lost sons and daughters.

Destroy Every Closet

City politician **Harvey Milk** was well-loved in San Francisco during his life, but after his assassination, many people have been inspired to live up to his eerily prescient command: "If a bullet should enter my brain, let that bullet destroy every closet door in the country." He recorded this statement on a tape that was to be played only if he was killed.

Milk moved to San Francisco in 1972 and opened a camera shop in the Castro. A natural leader, he became known as the Mayor of Castro Street, and was elected to the board of city supervisors in 1977, the first openly gay elected official of any large city in the US.

Harvey Milk had a friend in Mayor **George Moscone** (see photo). The two progressive politicians often verbally sparred with Supervisor **Dan White**, a former police officer who was the only dissenting vote for the 1978 gay rights ordinance that made it illegal to fire anyone in the city of San Francisco on the basis of their sexual orientation. After the ordinance passed, the anti-gay hate mail and death threats poured in, which some think prompted Milk to record his famous words, although others say he made the recording a full year before his death.

The pro-business White abruptly quit his post on the board of city supervisors on November 10; he was in financial trouble, and had taken a lot of heat for his views in liberal San Francisco. On November 27, White slipped into City Hall with a loaded revolver, lured Moscone into a private room, and killed him. He did the same to Milk. Future mayor **Dianne Feinstein**, president of the board of supervisors at the time, was the one who discovered Milk's body.

"People wept openly in the streets. Strangers hugged each other, trying to offer comfort, but there was no comfort," says Donald Eckert, who lived in the Castro at the time with his partner and was a friend and neighbor of Milk. "Clutching a special edition of the paper, Frankie and I went back to Henry Street. There was a police car parked in front of Harvey's house down the block. Police presence remained on our street until after the funerals."

That night there was a spontaneous 50,000-person candlelit march from the Castro to City Hall to mourn the two men. "This march was one of the most awesome events in my life. Five percent of the population of the entire city was present on a moment's notice and in spite of the mass of humanity, the silence was deafening," says Eckert, who added that Joan Baez was there in person and the crowd joined her when she sang *Amazing Grace*.

Dan White (see photo) was caught within hours, and eventually received a light sentence by claiming he was suffering from severe depression and not entirely responsible for his actions. His lawyers said that the health nut's excessive consumption of Twinkies proved the depth of his angst, which has come to be known as the **Twinkie Defense**, even though it's often mischaracterized as a claim that the cream-filled snack cakes made White go insane.

Three weeks in the fall of 1978 rocked the city:

November 18:
In Jonestown, Guyana, **Jim Jones** leads his San Francisco-based People's Temple in a mass murder-suicide; 913 die, including 276 children.

November 19:
The first US **Take Back the Night** march, by women protesting violence against women, occurs in San Francisco.

Photo: Donald Eckert

November 27:

Mayor **George Moscone** and openly gay city supervisor **Harvey Milk** are assassinated by former supervisor **Dan White**.

December 4:

Dianne Feinstein becomes San Francisco's first woman mayor. She served for the next ten years and eventually became a US Senator.

The **White Night Riots**, sometimes referred to as the **Second Gay Riots** (in homage to the famous 1969 **Stonewall Riots** in New York), broke out the night of May 21, 1979, after Dan White received only a five- to seven-year sentence for killing Harvey Milk and George Moscone. White had slipped into City Hall with a large amount of ammunition and shot both men again at close range after they lay dying or dead, clear evidence for most people that the murders were premeditated.

An angry crowd of people upset by the sentence gathered in the Castro and eventually moved to City Hall. There, the crowd turned violent and started vandalizing the building. "City Hall was trashed," says Donald Eckert, an eyewitness to the riots. "Several hundred police in riot gear stood in formation at the corner, watching the activity, but they were not allowed to respond, a wise decision on the part of the administration. For some reason, they had parked police cars at the other end of the block. No one really wanted to destroy City Hall. They just wanted to make a statement. However, when the activists went after the cars, cheers of approval came from the crowd."

All told, 12 cars went up in flames and more than 150 people were arrested. The police, humiliated by the fierce resistance they met at City Hall, showed up in the Castro hours later to exact revenge. They were unsuccessful at dispersing the crowd that had regrouped after the City Hall riots, and found that more people were joining the resistance, so the police trashed a Castro institution known as the **Elephant Walk**. It's now **Harvey's**, in honor of Harvey Milk (*500 Castro St., 415-431-4278*); legend has it that Mayor **Dianne Feinstein** had lunch at the Elephant Walk the next day to show her support of the gay community.

Dan White wound up serving five years in prison. On January 6, 1984, the day of his release, there were demonstrations and gatherings in the Castro, and members and friends of the gay community were told to stay home from work that day in a show of solidarity.

After spending some time in Los Angeles, White eventually moved back to San Francisco, even though Mayor Feinstein had asked him never to set foot in San Francisco again. He admitted to a close friend that there were others he was planning on killing that day – proving his murder was premeditated and explaining the amount of ammunition he was carrying – including future mayor **Willie Brown**. In October 1985, Dan White committed suicide; he went into a garage, started his car, and sat there until the carbon monoxide fumes ended his ignoble life.

The Revolution was Televised

The Symbionese Liberation Army (SLA) was an armed leftist group that wanted to create the "Symbionese Nation" – a place where all races enjoyed a mutually beneficial, symbiotic relationship. The group started their radical reign of terror by assassinating a school district official in Oakland in November 1973. When one of the SLA members involved was sent to prison, the group responded by kidnapping **Patty Hearst**, a young newspaper heiress, from her Berkeley apartment. They planned to do a prisoner swap, but in a surprising development, the prisoner became a member of the gang.

In Memory of Harvey Milk

The city's convention center is named for George Moscone, but the list of institutions named for Harvey Milk is long:

Eureka Valley-Harvey Milk Memorial Branch Library.

Harvey Milk Recreational Arts Center has a photography dark room for city residents.

Harvey Milk Civil Rights Academy, an alternative public school in the heart of the Castro.

Just a little more than two months after her February 1974 kidnapping, Hearst was spotted on a video camera at the **Hibernia Bank**, now a video rental store, on the corner of 22nd Avenue and Noriega Street in San Francisco. The image of the kidnapped heiress toting a machine gun during a bank robbery was shown by media outlets around the world; she had changed her name to **Tania** and called her family "capitalist pigs."

The SLA demanded that the wealthy Hearst family distribute $2 million worth of food and clothing to the poor people of the Bay Area, which they did. The police finally caught up to Hearst at Precita and Morse Streets in San Francisco in September 1975. Saying she had been brainwashed by her captors and was forced to help them rob the bank, Hearst started the uniquely American practice of wearing clothing that literally made a statement – during her trial, she wore a "Pardon Me" T-shirt. The back of it read, "Being kidnapped is always having to say you're sorry."

Hearst was convicted and served almost three years before President **Jimmy Carter** commuted her sentence. More than 20 years later, President **Bill Clinton** pardoned her on his last day in office – which, two decades after the fact, seemed a strange ending to a strange saga. Perhaps appropriately, that cinematic master of strangeness, director **John Waters**, has cast Hearst in a number of his films.

Things didn't end quite so well for a number of the less well-connected members of the SLA. In May 1974, hundreds of police descended on a house the SLA commandeered the night before in Los Angeles; a two-hour shootout ensued and ended when the house burst into flames, Waco-style. Six SLA members were dead, including the group's leader. Hearst apparently watched the whole thing live on television.

From 1999 to 2002, police scooped up a number of former SLA members who were wanted on outstanding charges. Most of them had been living as parents and spouses with jobs a little less radical than in their SLA days.

Harvey Milk High School, a place for LGBT students in New York City.

Harvey Milk Institute focuses on queer arts, culture and education.

The Harvey Milk Lesbian, Gay, Bisexual, Transgender Democratic Club.

Harvey Milk Plaza, outside of the Castro Street Muni station.

The **Black Panther Party** was founded in Oakland in 1966 by **Bobby Seale** and **Huey Newton** and was blamed for many of the race riots and disturbances that wreaked havoc in the US through the late '60s and '70s, although larger social forces, as well as FBI instigators, are more likely the real culprits.

As a matter of fact, although the Black Panthers did spread the notion of "Black Power," they didn't do so to the exclusion of other races, and actually existed in harmony with like-minded groups regardless of race. Their principal claim was that black people were being unfairly used and abused by the white powers that be, as exemplified by the Vietnam War, when the poor and the black were shipped off in droves and many came home in boxes.

The Black Panthers drew the ire of Oakland police by following them around the city armed with guns and copies of the law. There was nothing the police could do, because the firearms were registered and in plain sight – legal according to California law at the time. When the Panthers' activities inspired politicians to change the laws, members of the group burst into the California State Capitol Building in Sacramento with rifles slung over their shoulders. As they were being herded out, one of them told a reporter, "We're the Black Panthers. We're black people with guns. What about it?"

The Panthers were most famous for promoting the cause of black militancy that many in the black community, especially angry young men, could relate to better than the message of pacifism espoused by **Dr. Martin Luther King, Jr**. It also helped that the Panthers believed in food *and* bombs – they offered free breakfasts to children, undertook a huge sickle-cell anemia testing initiative, and gave free drug and alcohol counseling to whoever wanted it.

Official Black Panther Party 10-Point Plan

• We want freedom. We want power to determine the destiny of our Black Community.

• We want full employment for our people.

• We want an end to the robbery by the white man of our Black Community.

• We want decent housing, fit for shelter of human beings.

• We want education for our people that exposes the true nature of this decadent American society. We want education that teaches us our true history and our role in the present-day society.

• We want all black men to be exempt from military service.

- We want an immediate end to police brutality and murder of black people.

- We want freedom for all black men held in federal, state, county, and city prisons and jails.

- We want all black people when brought to trial to be tried in court by a jury of their peer group or people from their black communities, as defined by the Constitution of the United States.

- We want land, bread, housing, education, clothing, justice, and peace.

Newton, harassed by Oakland police for years, shot and killed an officer in September 1968; he said it was in self-defense, but was convicted and sentenced to 15 years. However, after appeals, the state eventually dropped its case and let Newton go. Unfortunately, Newton became afflicted with the drug and alcohol problems that the Black Panthers were trying to eradicate in Oakland.

As a matter of fact, some say that Newton was trying to use the might of the Panthers to take over the drug trade in Oakland. He was accused of murdering a 17-year-old prostitute in 1974. The sad fact is, after spending years as a target for angry and scared white police officers, Newton was killed in August 1989 in a drug deal that went bad in Oakland.

Seale, who was one of the Chicago Eight and was charged with inciting the riots at the infamous 1968 Democratic National Convention, is one of the few original Panthers who was neither killed in a police shootout nor is in jail. He remains a community activist, and has joked on camera about the Mao's Little Red Books that the Panthers were famous for selling to Berkeley students. Seale says that he and other Panthers would go into San Francisco's Chinatown and buy the books for $1, which they'd then sell to naïve Berkeley students, star-struck by the famous revolutionaries, for three times the price. Seale has said that many Panthers didn't even read the book, but found that peddling it was easy money.

The Winter of 2004 saw thousands of gay and lesbian couples married at City Hall, thanks to the surprisingly progressive Mayor **Gavin Newsom** (see photo). Although he had been maligned as a limousine liberal in the 2003 mayoral election (also popular was Green Party candidate Matt Gonzalez, someone who lives in an apartment and deals with many of the same issues as normal San Franciscans), Newsom electrified San Francisco when he declared that City Hall would start issuing marriage certificates for same-sex couples, in defiance of both state and federal law.

Although some in Newsom's own party said that elevating gay marriage to the national stage would give ammunition to Bush supporters to win a second term in the White House, most agreed that it was the right thing to do, consequences be damned. Besides, as many supporters pointed out, there's never a good time to crusade for civil rights in the eyes of the status quo.

Almost 4,000 same-sex couples were married (including **Rosie O'Donnell** and her partner **Kelli Carpenter**, see photo), with many city employees deputized to perform marriages nearly around the clock. A huge line snaked around City Hall. People of all orientations were just beside themselves. George W. Bush was in the White House and the Iraq war was becoming the mess that many predicted it would be; locals were starved for some good news, and the Winter of Love put San Francisco back on the map as the peninsula that could change the world.

A GOOD LAWYER IS HARD TO FIND

Angela Davis, a well-known **Black Power** advocate and **Black Panther** associate, and **Patty Hearst**, hostage turned freedom fighter, have a man in common. **Terrence Hallinan**, prosecutor of Fajita Gate (see page 237), was the lawyer for both Hearst and Davis. Davis was up on charges for supposedly taking part in an attempted jail break in Marin County that resulted in a murder. A gun registered in her name was used, but she was tried and acquitted. Davis has lived on and off in the Bay Area, and is still an activist, writer, and teacher; she also ran for vice president of the United States on the Communist Party ticket.

1865:

In April, police used the telegraph system for the first time under emergency conditions to organize a response to riots that followed the news of the assassination of President Abraham Lincoln.

1934:

On May 9, striking maritime workers rioted after an alliance of their employers tried to break the strike that effectively shut down shipping on the West Coast. On July 5, zealous police officers killed two strikers, Nick Bordoise and Howard Sperry. More than 100 people were injured in what came to be known as the **Battle of Rincon Hill**. To this day, tourists at Fisherman's Wharf are often surprised by the chalk outline of two bodies on a sidewalk – a remembrance in front of the **Longshoreman's Memorial Building** (400 North Point St., 415-776-8100).

But on March 11, 2004, nearly a month to the day that the first same-sex wedding certificate was issued in San Francisco, the California Supreme Court ruled that the 3,955 same-sex marriage licenses were invalid. Although it was a profoundly disappointing decision, many couples, and more than a few gay rights advocates, said that the Winter of Love showed the world images of "normal" people who only wanted to legally cement their long-standing partnerships.

The Rumor Mill

The City by the Bay has its share of urban rumors and notorious accusations. Some of the rumors have turned out to be local riffs on popular urban myths, while others were just the work of con artists.

Although the location varies, legend has it that **Charlie Chaplin** entered a Chaplin look-alike contest in an old San Francisco theater. He lost, and apparently he bitterly complained that none of the contestants did his trademark walk correctly.

In 1963, a man returned to his parked car to find it severely damaged, with a note on it that read: "I hit your car, and because a large crowd is starting to gather around me I have to write this note to appear I'm giving you my insurance details, which as you can see, I haven't done." This urban myth has popped up all over the US ever since *San Francisco Chronicle* columnist **Herb Caen** reported an incident like this that supposedly happened to a friend of his.

Who or what is **Monkey Knife Fight**? If Koko the gorilla (who lives in the Bay Area) can paint, isn't it conceivable that monkeys could create graffiti? Probably one of the city's most intriguing unsolved mysteries is who (or what) is behind the popular stenciled graffiti that has been spotted all over town that simply reads: "Monkey Knife Fight." It is so popular that it spawned rhymed imitators like "Junky Wife Bite." Yes, there's a number of bands with the name and a beer from Pennsylvania named after cutlery-wielding simians, but even the bravest reporters have not gotten to the bottom of this barrel of brawling monkeys.

In a public relations nightmare for **Wendy's**, in 2005 a woman in San Jose claimed to have found a finger in her bowl of chili from the fast-food chain. Bay area

Wendy's restaurants saw business decline dramatically until the woman, **Anna Ayala**, who it was discovered had a fondness for suing big companies, was arrested by police for planting the finger. Her husband apparently got the digit from a coworker who had had an accident at work – the body part was apparently going to be used to make money to settle a gambling debt.

Flight 93

On September 11, 2001, 37 passengers, many of them residents of the Bay Area, were on United Flight 93 from Newark, NJ, to San Francisco. When four men who had been sitting in first class announced that they had a bomb and were taking control of the plane, worried passengers who made cell phone calls to relatives were told that two planes had been crashed into New York City's Twin Towers.

1966:
The **Hunter's Point Riot** broke out on September 27 when a white officer shot and killed a 16-year-old black youth as he was fleeing the scene of a car theft.

1992:
San Francisco Mayor **Frank Jordan** declared a state of emergency when looters descended on downtown San Francisco on April 30 after the not guilty verdict for the Los Angeles police officers who beat **Rodney King**. More than 100 businesses were damaged or looted and more than 1,000 people arrested. Police Chief **Richard Hongisto** was fired after he ordered his officers to clear the racks of 2,000 copies of an issue of the gay newspaper *Bay Times*, which criticized his tactics against King demonstrators and published a cartoon of him playing with his night stick in a suggestive manner.

According to the *9/11 Commission Report,* some passengers told their loved ones via cell phone that they would try to overpower the hijackers, and apparently, almost everyone on board did what they could – one flight attendant even boiled water to throw on them.

At least three of the men who said they were going to fight had deep connections to the Bay Area: **Todd Beamer** was a New Jersey resident who went to high school in the Bay Area city of Los Gatos; **Mark Bingham** (see photo) owned a public relations company in San Francisco, played on a gay rugby team, and was also a Los Gatos alum; and **Tom Burnett** was an executive at a local medical device company.

Beamer's famous last words, "Let's roll," was in fact more likely "roll it," referring to the food cart that investigators think the men tried to use to batter the cockpit door open to get to the terrorists. They apparently weren't successful at getting the door open, but the terrorists, scared that the passengers would regain control, crashed the plane in rural southwest Pennsylvania.

Eyewitnesses say the impact created a long, shallow crater, and that debris was strewn over three acres. No one survived, but everyone agrees that if it had not been for the bravery of the passengers, many more would have died if the plane had reached its diverted destination of Washington, D.C.

Mark Bingham has become a new icon for the gay community – six feet, four inches tall and brave to a fault. Bingham's longtime partner has said that Bingham twice protected him from muggings, one at gunpoint.

The United Airlines Newark-to-San Francisco route has been renumbered and is now known as Flight 81.

2003:

The **Oakland Raiders'** Super Bowl loss resulted in rioting in downtown Oakland on the night of January 26. The rioters raged for five hours, dispersing when police showed up only to regroup elsewhere. The riots encompassed nearly 50 city blocks – 12 cars were destroyed and a number of businesses looted.

2003:

Protesters shut down sections of the Financial District on March 20, the day the first bombs started falling on **Baghdad**. Occasionally the protestors turned violent, and more than 1,000 people were arrested. The events of that day were the most serious, but numerous anti-George W. Bush, anti-war protests continued throughout 2003.

The worst mass killing San Francisco has ever witnessed occurred on July 1, 1993. In just 15 minutes, **Gian Luigi Ferri** – who had an investment recently go sour and blamed bad legal advice he'd gotten from the law firm of Pettit & Martin years earlier – killed eight people and wounded six others with two semi-automatic weapons and a pistol at the firm's offices at 101 California Street (see photo). The killer traversed several different floors of the 48-storey building during his rampage, increasing the confusion and mayhem.

One of the victims, **John Scully**, saved his wife's life by shielding her with his body; he was shot six times, and ultimately died. A secretary for another law firm,

EMPEROR NORTON'S DECREES

Emperor Norton (see page 254) declares himself emperor and gives his decree to a newspaper editor to publish, September 1859:
At the peremptory request of a large majority of the citizens of these United States, I, Joshua Norton, formerly of Algoa Bay, Cape of Good Hope, and now for the past nine years and ten months of San Francisco, California, declare and proclaim myself Emperor of these US, and in virtue of the authority thereby in me vested, do hereby order and direct the representatives of the different States of the Union to assemble in the Musical Hall of this city on the 1st day of February next,

Deborah Fogel, was shot, and lay unassisted for an hour before she bled to death – resulting in public outrage that the police were not able to secure the scene and safely get paramedics to her in time. The killer shot himself in a stairwell.

The shootings instigated many changes in San Francisco and helped pass a nationwide ban on the manufacture and sale of assault weapons (which expired in 2004). **Dianne Feinstein**, who has seen more than her share of gun-related violence in San Francisco, has been a strong proponent of the federal ban and is one of the politicians who helped push for the 1994 federal law.

101 California, as locals refer to the massacre, changed the way police train for situations in high-rise buildings as well as security procedures at many offices in the Financial District. The state of California has some of the strictest gun laws in the country, and while federal laws have lapsed, local politicians have made sure that purchasing a gun here is as difficult as possible in the context of much of America's pro-gun attitudes.

These laws didn't stop **Sean Penn**, bad-boy of the silver screen, from packing heat. He calls the Bay Area home and in April 2003 discovered that his car had been stolen in broad daylight while he lunched at a Berkeley restaurant. Police eventually recovered his 1987 Buick, but the two handguns Penn kept in the car were gone for good. Penn has a permit to carry a concealed weapon, so no charges were filed – though eyebrows were raised at his choice of car. Penn has since turned his attention towards writing about other people with guns – he recently filed dispatches from Iraq for the *San Francisco Chronicle*.

then and there to make such alterations in the existing laws of the Union as may ameliorate the evils under which the country is laboring, and thereby cause confidence to exist, both at home and abroad, in our stability and integrity.

Proper name of City by the Bay, 1859:
Whoever after due and proper warning shall be heard to utter the abominable word "Frisco," which has no linguistic or other warrant, shall be deemed guilty of a High Misdemeanor, and shall pay into the Imperial Treasury as penalty the sum of twenty-five dollars.

The King of Characters

Locals hate it when people call the city "Frisco," a resentment that was started by self-proclaimed **Emperor Norton**, a man who in the 1800s printed his own money and wrote his own laws, one of which made it a crime to call the city anything other than its full name. Like the best of the San Francisco characters, residents adopted him as their own.

Born Joshua Abraham Norton in England, he came to San Francisco at the height of the Gold Rush from South Africa, where he lived with his well-to-do parents. He had not yet declared himself an emperor, though as one of the many men who were making a fortune in San Francisco at that time, he was rich enough to lead a royal existence. Although it's said he had accumulated $250,000 by 1853, some bad investments led to bankruptcy in 1857. He disappeared for a while, but returned thinking he was royalty.

Norton is proof that if you act like something is a fact for long enough, people will start to play along. His uniform was donated by the army post at what's now Presidio Park. Bars and hotels accepted his self-printed money as legal tender. And after an incident where a police officer tried to lock Norton up for being crazy, the resulting public outrage prompted the department to instruct its officers to salute the emperor whenever they saw him. The city also supposedly provided him free room and board for life to make up for the insult.

His legend continued to flourish. Restaurants he frequented advertised that he was a regular guest to attract more business, and

plays and operas reserved seats for both Norton and his two dogs, Bummer and Lazarus. When one of the dogs died, Mark Twain wrote his obituary: "Full of years, and

More Local Color

Sam Brannan

Brannan was a Mormon entrepreneur who liked his drink and was a proponent of free love before the phrase existed. He convinced 230 Mormons to come with him from the East Coast; the group arrived here in 1846 (when the town was still called Yerba Buena, though it was renamed to San Francisco the next year) and tripled the population of the sleepy town. Brannan and his followers laid down the infrastructure — by constructing buildings and opening stores — that put the Gold Rush in motion. According to legend, after visiting a gold mine near Sacramento, he returned to San Francisco, bought honor, and disease, and fleas."

Norton inspected his empire every morning and by all accounts was a charming, friendly man and a good listener with a good heart. On one occasion, he used his standing to step in front of a group of anti-Chinese demonstrators who were about to take out their anger on a group of Chinese immigrants. Norton also made it a point of attending different religious services every week so that it didn't seem like he favored any part of his constituency. He would ask people about any problems in their neighborhood and relay citizen concerns to newspapers and public officials. He was also called on to settle disputes between neighbors, as his fairness was legendary.

Norton, although maybe a little out of joint by some standards, was ahead of his time in many ways. One of his decrees was to build a bridge between Oakland and San Francisco (there is now some talk of renaming the **Bay Bridge** the Emperor Norton Bridge). He also decreed that scientists spend time researching how to build machines that fly, called for a "universal religion" that he hoped would end religious wars, and tried to create what we'd now call the United Nations, which started in San Francisco in 1945.

Norton sent advice to leaders around the world. **King Kamehameha** of what are now the Sandwich Islands liked the Emperor's missives so much that it's said he refused to deal with the US government later in his life and only recognized Norton's empire. Norton even corresponded with England's **Queen Victoria**, and rumors were rampant that he was going to marry her some day and that he was actually sitting on a monumental fortune.

Norton died on January 8, 1880, on the corner of California and Grant Streets. The *San Francisco Chronicle* proclaimed in a headline banner: "Le Roi Est Mort," the king is dead. Some 30,000 San Franciscans paid their final respects. The day after his funeral there was a total solar eclipse, and people were convinced it was a sign of Norton's passing. Upon cleaning out his room, it was discovered that other than a big collection of hats, he didn't own much at all and was in fact penniless. Norton, "Emperor of the United States and Protector of Mexico," is today buried in Colma, south of San Francisco.

every shovel he could find, and ran through the streets shouting that there was gold for the taking in the nearby hills; he then resold the shovels at outrageous prices that would-be miners were eager to pay.

Brannan was excommunicated because he kept his followers' tithes for himself and his projects. When representatives from the Mormon Church in Utah asked for the money that they thought should really belong to headquarters, Brannan infamously said, "You go back and tell Brigham Young that I'll give up the Lord's money when he sends me a receipt signed by the Lord."

At the height of the dot-com boom, three young entrepreneurs in San Francisco decided to go against the grain of celebrity culture and create trading cards that profiled normal people. A big hit in a place where people pride themselves on expecting some substance with their style, **PeopleCards** "democratized celebrity," says the company's cofounder, **Brant Herman**.

"I had always been a trading card fan, but one day I heard something about Steve Martin getting in a fender-bender on the radio news," Herman told us. "That set me off, and I thought it would be just as relevant and interesting, if not more so, to hear about Joe Schmo's fender-bender. Then I looked for mediums that might be good for revealing that, and trading cards struck me as a medium that is only cardboard, but when the faces of famous people are on them, they become extremely valuable."

Along with **Todd Herman** and **Brian Mullin**, Herman propelled PeopleCards to the national stage with a number of media interviews. Soon, though, the combination of people not "getting it," the economic downturn, and events of 9/11 shut down the homage to everyman. "In San Francisco, people seemed to get it more," Herman said. "Across the country, however, many people simply furrowed their brow and wondered why normal people would be important."

Frank Chu

Chu is a fixture downtown with his ever-changing picket signs — some of which call for the impeachment of Clinton. The modern heir to Emperor Norton, Chu has a bar named after him where he drinks and eats for free, the **12 Galaxies** *(2565 Mission St . 415-970-9777, 12galaxies.com)*, and can often be seen at social gatherings and launch parties around town. He's without a doubt San Francisco's most recognizable local celebrity.

That Double Vision

No, the medicinal marijuana in the air isn't making you see double. Known to frequent the Union Square shopping area are two grey foxes who dress exactly the same – Vivian and Marion Brown, commonly referred to as the **Brown Twins**. They've appeared in a number of TV commercials, and win "most identical" at twin conventions all the time.

Another showbiz pair that moved to the Bay Area are the **Borden Twins**, Rosalyn "Roz" and Marilyn Borden. They used to have a Bay cruise tour company where the sisters – who appeared on TV shows including *I Love Lucy* (they played Teensy and Weensy), *Maude*, and *Rhoda* – performed for the passengers. Rosalyn passed away in 2003.

In 1996, **Sean** and **Sam Manuel** were both drafted by the San Francisco 49ers football team. When Sam was eventually dropped by the team, Sean quit his lucrative contract, saying he wouldn't play for the team if his brother wasn't with him, surprising many. "Money doesn't mean that much," Sean was quoted as saying.

Marijuana Man

Marijuana Man can be seen on the commute between downtown and the Haight. He usually has a long train of dried marijuana leaves draped over his head, and also wears pro-pot T-shirts.

Pink Man

This man who regularly wears a pink unitard is often spotted on his unicycle downtown and in nearby neighborhoods. We've also seen him at a tradeshow in San Jose, working the floor in his usual get-up.

Living

Photo: Helene Goupil

Although the dot-com boom was a prosperous period for San Francisco residents, most locals are secretly happy it's over. With people working 20 hours a day, housing prices and the cost-of-living went sky high and stress levels were beyond measure. Today, life in San Francisco is much more relaxed, and as soon as you walk outside of the busy Financial District, it's possible you could forget you're in a big city. But according to the 2000 US Census, San Francisco is the nation's fifth most populated metropolitan area with a large international community – 37 percent of the population were born in a foreign country.

Photo: FredAlert

Sisters Are Doing It for Themselves

Once upon a time, in 1976, three male performers in Iowa were staging their version of *The Sound of Music*. To help out, local Catholic nuns lent them some old habits for use in the play.

In 1979, the men in habits arrived in San Francisco. They first got together to perform cheers at local games. These "shows" made the group popular and they were frequently asked to make appearances at parties and fundraisers. Later named the **Sisters of Perpetual Indulgence**, the performers took advantage of their popularity to host fundraisers for local charities. Today, there are approximately 30 members, including Sister Anal Receptive, Sister Lily White Superior Posterior, and Sister Lolita Me Into Temptation. The Sisters are a partying bunch, but they are also very active in raising funds for AIDS organizations and other local non-profits. Orders have since formed in major cities worldwide.

thesisters.org

Quake City

The San Andreas Fault was named in 1895 by geologist A.C. Lawson after San Andreas Lake, about 20 miles south of San Francisco. The last big earthquake hit the Bay Area in 1989; experts say that another major one could hit by 2030. Although most people are aware of this prediction, most remain unprepared. Here's what to do in case it happens:

• If you are indoors, stay inside. Drop, cover, and hold on. Stay away from windows and doors.

• If you are outdoors, stay away from buildings, trees, and power lines. Drop to the ground until the shaking stops.

• If you're in a car, slow down, and drive to a place away from buildings, trees, and power lines. Turn on emergency flashers and stop. Do not stop on overpasses, underpasses, or bridges.

festivals and fairs

A list of fun, crazy, even naughty happenings around town.

Castro Street Fair
    An October fair where people enjoy outdoor concerts, arts and crafts, food, and lots of beer; the festival is a fundraiser for Castro charities. *castrostreetfair.org*

Photo: FredAlert

Folsom Street Fair
    Anything goes at the largest leather, alternative, and fetish street fair in the world. Count on public spankings, lots of nudity, and gag masks. All proceeds raised are directly returned to San Francisco charities; in 2004, $265,000 was donated. This street fair happens the last weekend in September. *folsomstreetfair.com*

Facts of (San Francisco) Life

Interesting figures culled from the 2000 US Census on San Francisco city and County, with additional estimates:

2000 census population:
776,733

Male: 50.8 percent
Female: 49.2 percent

White: 49.7 percent
Asian: 30.8 percent
Hispanic/Latino: 14.1 percent
Black: 7.8 percent
American Indian and Alaska Native: 0.4 percent
Other races: 6.5 percent
Two or more races: 4.3 percent

Age: 18 to 64: 71.8 percent
Age: 65 and over: 13.7 percent
Median age: 36.5

How Weird Street Faire

Thousands of people in costumes head to Howard and 12th Streets to dance the day away at America's longest running electronic music street festival; the event is a fundraiser for the World Peace Through Technology Organization.

howweird.org

Lazy Bear Weekend

A mid-July celebration and fundraiser for many charities, this event is for bears, bear lovers, and big partiers.

lazybearweekend.com

Lesbians in Russian River

Women-only parties are organized in May and September.

russianriverwomensweekeends.com

North Beach Festival

65,000 people attend this festival, one of the oldest arts and crafts fairs in the nation. The event includes a juried arts and crafts show, Italian street chalk art, music, a beer garden, an animal blessing, and a poetry stage.

sfnorthbeach.org

Northern California Cherry Blossom Festival

Annual spring event that takes place in Japantown; it includes tea ceremonies, martial arts, drumming, traditional dance, and a parade.

nccbf.org

Up Your Alley

This street event boasts even more leather and leashes than the Folsom Street Fair. It's organized by the Folsom Street Fair people and takes place the last weekend of July on Dore Alley, between Folsom and Howard Streets, and the adjoining block of Folsom Street between 9th and 10th Streets.

folsomstreetfair.com/alley

Land area:
47 sq. mi. (122 sq. km)

Altitude:
Highest, 925 ft.; lowest, sea level

Avg. daily temperature:
Jan., 51.1° F; July, 59.1° F

Churches:
540 (all denominations)

City-owned parks and squares: 200+

Radio stations: 29

Television stations: 10

Civilian labor force: 448,432

Unemployed: 3.0 percent

Per capita personal income:
$34,556

While most major cities devote a day each year to Gay Pride celebrations, San Francisco, often called "Gay by the Bay," celebrates pride most days of the year. The majority of events are held in June, which is officially Gay Pride Month (sfpride.org).

Kicking off the festivities is **Gay Day at Paramount's Great America** theme park every Memorial Day weekend (*4699 Great America Pky., Santa Clara, 418-988-1776, pgathrills.com*), followed by the **San Francisco International LGBT Film Festival** (*415-703-8650, frameline.org/festival/29th*), and the **Transgender Community Awards**, held at the **San Francisco LGBT Community Center** (*1800 Market St., 415-865-5555, sfcenter.org*). The day before the big **Pride Parade** – held the last Sunday in June each year – along Market Street are the **Dyke March** (*415-241-8882, dykemarch.org/SFO*) and **Pink Saturday**, a drunken fest in the Castro benefiting charities.

For more information, check out *Pride* magazine (*pridemagazine.com*), available in most independent bookstores starting late May.

pride throughout the year

Of course, San Francisco being what it is, there are numerous gay and lesbian events throughout the year, not just during Pride Month in June.

AIDS Candlelight Vigil

The vigil, now the largest grassroots AIDS event in the world, started here in 1983 when the Castro was starting to lose many residents to the AIDS virus. The march was organized to remember those who had passed away, support those who were living, and educate the public. It takes place each year on the third Sunday of May.
aidscandlelightvigil.org

Change(s) in the Weather

With several microclimates in the area, it's recommended that you keep a sweater in your bag at all times because temperatures can vary greatly depending on what neighborhood you're in.

May and September generally bring sunny days, and often there are summer-like temperatures for about a week every March; the problem is, you never know which week it will be. The rest of the time, be wary of what looks like a nice day because low temperatures could be right around the corner.

Geezer's Ball

An annual ball where mature Bay Area gay and bisexual men celebrate "aging well and living well."

Gus Presents

Local clubs host monthly gay dance parties with titles such as the "Underworld Drop Your Pants And Dance," "Sanctuary," "Giant T-Dance," and the popular "Colossus" of Pride Weekend.
guspresents.com

Harvey Milk/George Moscone Memorial

November 27 marks the day the first openly gay supervisor, Milk, and Mayor Moscone were killed at City Hall by ex-supervisor Dan White in 1978. A candlelight march is organized every year on the anniversary of their deaths.

National Queer Arts Festival

This festival takes place in June and includes performances and visual arts exhibitions by gay artists; it's organized by the Queer Cultural Center and the San Francisco LGBT Community Center.
415-864-4124, queerculturalcenter.org

Sundance Stompede

An annual country-western dance weekend for the LGBT community and its friends; the festivities include a welcome dance, a hoedown, and the Stompede Ball.
stompede.com

The Academy of Friends

What started as a private Oscar Night party in 1980 is now the biggest Oscar Night party outside Hollywood. The event raises funds for Bay Area HIV/AIDS service organizations.
415-995-9890, academyoffriends.org

yoga, *au naturel*

Photo: Judith Greenburg

San Francisco is known for its liberal ways, so it may not be a surprise to some that in September 2004, city prosecutors decided that it wasn't illegal to practice yoga naked in public spaces. George Monty Davis, also known in the Fisherman's Wharf area as "the naked yoga guy," had been charged with indecent exposure. He was known for regularly dropping his pants, shirt, and underwear at the Wharf and comfortably striking naked yoga poses in public. According to Debbie Mesloh, a spokeswoman for the district attorney's office, "Simply being naked on the street is not a crime in San Francisco.... To bring a case, a person would have to exhibit lewd behavior, block traffic or impede pedestrians on a sidewalk, something along those lines."

As a result of the hoopla, yoga studios started offering naked yoga lessons such as the Sunday class at the **One Taste Urban Retreat Center** *(1074 Folsom St. at 7th St., 415-503-1100, onetastesf.com)*. It takes place indoors – perhaps a good way for shy students to work up the courage to join naked Davis in his outdoor stretches.

For a it's-so-hot-in-here-I-wish-I-were-naked yoga experience, try Bikram Yoga at **Funky Door Yoga** *(186 Second St., 415-957-1088; 1749 Waller St., 415-668-2227; 1336 Polk St., 415-673-8659; 2567 Shattuck Ave., 510-204-9642, funkydooryoga.com)* or at **Mission Yoga** *(2390 Mission St., 415-401-9642, missionyoga.com)*. Created by Bikram Choudhury, a yoga teacher from India, Bikram classes take place in a heated room where the average temperature is 100 degrees Fahrenheit.

IT'S FREE ... REALLY
The **Really Really Free Market** is a non-commercial event where communities get together to share and/or exchange skills and objects; some people get rid of things they no longer use, others find stuff to take home, and everyone walks away happy. The market takes place at Dolores Park the last Saturday of every month.
reallyreallyfreemarket.org

Photo: Rodolfo Arpia

CRIME AND PUNISHMENT

A recent survey shows that San Francisco was the ninth safest American city with a population of 500,000 people or more. Crime still happens here, of course, but looking at the *San Francisco Observer*'s daily Crime Log column — a summary of arrests in each neighborhood — will show you that San Franciscans are a pretty good bunch.

sfobserver.com

Stretch and bend to your heart's content at these studios:

A Body of Work
569 Ruger St., 415-561-3991, abodyofwork-sf.com

Bernal Yoga
461 Cortland Ave., 415-643-9007, bernalyoga.com

Greenpath Yoga Studio
2242 Lombard St., 415-775-7545, greenpathyoga.org

The Mindful Body
2876 California St., 415-931-2639, themindfulbody.com

Satori Yoga Studio
40 1st St., 415-618-0418, satoriyogastudio.com

Yoga Loft
321 Divisadero St., 415-626-5638, theloftsf.com

Yoga Tree
1234 Valencia St., 415-647-9707; 780 Stanyan St., 415-387-4707; 519 Hayes St., 415-626-9707; Yoga Flow Castro: 97 Collingwood St., 415-701-9642, yogatreesf.com

Today, the **San Francisco Zen Center** *(300 Page St., 415-863-3136, sfzc.com)* is a tranquil place where hundreds of residents, beginner to advanced, gather to meditate. However, things weren't always so Zen here.

The center was founded in 1962 by Shunryu Suzuki Roshi, author of *Zen Mind, Beginner's Mind* with the help of some of his first students – including one named **Richard Baker** (see photo). Baker succeeded Suzuki Roshi when he passed away in 1971, at which point things began to change at the Zen Center.

Baker found himself at the head of a booming business and some believe that the power got to his head. As the years went by, Baker started living a life that appeared at odds with the earthy lifestyle preached at the center – he drove a BMW, spent time with the likes of Jerry Brown and Linda Ronstadt, and cheated on his wife numerous times; he justified his actions by explaining that unenlightened people sometimes could not understand the actions of an enlightened person like himself.

The Zen Center chose to look the other way, but in 1983, Baker went too far. At the Peace Conference at Tassajara, a retreat center, Paul Hawken, Baker's then best friend, found out that his wife Anna and Baker were having an affair. Hawken, a generous contributor to the Zen Center, threatened a legal battle, and Baker was forced to resign.

The now-uncontroversial San Francisco Zen Center offers meditation classes and retreats. Guests may stay for one night or more in one of the Zen Center's rooms.

Holiday Hams

We're not a religious bunch here and we love to dress up, or down, so most traditional holidays are spent with friends or at one of these unusual events.

Chinese New Year

While the biggest Chinese New Year's parade outside of Asia takes place in San Francisco's Chinatown in February, teams run around looking for hidden messages and clues placed by Jayson Wechter of **San Francisco Treasure Hunts** *(sftreasurehunt.com)*. Every year, the Chinese New Year Treasure Hunt is organized to benefit the Hamilton Family Center, a homeless support organization.

Christmas (and more)

Each December since 1994, drunken Santas bring a naughty Christmas spirit to the city by bar-hopping until they drop *(santarchy.com)*. The **San Francisco Cacophony Society** *(sfcacophony.org)* is responsible for the debauchery; the group also organizes pranks and marches

throughout the year like the **Saint Stupid's Day Parade** (saintstupid.com/event.html) on April 1 where people dress like fools and parade up Columbus Street to Washington Square Park, and **Brides of March** (bridesofmarch.org, see photo), where men and women party it up while wearing old wedding gowns. You can also find the Cacophony group at the Easter **Bunny Jam** (bunnyjam.com), "a costumed Easter art hopening."

Easter

The Sisters of Perpetual Indulgence (thesisters.org) host annual **Easter Bonnet** and **Hunky Jesus** contests on Easter Sunday at Dolores Park. Participants line up in Jesus costumes in the hope of winning the title of Hunky Jesus of the year.

Photo: FredAlert

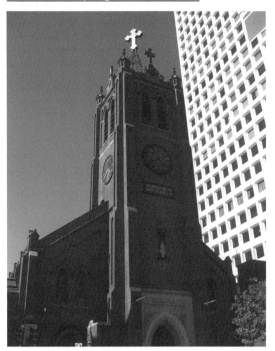

Note to jazz aficionados: Next time you walk down Divisadero Street, stop by Joe Pye, a clothing store (351 Divisadero St.) for a moment of silence. This building once housed the city's beloved **Saint John's African Orthodox Church**. Started by Bishop Franzo King in 1971, this church worshipped a saint you won't find in the Bible – the late musician **John Coltrane**. Nicknamed the **Church of John Coltrane**, a parish full of hipsters and music lovers would crowd the small locale every Sunday to watch jazz jam sessions. Sure, there was a sermon, but the show is what most people came for. The church unfortunately had to move out in 2001 when the landlord doubled their rent.

Still at its original location is **Old St. Mary's** (see photo) (660 California St., 415-288-3800, oldsaintmarys.org), the first Catholic cathedral to be built west of the Mississippi. The church was built using bricks shipped from New England via Cape Horn, and pre-cut granite blocks transported from China.

Faith in activism and separation of Church and State is what keeps the **San Francisco Atheists** (sfatheists.com), a chapter of the American Atheists, going. The group gets together with other Bay Area atheists and organizes protests, speeches, and events.

 Remember the days where you could make jokes about meeting your girlfriend online on one of those dating websites? Today's Bay Area singles don't find your tactless jokes funny, as many of them are members of one if not several online communities. And these communities aren't only for singles: well-read family types have been connecting on **The WELL** (well.com), an online community where members discuss current events and literature, among other subjects, since the 1980s. The first WELL computer and modem rack were located in Sausalito, just past the Golden Gate Bridge, near the classic rustic houseboat harbor.

Also based here is **Friendster** (friendster.com), a website started by Jonathan Abrams in 2002, that aims to "make the world a smaller place by bringing the power of social networking to every aspect of life, one friend at a time."

Tribe.net is a newcomer to the online community scene that is also widely used to post jobs, events, and the like.

Right outside of the city you'll find **LinkedIn** (linkedin.com) where you can bond online with people like Pierre Omidyar, founder of nearby eBay, one of the website's 40,000 members.

And if you need an online address book to keep up with everyone you meet on and offline, San Francisco-based **Ringo** (ringo.com) lets you log in for free.

SCARY SAN FRANCISCO

Even though any event in San Francisco usually means there will be people walking around naked or in costumes, nothing beats **Halloween**; thousands of people walk the Castro showing off their wild accoutrements. Two things you should remember: don't plan on meeting friends there, as the huge crowds make it impossible to find anyone; and if you want to drink, do it in bars or practice hiding bottles because the Castro street party is now a non-alcoholic event. *halloweensf.com*

The Castro is not the only way to do Halloween in the city (and not only on October 31). Here are two of the events happening around town:

The Haunted Haight Walking Tour reveals stories about the ghosts, witches, and macabre history of this famous San Francisco district. *Meets Fri. through Mon., 7 p.m., 1573 Haight St., 415-863-1416 hauntedhaight.com*

The Vampire Tour of San Francisco shows visitors the haunts of Nob Hill. Costumes are welcomed on Halloween night. *Meets Fri. and Sat., 8 p.m., on corner of California and Taylor Sts., 650-279-1840 sfvampiretour.com*

The Birth of Craigslist

Photo: Ann Ly, courtesy of craigslist

In 1995, **Craig Newmark**, a San Francisco computer programmer, started sending e-mails to friends to let them know about cool events happening in the Bay Area. Friends of friends asked to be added to the mailing list; soon, the number of people on the list became so large that Newmark had to upgrade to a list server. He then decided to create a website that was a kind of online classified section, where visitors could find event listings, jobs, stuff for sale, and apartments, which in the late 1990s were tough to find because of the dot-com boom. Today, **Craigslist** *(craigslist.com)* is the one word you need to remember should you decide to move to San Francisco (or anywhere for that matter; most major cities in North America have their own "craigslistings"). Craig Newmark still lives and works in San Francisco; you might find him hanging out at **Reverie Coffee Café** *(848 Cole St., 415-242-0200)*.

It's for My Eyes

Photo: Annette Birkenfeld

Getting high may not be a way of life for most people, but it definitely at least counts as a hobby for many Bay Area locals. And if you live in San Francisco, be ready for plentiful and high quality marijuana from Humboldt County as well as local dispensaries where one can obtain Ziploc bags of pot simply by showing your medical marijuana card. This is a very good thing or very bad thing, depending on your point of view.

Part of the reason so many pot clubs have opened here recently is because adjacent cities, including Oakland, now commonly called Oaksterdam, started limiting the number of pot dispensaries there. It's said that San Francisco now has more pot clubs than McDonald's — the official count is 43.

A recent *San Francisco Chronicle* article reported that in 2000, 754 city residents received medical marijuana cards the first year they were available. As of early 2005, 8,200 city residents had valid cards, and about 25 cards are issued each day. So how do you get one? You'll need a physician's statement that says why you need it and for how long (there is a two-year limit), proper ID, proof that you live in SF, and a $25 fee. Applications are available from your doctor's office or at the **San Francisco Department of Public Health** *(101 Grove St., 1st floor, bet. Polk and Van Ness, across the street from City Hall, dph.sf.ca.us/Services/ MCIDInfo.htm)*. With the card, the law states that "a qualified patient or primary caregiver may possess no more than eight ounces of dried marijuana per qualified patient. In addition, a qualified patient or primary caregiver may also maintain no more than six mature or 12 immature marijuana plants per qualified patient."

Some Odd Jobs

San Franciscans have found ways to avoid full-time work and still pay their bills. It's still possible to work odd jobs (like those listed below) and get by — at least while rents stay at post-boom levels.

Market Research

If you need some cash right away, market research study groups can help out. Participants get paid $50 to $200 for sessions up to two hours long. The market research company will usually provide snacks and sodas, and gives you a check at the end of the session. Although you can't participate every week, once you're in their database, some companies may contact you again. The "ETC." section of *craigslist.org* is a good place to check for upcoming sessions.

Peachy's Puffs and Tuffs

Peachy's Puffs was launched here by Peachy D'Ambrogio in the 1980s to bring back the cigarette and candy girl service that were the mainstays of old movie theaters and nightclubs.

If you've got what it takes to sell glow-in-the-dark toys, fake roses, and cigarettes, Peachy's Puffs is a good way to make a few bucks, especially if it's flexibility you're looking for. Once the company knows you, employees can take extended time off; when you're ready to work again, just give them a call. The company also provides merchandise, transportation, costumes, and accessories. You can expect to make $10 - $30 per hour on average. And guys: don't despair, you too can work here. Peachy's Tuffs, men dressed in zoot suits, are often hired for company parties.
peachyspuffs.com

The Dark Crystal

We're not trying to get all preachy here, but crystal meth is a huge problem in San Francisco, especially in the gay community. If you doubt it, just notice how the billboards and public service posters change once you step into the Castro.

A 2003 survey showed that 16 percent of 388 men used the drug the last time they had anal sex. A recent report showed that up to 40 percent of gay men in the city have tried meth, while a study conducted during 2002 at one high-risk clinic found that 25-30 percent of those with new HIV infections had used the drug in the previous six months.

Those looking for help can go to *tweaker.org* and *lifeormeth.org*; meetings are listed at *crystalmeth.org*

Got Health?

The **Haight-Ashbury Free Clinic** (*558 Clayton St., 415-487-5632, hafci.org*) was the first clinic in the United States to offer free healthcare when it opened in the 1960s. While Gray Line buses offered "Hippie Hop" tours that drove tourists around the Haight so they could see wild hippies up close, David Smith, a young doctor, became increasingly concerned by the number of overdoses he witnessed.

He opened the clinic so that the kids on Haight Street suffering from drug and alcohol addiction as well as mental and physical problems could get the help they needed. The clinic offers a safe place for anyone who doesn't have health insurance, as well as programs such as Rock Medicine, a volunteer-run on-site medical service for concerts and public events, substance abuse treatment services, and jail psychiatric services.

The establishment was the first to promote the use of bleach to clean needles used by drug addicts. In 1989, while in town for a concert, Nirvana band members got treated for the flu there and legend has it that when Kurt Cobain saw the campaign, he decided to name their next album *Bleach*.

The **San Francisco Free Clinic** (*4900 California St., 415-750-9894, sffc.org*) also offers free healthcare.

The Temp Life

Temp agencies are a good way to get started in the job market when you first move to the Bay Area, or help to bring in a little extra money when cash is low.

ABA
33 New Montgomery St., Suite 800, 415-434-4222, abastaff.com

The Job Shop
163 Second St., Suite 400, 415-226-8610, jobshopsf.com

The Right People
1 Sutter St., 415-705-5333, rightpeople.com

There's a food store for everyone. Here are some of the specialty ones, where you can pick up gourmet goodies to go:

At **Bi-Rite Market** *(3639 18th St., 415-241-9760, biritemarket.com)*, a Mission district market that has been run by the same family since the 1960s, you'll find paninis, cold-smoked salmon, and baskets of fruits and vegetables.

Cowgirl Creamery Cheese Shop *(1 Ferry Building, #17, 415-362-9354)* has the widest selection of cheese in the city, and with **Acme Bread** *(#15, 415-288-2978)* next door, there's a picnic just waiting to happen. But the long weekend lines can be discouraging – as an alternative, go to **Country Cheese** (see photo) *(415 Divisadero St., 415-621-8130)*, a spacious operation where you'll find friendly staff and some of the best-priced cheeses and pâtés around.

Lucca Ravioli Co. (1100 Valencia St., 415-647-5581) will take care of any Italian food cravings, and as for Asian food, there's no better place than Clement Street. **Richmond New May Wah Supermarket** (711 Clement St., 415-221-9826) is a local favorite for fresh herbs, banana leaves, and inexpensive seafood. If it's Japanese you want, seaweed salad, sushi, and other Japanese delicacies can be picked up at **Nijiya Market** (1737 Post St., 415-563-1901).

You can satisfy your sweet tooth with croissants, éclairs, and other pastries at **Tartine Bakery** (600 Guerrero St., 415-487-2600, tartinebakery.com) or at **Bay Bread Boulangerie** (2325 Pine St., 415-440-0356).

For California-cuisine ingredients, head to **Rainbow Grocery** (1745 Folsom St., 415-863-0620, rainbowgrocery.org), also vegetarian- and vegan-friendly. **Good Life Grocery** (448 Cortland Ave., 415-648-3221) offers organic products, and they have a great selection of meats. The worker-owned co-op **Other Avenues** (3930 Judah St., 415-661-7475, otheravenues.org), **Village Market** (4555 California St., 415-221-0445), and **Harvest Urban** (191 - 8th St., 415-621-1000, harvesturban.com) are also great places to shop for fresh products.

If you're in the mood for smoked herring, homemade sour cream, pastries, and cured meats, you'll love the Russian markets on Geary Blvd. such as **New World Market** (5641 Geary Blvd., at 21st Ave., 415-751-8810). On 24th Street, Mexican food lovers can stop in any restaurant or store to sample fresh tortillas, tamales, chilis, and salsas.

Tel Aviv Strictly Kosher Market (2495 Irving St., at 26th, 415-661-7588) sells kosher meat, barbecued chickens, knishes, piroshkis, and Kosher wines from around the world, and **Salama Halal Meat** (604 Geary St., 415-474-0359) specializes in meats that conform to Islamic dietary requirements.

For everything else including oils, sauces, and great gourmet goods, there's **Yum** (1750 Market St., 415-626-9866, yumfoods.com).

A list of retail stores that sell organic produce can be found at omorganics.org.

DOG DAY AFTERNOONS

Gone are the days where you and Sparky could run free through the park. Dog organizations fight hard to keep "off-leash" areas in parks around town. As of writing, there are 21. A list and map can be found at sfdog.org.

farm food

Photo: Judy Watt

At farmers' markets in the area, you can pick up the freshest produce, direct from the source. If they are open seasonally, they are usually in business between April/May and November.

Alemany

Sat. year-round, 5 a.m.-5 p.m., 100 Alemany Blvd., at Hwy 101 and Hwy 280 interchange, 415-647-9423

Bayview Hunters Point

Sat. seasonally, 9:30 a.m.-1:30 p.m., Third and Oakdale Sts., near the Bayview Opera House, 415-355-3723

The Cannery

Sat. seasonally, 9 a.m.-3 p.m., Del Monte Square, 2801 Leavenworth St., 415-771-3112

Ferry Plaza

Sat. year-round, 8 a.m.-2 p.m., Tues. year-round, 10 a.m.-2 p.m., Thurs. seasonally, 4-8 p.m., Sun. seasonally, 10 a.m.-2 p.m., Ferry Building, Embarcadero, at the foot of Market Street; 415-291-3276

Home Movies

Where to get your DVDs and videos.

Choi's Home Video

Thankfully, the opening of a nearby Blockbuster video hasn't put this store out of business. Help the guy out, keep going to this shop. *1410 Lombard St., 415-441-5610, choisvideo.com*

Famous Sports Videos III

For times you're in the mood to watch nothing but sports, this is the place to go. If you want a movie, don't bother, they don't have any. *2456 Chestnut St., 415-440-2510*

Japan Video & Media Inc.

There's a wide selection of animé and movies from Asia, for sale or rent. *1737 Post St., 415-563-5220*

Fillmore Street

Sat. usually Apr.-Nov., 9 a.m.-1 p.m., Fillmore and O'Farrell, 800-949-3276

Heart of the City

Wed. year-round, 7 a.m.-5:30 p.m.; Sun., 7 a.m.-5 p.m., Market St., between Seventh and Eighth Sts., 415-558-9455

Noe Valley

Sat. year-round, 8 a.m.-1p.m., 3861 24th St., between Sanchez and Vicksburg Sts., 415-248-1332

Le Video

A great place for cult French movies and independent films.

1231 9th Ave., 415-566-3606, levideo.com

Naked Eye News & Video

Ask the owner of Naked Eye for recommendations — he's seen all the videos he rents, several times.

607 Haight St. #A, 415-864-2985

Video Cafe

This is a 24-hour café and video store rolled into one.

5700 Geary Blvd. at 21st Ave., 415-387-3999

Wired

The **Horseshoe Coffee House** *(566 Haight St., 415-626-8852)*, the first Internet café in the United States, is a good place to get online, but the city also has a lot of wi-fi enabled places. A list can be found at *wi-fihotspotlist.com*.

with a little help from your friends

Eating out can be pricey, and besides, sometimes all you want to do is stay home and watch a movie. A good dinner without the hassles of cooking from scratch can be had thanks to some local prepared foods companies. You simply follow basic instructions on the box, and voilà – dinner's on the table.

Besos

685 Harrison St., 415-495-5460, besosfoods.com

Boulette's Larder

Ferry Building Marketplace, 415-399-1155, bouletteslarder.com

But if you don't even feel like turning on the stove, you can get a great meal delivered to you by calling **Dining In**, a personal chef service *(415-255-2433, dininginsf.com)*, or **Wally's Food Company**, which delivers pre-made gourmet meals for every occasion *(415-771-1395, wallysfoodco.com)*.

FREEDOM EATERS

Eating right can become a political statement here – when many Americans stopped eating and buying French products because of the French "non" to the Iraq War, a small group in San Francisco protested the boycott by pointedly patronizing French bistros and restaurants on Friday evenings. The protest, which was called "French Friday," was led by **Gerald Lenoir**, a Frenchman by birth who lives in Berkeley. Not to worry, though, you can still eat French food here simply because you like it.

fresher-upper

During the dot-com boom, **delivery services** like Kozmo would bring you almost anything you needed to your doorstep, from books to ice cream. Webvan, another popular delivery company, specialized in grocery delivery. Unfortunately, these companies went with the dot-com bust and residents had to get used to getting stuff on their own again. Bigger grocery stores like Safeway (safeway.com) and Albertson's (albertsons.com) each recently started offering their own delivery service in the area. Local customers can now order online, choose a delivery time frame, and forget about the days they had to lug heavy bags of groceries on public transportation.

Some Bay Area farms are offering the same convenience for organic produce. Customers can choose to have a box of select fruits and vegetables delivered to their home or office as often as once a week. Most websites include recipes in case you need ideas on what to do with the box's contents.

Eatwell Farms
eatwell.com

Farm Fresh to You
farmfreshtoyou.com

Organic Express
organicexpress.com

Planet Organics
planetorganics.com

Terra Firma Farm
terrafirmafarm.com

WestSide Organics
westsideorganics.com

Winter Creek Gardens
wintercreekgardens.com

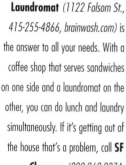

LICK IT CLEAN

Got nothing to wear and nothing to eat? **Brainwash Café and Laundromat** *(1122 Folsom St., 415-255-4866, brainwash.com)* is the answer to all your needs. With a coffee shop that serves sandwiches on one side and a laundromat on the other, you can do lunch and laundry simultaneously. If it's getting out of the house that's a problem, call **SF Cleaners** *(800-960-9274, sfcleaners.com)*; you'll pay more, but you'll get free pick up and delivery.

do it up

Hair salons where you can eat, enjoy art, and always come out looking fabulous.

dekko

One of the only live/work loft salons in town.
1325 Indiana St., Ground Level, 415-285-8848

Edo

Razor haircuts and edgy styles mix with art exhibits of local artists in what used to be a Baptist church.
601 Haight St., 415-861-0131, edosalon.com

Elevation Salon and Café

This salon's got it all: cool hair stylists, a beauty bar, a café, and wireless Internet. It's so hip we're too ashamed to walk in with our cheap do's.
451 Bush St., 415-392-2969, elevationsalon.com

Glamarama

Deena Davenport opened this salon to offer a safe and friendly place for the transgender community to get their hair done. They also sell wigs and offer wig styling.
417 South Van Ness Ave., 415-861-4526,
glamarama.com

Romantasy

This isn't a salon per se but more of a makeover place to help bring out customers' feminine side. Romantasy's Gender Image Salons teaches those new to cross-dressing how to apply makeup, do their hair, and get ready for a night on the town.
415-585-0760, romantasy.com

CALL FOR A GOOD TIME

Once a week since 2001, Kate Pocrass records a suggested journey on her answering machine for people interested in visiting a different part of the city. To hear the week's destination, call **Mundane Journeys** at 415-364-1465. Have your pen and notebook handy, as she'll tell you where to go, what to look for, and how to get there.
mundanejourneys.com

what's going on?

Know who to see and where to go by reading local blogs and newsletters.

Dailycandy.com

A daily e-mail newsletter that gives you the low-down on one cool company/person/destination.

Flavorpill.net

A weekly e-mail newsletter that lets you know events worth checking out that week.

Sfist.com and Sf.metblogs.com

Two blogs that focus on everything San Francisco.

PRETTY IN PINK

Freetah B., a local drag queen, drives people in style in her sweet baby, a pink limousine *(415-986-7465, pinkladylimo.com)* with pink faux-fur seats. **Pink Lady Limo** offers bachelorette parties and city tours.

The Banker and the Bear

A banker and a bear is all the **San Francisco Zoo** *(1 Zoo Road, 415-753-7080, sfzoo.org)* needed to come to life. In 1889, **William Randolph Hearst** got into a heated conversation with Allen Kelly, one of his reporters at the *San Francisco Examiner*, about the existence of grizzlies in California; Hearst challenged the journalist to go out and find one. So Kelly set off for the Ventura County mountains and after five months of searching, he was finally able to trap a bear and bring it back. Kelly and the *San Francisco Examiner* party were greeted by no less than 20,000 residents upon their return to the city.

The bear, later named Monarch, lived in Woodward's Gardens and in Golden Gate Park and sired two cubs. Although Monarch never lived in the zoo's current location, he inspired Herbert Fleishhacker, a wealthy banker, to build the San Francisco Zoo, which opened in 1929.

homes, sweet homes

Not a Buyer's Market

Buying a house in San Francisco is as tough as trying to find a parking spot in the narrow residential streets for your family van. A two-bedroom, 1,000-square-foot starter home is considered a steal at $750,000. And that's just the starting price; interested buyers usually have to bid higher – sometimes up to $200,000, more – and hope that will get them ahead of everyone else.

If you are willing to suffer the headaches and want to buy a home in the Bay Area, you should familiarize yourself with at least two techniques:

The pre-emptive offer: serious home buyers won't wait until the date on which you can officially make an offer. They figure how much they can afford above the listed price and make an offer that sellers just can't refuse.

The sharp bid: although many agents find this technique unethical because bidding information is disclosed, it's still a common way to get ahead. Buyers wait to hear other bids and offer to pay X dollars more than the highest one.

House No. 1

The first home to be built in San Francisco was at 823 Grant Avenue. It was owned by William A. Richardson, a former British sailor who worked as a middleman between the seamen and land owners. The original house is long gone, but a plaque has been placed on the wall that reads, "The birthplace of a great city, here, June 25, 1835, William A. Richardson, founder of Yerba Buena (later San Francisco), erected its first habitation...."

Living High

According to a 2005 study by *Forbes* magazine, San Francisco has five of the most expensive zip codes in the country – including *the* most expensive, just outside of the city in Atherton (94027). The Marina District and Cow Hollow ranked highest in the city with a median price of $1,183,307. The Inner Richmond and Presidio Heights, Castro/Noe Valley, St. Francis Wood/Ingleside/Miraloma Park, and the Outer Richmond/Seacliff area were also named.

Kid Stuff

According to 2000 US Census estimates, San Francisco has the lowest percentage of children of any major US city: only 14.5 percent of the city's population is 18 and younger, which is less than its big brother New York at 24 percent, and less than retirement haven Palm Beach, Fla. at 19 percent. Kids are even outnumbered by dogs: there are 112,000 children and 120,000 dogs (according to the San Francisco Dog Owners Group).

Despite the numbers, there are still plenty of things for kids to do around here.

Artery
Art classes for kids and parents.
1311 Church St., 415-285-0235, arterysf.com

Gay Getaways

Children's Art Center

A non-profit organization that offers workshops and classes.
Fort Mason, Building C, 415-771-0292, childrensartcenter.org

Circus Center

A training center for the arts of the circus, for children and adults.
755 Frederick St., 415-759-8123

Exploratorium

A fun-filled and hands-on science and art museum.
3601 Lyon St., 415-563-7337, exploratorium.edu

Photo: Celine Moravec

Glitter & Razz Productions

Offers plays and workshops.
415-378-0371, glitterandrazz.com

In 1978, Peter Pender bought the old Murphy's Ranch Resort, which the Murphy family had opened in 1905 near Guerneville, and reopened it as **Fifes Guest Ranch** *(16467 River Rd., Geurneville, 707-869-0656, fifes.com)*, the first gay resort in the area (see photo). Other resorts in the area followed and Russian River, in West Sonoma County (North of San Francisco), became a popular gay getaway. Refurbished in 2001, Fifes gives city dwellers plenty of choices in relaxation; parties happen at the pool, in the woods, or anywhere you want to take it. For a more rustic weekend with no phones, TV, or clothes (it's clothing-optional), try **Highlands Resort** *(14000 Woodland Dr., Geurneville, 707-869-0333, highlandsresort.com)*, a quieter property with tents and cabins. **Russian River Resort** *(16390 4th St., Geurneville, 707-869-0691, russianriverresort.com)* also offers a cozy clothing-optional setting with a happening hot tub.

Going, Going, Gone

According to the 2000 US Census, San Francisco's population declined by 1.5 percent between July 2001 and July 2002, making it the fastest shrinking city among 242 American cities with more than 100,000 people. So where is everyone going? It looks like people are going where the sun is – Southern California and the Southwest have seen the biggest population increases.

If You Must Leave

Public transportation can get you almost everywhere in and around the city, but if you want to get away for a few days, there are options other than renting a car.

If you're 23 or older with a valid driver's license (foreign travelers also need a passport with valid exit visa), you can drive a car from your location to another for free with **Auto Driveaway Co.** (28402 Century St., Hayward, 510-782-4999, driveawayco.com/carsavailable.html). Car owners (usually those moving to another city) leave their cars with the company, which then arranges for it to be driven to the designated destination. You may not get to go where you want, but it's a great way to enjoy an impromptu road trip. You'll receive the first tank of gas free, and a certain number of days to complete the trip.

City Car Share (415-995-8588, citycarshare.org), a car rental co-operative that was created to encourage shared car use, also is a good way to get around, although it's best for short distances. Members pay a $10 monthly fee and are charged $4 per hour and 44 cents per mile including gas, insurance, and reserved parking.

If you're looking for alternatives to your daily commute, check options at sfenvironment.com.

Firing It Up in the Desert

Labor Day weekends can sometimes be quiet here because many San Franciscans are in the middle of the Nevada desert taking part in **Burning Man** (burningman.com), an outdoor art festival and temporary community based on self-expression and self-reliance. **Larry Harvey** is the leader of this massive human exodus to the desert. Although the press is sticking to the story of a man who started the festival by gathering all his friends on the beach as a way to forget a painful break-up in 1986, Harvey says that, more importantly, it was "an act of radical self-expression."

Even though Harvey's father may have been a tall carpenter, the giant wooden man who ends up being burned at the end of each yearly event has nothing to do with him, according to Harvey.

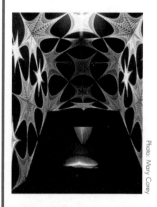

Photo: Mary Corey

Gregangelo Museum
A fun house filled with wacky furniture and wall décor inspired by sacred places around the world.
Call for an appointment,
415-664-0095, gregangelo.com

Musée Mecanique
Get those quarters ready for old-time arcade games and mechanical shows with dolls that represent events such as the French revolution.
Pier 45 at the end of Taylor St.,
415-346-2000

Ripley's Believe It or Not! Museum
Oddities abound at the local cartoonist's museum. Robert Ripley was from Santa Rosa, just outside the city, and was the first cartoonist to become a millionaire.
175 Jefferson St., 415-771-6188,
ripleysf.com

wine country

Photo: William Faulkner

The Rooftop at Yerba Buena Gardens

Includes **Zeum** (a center that encourages children to express themselves through art), an ice skating and bowling center, a child development center, a 1906 carousel that used to be at Playland-at-the-Beach, and gardens. *221 Fourth St. at Howard St., 415-777-2800, zeum.org*

750 Folsom St., 415-777-3727, skatebowl.com

Wax Museum

145 Jefferson St., 800-439-4305, waxmuseum.com

On weekends, wineries in Sonoma and Napa Valley see urban dwellers from San Francisco drive out to sample and buy local wines, in an effort to contribute to the local economy, we're sure. To feel a little less of a wino on vacation, bone up on some of the wine trivia that follows here. You'll impress people you meet on your winery tour, if you can keep your names and dates straight, of course.

Sonoma Valley

On July 4, 1823, Padre José Altamira founded **Mission San Francisco Solano**, California's northernmost Franciscan mission, the only one established in California when it was still a Mexican territory. (In 1821, Mexico gained its independence from Spain and Alta California became a territory of the Republic of Mexico.) In 1834, Commandant M. G. Vallejo carried out secularization orders, and the mission became a church serving the Pueblo and Sonoma Valley until it was sold in 1881. *Located in Sonoma State Historic Park, NW corner of Spain at First St. East in Sonoma, members.napanet .net/~sshpa*

The birthplace of California wine is **Buena Vista Winery and Vineyards**, which was founded in 1857 by Count Agoston Haraszthy, who traveled around Europe in 1861 and returned with grapevine cuttings which he used to start his vineyards. With the help of his workers, he dug storage tunnels into the limestone rock, now a common technique in nearby Napa Valley wineries. *18000 Old Winery Rd., two miles NE of Sonoma, 707-938-1266, buenavistawinery.com*

Napa Valley

The first valley residents were the Wappo Indians, who named the valley "Napa," which meant a land of plenty due to the abundance of salmon, wildcats, elk, black bears, and grizzlies, not to mention wild grapes.

Calvert Yount had an interest in the grapes and realized he could make a living out of them. In 1836, he established the first homestead in what is now Yountville and planted vineyards. Around the same time, John Patchett planted a vineyard in nearby St. Helena, Dr George Crane promoted the planting of grapevines through a series of newspaper articles, and Hamilton Walker Crabb experimented with more than 400 grape varieties.

Charles Krug opened Napa Valley's first commercial winery in 1861 (now called **Charles Krug - Peter Mondavi Family Winery**, *(2800 Main St., St. Helena, 707-967-2220, charleskrug.com)*. By 1889, there were more than 140 wineries in operation in Napa, including

Do Your Homework

According to the 2000 US Census, there are 112 languages spoken in the Bay Area, and in San Francisco County alone, 45.7 percent speak a language other than English at home. Enrolling your kids in international schools can come at a steep price but if you're relying on your pride and joy to act as a guide and translate everything for you next time you're vacationing abroad, check out some of the Bay Area's international schools.

Chinese-American School
150 Oak St., 415-865-6000, cais.org

French-American International School of San Francisco

150 Oak St., 415-558-2000, fais-ihs.org

German-American International School

275 Elliott Dr., Menlo Park, 650-324-8617, germanamericanschool.org

Lycée Français La Pérouse

755 Ashbury St., 415-661-5232; 330 Golden Hind Passage, Corte Madera, 415-924-1737, lelycee.org

Russian-American International School

1250 Quintara St., 415-837-0901, russianamericanschool.org

Schramsberg, founded in 1862 (*1400 Schramsberg Rd. at Peterson Dr., Calistoga, 707-942-4558, schramsberg.com*), **Beringer** in 1876 (*2000 Main St., St. Helena, 707-967-4412, beringer.com*), and Inglenook in 1880, which was purchased by Francis Ford Coppola in 1995. Coppola settled at the winery with his family, renovated the chateau, and opened an museum upstairs full of props from his films. He changed the name to **Niebaum-Coppola Winery** (*1991 St. Helena Highway, Rutherford, 707-968-1100, niebaum-coppola.com*) after Gustave Ferdinand Niebaum, the founder of the Inglenook winery.

index

index

index

index

index

index

index

index

index

index

index

index

HELENE GOUPIL and JOSH KRIST are editor and publisher, respectively, of *InsideOut* Travel Magazine, an online publication that caters to the traveler/adventurer at heart. Helene, Josh, and *InsideOut* (*www.insideoutmag.com*) are based in San Francisco.